Heloise & Abelard

Heloise & Abelard

A NEW BIOGRAPHY

JAMES BURGE

HarperSanFrancisco
A Division of HarperCollins*Publishers*

HarperCollins books may be purchased for educational, business, or sales promotional use. For information please write: Special Markets Department, HarperCollins Publishers, Inc., 10 East 53rd Street, New York, NY 10022.

HarperCollins Web site: http://www.harpercollins.com
HarperCollins®, ⛪ ®, and HarperSanFrancisco™ are trademarks of HarperCollins Publishers, Inc.

FIRST EDITION

Library of Congress Cataloging-in-Publication Data has been ordered and is available upon request.

ISBN 0–06–073663–1 (cloth)

05 06 07 08 09 RRD(H) 10 9 8 7 6 5 4 3 2 1

Petro et Heloyse Jacobus salutem

For my family: Kate, Zoë, and Chloë

Contents

Acknowledgments

CKNOWLEDGMENTS must go to Penguin Books for permission to use the translations of the later letters by Betty Radice in *The Letters of Abelard and Heloise* (© Betty Radice 1974). The translations of the "early letters," which were originally edited by Ewald Köntsgen, are by Constant Mews and Neville Chiavaroli from *The Lost Love Letters of Abelard and Heloise: Perceptions of Dialogue in Twelfth-Century France* (London: Palgrave Macmillan, 1999). Any errors that I may inadvertently have introduced are, it goes without saying, all my own work. Thanks to Brenda Cook and Sylvia Barnard for sharing with me their translation of the *Carmen ad Astralabium* and to Harold Perkin, Olga Prendergast, Carine Minne, and Matthias von der Tann who were so generous with their time and assistance. At a personal level my gratitude goes first of all to my wife, Kate, for many things, especially her ability to say the right thing even when prompted. Thanks are due also to Peter Carson of Profile Books whose patience allowed the writing of this book to become an educational experience, and to my agent, Sheila Ableman, without whose boundless enthusiasm and encouragement this project certainly would not have started and might not have finished.

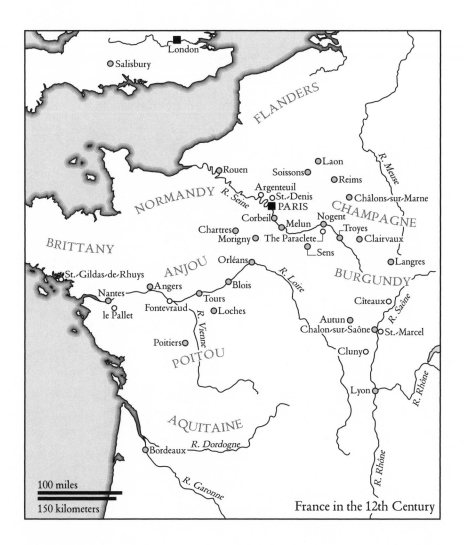

France in the 12th Century

100 miles

150 kilometers

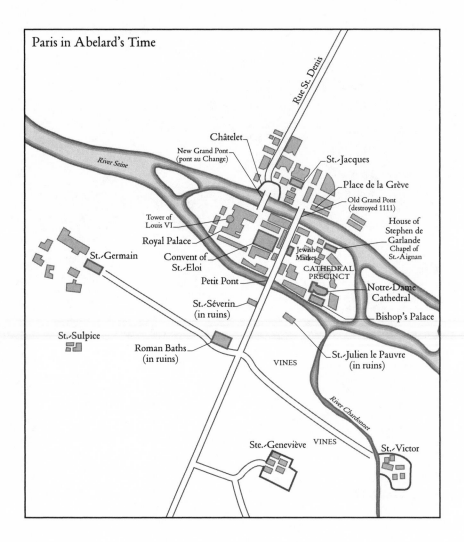

Paris in Abelard's Time

Rue St. Denis

Châtelet

New Grand Pont
(pont au Change)

St. Jacques

River Seine

Place de la Grève

Old Grand Pont
(destroyed 1111)

Tower of
Louis VI

House of
Stephen de
Garlande

Royal Palace

Chapel of
St. Aignan

St. Germain

Convent of
St. Eloi

Jewish
Market

CATHEDRAL
PRECINCT

Petit Pont

Notre Dame
Cathedral

St. Séverin
(in ruins)

Bishop's Palace

St. Sulpice

Roman Baths
(in ruins)

St. Julien le Pauvre
(in ruins)

VINES

River Chardonnet

Ste. Geneviève

VINES

St. Victor

List of Illustrations

Chronology of the Lives of Heloise and Abelard

The order of events in the story is well established but many of the dates pertaining to the couple are certain only to an accuracy of one or two years. In the case of the birth date of Heloise there is even more uncertainty; the year given below is a best guess.

1079	Peter Abelard born, le Pallet, Brittany
1081	Bayeux tapestry completed
1093–99	Abelard taught by Roscelin at Loches
1095	First crusade launched by Pope Urban II at Clermont-Ferrand (November 27)
1095	Heloise born
1098	Cistercian Order founded
1100	Abbey of Fontevraud founded by Robert of Arbrissel
1100	Abelard arrives in Paris, joins the school of Notre-Dame
1102	Abelard sets up his own school at Melun
1104	Stephen de Garlande ousted from power
1104	Abelard moves his school to Corbeil. Later returns to Brittany
1107	Dissolution of convent of St.-Eloi
1108	William of Champeaux becomes a canon at the abbey of St.-Victor
1108	Stephen de Garlande appointed chancellor by Louis VI
1108	Abelard returns to Paris, sets up a school at the abbey of Mont Ste.-Geneviève

1112	Abelard goes to Brittany to attend his mother's investiture as a nun
1113	Abelard enrolls in the school of Anselm at Laon, and is soon asked to leave
1114	Abelard returns to Paris to become master of the school of Notre-Dame
1115	Bernard founds the abbey of Clairvaux
1115–16	Abelard and Heloise become lovers. "Early letters" written
1116	Heloise becomes pregnant and is removed to Abelard's family in Brittany
1116	Astralabe born
1116	Abelard and Heloise marry in secret in Paris
1117	Castration of Abelard. Abelard becomes a monk at St.-Denis, Heloise a nun at Argenteuil
1118	Order of Knights Templar founded
1121	Council of Soissons. Abelard forced to burn his book on the Trinity
1122	Abelard flees from St.-Denis to Nogent after a row about the identity of the saint
1122	Abbot Adam of St.-Denis dies (February 19), and is replaced by Abbot Suger (March 12)
1122	Abelard founds the monastery of the Paraclete
1127	Disgrace of Stephen de Garlande
1127	Abelard becomes abbot of St.-Gildas de Rhuys, Brittany
1129	Suger accuses nuns of the convent of Argenteuil of immorality and claims the convent belongs to St.-Denis
1129	Heloise moves to the Paraclete
1132–16	Abelard writes the autobiography and the couple exchange the "later letters"
1136	John of Salisbury attends Abelard's lectures at Ste.-Geneviève
1137	Prince Louis (later Louis VII) marries Eleanor of Aquitaine (August 1)
1137	Death of Louis VI. Accession of Louis VII

1137	Abbot Suger begins work on the refurbishment of St. Denis
1137–40	Composition of *Ethica*, "Hymns for the Paraclete," *Problems of Heloise* and "Laments"
1140	Council of Sens. Abelard accused of heresy
1140	Abelard stays at Cluny. "Reconciliation" with Bernard of Clairvaux
1142	Abelard moves to St. Marcel
1142	Abelard dies (April 21)
1147	Bernard of Clairvaux preaches the second crusade
1147	Pope Eugenius III issues a bull confirming the possessions of the Paraclete
1150	Astralabe is a canon at Nantes
1151–63	Foundation of six daughter houses of the Paraclete
1162–65	Astralabe is abbot of Hauterive in what is now the Swiss canton of Fribourg
1163	Heloise dies (May 16)
1275	Publication of the story of Abelard and Heloise by Jean de Meung in the *Roman de la Rose*
1290	Publication of a French translation of the letters by Jean de Meung
1791	Dissolution of the Paraclete. Remains of Abelard and Heloise transferred to Nogent sur Seine
1800	Remains moved to Auguste Lenoir's Museum of French Monuments in Paris
1817	Remains moved to their current resting place, the cemetery of Père Lachaise, Paris

INTRODUCTION
The letters of two lovers

BELARD AND HELOISE lived 900 years ago. Their story — a mixture of spiritual quest, erotic passion, and horrific brutality — is probably the most memorable tale of all from the Middle Ages. It is certainly the one in which we are given the most insight into the thoughts and feelings of the protagonists. But we only know about the story at all because of two separate chance discoveries, both of collections of letters. The first discovery took place less than a hundred years after their deaths; the second has had to wait until the last three years to be recognized for what it was.

We do not know when the first find was made, but sometime in the century after Heloise's death somebody must have made a copy of a manuscript that she had left in the library of her convent, the Paraclete, near the town of Troyes in the county of Champagne in northern France. It passed into the hands of the poet Jean de Meung who, in 1275, became the first person to mention the couple in writing when he incorporated their story into his epic poem the *Roman de la Rose*. His account makes it clear that the story was contained in letters; he even comments on their frankness and honesty. From then on the tale of Abelard and Heloise begins to diffuse into the consciousness of the Middle Ages.

What de Meung had seen was a collection of eight letters that to this day remain the source of our knowledge of the bones of the story. There are five letters from Abelard, three from Heloise, all written in

Latin, which was the language of all writing at this period.

Other sources corroborate the story, but without these letters nobody today would be aware of the love affair. Abelard would still be remembered, but as a controversial philosopher of the Middle Ages whose career had culminated in a disastrous clash with ecclesiastical authority. Heloise would be little more than a name on an obscure twelfth-century manuscript. It is a tribute to her qualities, not least as a writer, that her three letters alone have made her famous.

The first letter of the collection is from Abelard. It is addressed not to Heloise, however, but to an unnamed monk. It is what was called in the Middle Ages a "letter of consolation," the idea being that the recipient should be so moved by the misfortunes of the writer that he himself would feel better about his own troubles. At 20,000 words it is really more of an autobiography, an account of Abelard's life to date. It has been known for centuries by the phrase that he himself uses, "The Story of My Misfortunes."*

This autobiographical letter tells, for the benefit of the anonymous monk, the story of the couple's meeting and falling in love, of the birth of the child they called Astralabe, and of their secret marriage. It tells also of the violence and tragedy that followed – a chain of events born out of a blood feud, misunderstandings, and dark desires – which culminated in a brutal attack on Abelard. As he slept he was set upon and castrated by thugs acting on the orders of Heloise's uncle, Fulbert. In the aftermath the couple separated and each entered monastic orders. The autobiography was written fifteen years after these events, at a time when Abelard was in exile in Brittany, living in a monastery that he detested, and where, according to him, the monks were trying to kill him.

It is not known precisely how Heloise came to read a copy of the autobiographical letter; perhaps Abelard even sent it to her as well as to the monk. Her letter to Abelard in response to this is the next in the

---

* "Historia Calamitatum Mearum." In this book I refer to this autobiographical letter for simplicity as "the autobiography." Its other title among historians is "Letter I."

series. She is reacting to a letter from the husband with whom she has not spoken for fifteen years, written to a third party, which tells the story of her own life. She writes to him, perhaps understandably, with a considerable amount of passion and so begins a dialogue that would continue for the rest of their lives, as they tried to make sense of what had happened. Abelard comes to see his fate almost as a gift: a chance to pursue the truth without distraction. Heloise, however, is unable to deny the essential rightness of the love they shared. This dialogue takes place in the context of Abelard's continuing – and ultimately disastrous – conflict with those in authority.

These letters captivate anyone who comes in contact with them. Not only do they contain the story of Abelard and Heloise but they are a unique resource for anyone interested in the thoughts and feelings of people from an age that is both so different from and yet so similar to our own. It would have been churlish to have asked Providence for anything more, yet there was more.

In 1980 Constant Mews, a young scholar in New Zealand, was looking at a modern edition of a rather obscure Latin book from the fifteenth century. It was a collection of examples of how to write letters: correct forms of address, good style, etc. It was a kind of self-help book, a response to the increase in literacy in the period, of interest at that time to those who wished to write an effective letter to their local bishop, for example. The man who had originally compiled it, one Johannes de Vepria, had followed a number of staid but worthy examples of good letter-writing form with something a little different: a section that he headed "From the Letters of Two Lovers." This was less formal and more passionate. De Vepria had started by copying just the openings and endings of the letters – elaborate greetings and farewells to serve as examples of fine style. At some stage it appears that he himself had become more interested in the content, for he started to include whole letters and even poems.

He had ended up with a collection of fragments, of various sizes, from 113 letters. He did not identify the correspondents but simply labeled them "Man" and "Woman."

Mews read: "To her sweet love, more sweetly scented than any spice, from she who is his in heart and body: I send the freshness of eternal happiness as the flowers of your youth fade." Mews knew the story of Abelard and Heloise well. He had studied their letters as well as Abelard's philosophical ideas. As he read the book he realized that it was possible that these letters constituted the most extraordinary time capsule. Both Abelard and Heloise mention that during the period of their affair (no more than two years) they wrote to each other every day. Heloise reminds Abelard how he "showered her in letters" during their courtship. Could he now be looking at copies of the very daily messages that they mention? He read, "How fertile with delight is your breast, how you shine with utter beauty, body so full of moisture, that indescribable scent of yours." It was not impossible.

The original Latin text had been prepared for publication in its modern edition by a German scholar, Ewald Köntsgen. In 1974, when the book was published, he had included a cautious subtitle for the final section: "Letters of Abelard and Heloise?" But he had not pursued his own question – he was cautious and unwilling to speculate further. He was a philologist whose main interest was in producing a perfect version of the Latin text.

Mews was fascinated by the possibility of what he might have found. He continued to study the letters for the next decade. If he was right it was the kind of discovery about which historians do not even dare to let themselves fantasize. It was almost of the order of a new play by Shakespeare or a lost gospel. Or was it a blatant forgery that could only bring ruin to an academic? This could not be a question of a modern forgery, however. The letters were obviously from an old source, on paper of the right period. Johannes de Vepria, the copyist, was known from other works of the fifteenth century. His handwriting was known to scholars; he even had a good reputation for accurate copying. Could the letters have been forged by him or by some-one before him? It seemed very unlikely: the collection was such a mess. Parts of it did not make sense; events and arguments did not always hang together. Someone at the time might well have decided to write letters from the standpoint of somebody else (to call such an act forgery would be the modern way of judging what was a not unknown medieval practice), but if they had done so the collection would have been more coherent. It would have been put together in a way that made an obvious moral point. There was no moral in the new letters.

Of the few other academics who had commented on the letters up until then, some had dismissed them as "literary exercises." But Mews could see that the letters plainly did not constitute a work of fiction of any kind known in the Middle Ages. They had not been constructed as a creative exercise by one person; they were too chaot-ic in their content. As a novel they are confused and irritating, but as historical evidence they are beyond price.

Could they be genuine letters but written by a different couple? Mews checked through facts he could glean from the de Vepria col-lection against what is known of Abelard and Heloise from the well-established letters. The man in the new letters is certainly a philosopher by training – he uses all the language of medieval philos-ophy, even terms that were particularly dear to Abelard in his schol-arly writings. He is also, like Abelard, famous – the woman thinks he is the most brilliant man of his time – and no stranger to controversy. The woman is his student, just like Heloise. But she is not just a stu-dent, she is his most able pupil, a woman of outstanding intelligence, well versed in classical literature. These are the very things for which we are told Heloise was famous in her lifetime. The woman makes it clear that, although she is French, the man is not – Abelard was a Breton. The couple are conducting the relationship in secret, living in constant fear of discovery, just like Abelard and Heloise. The couple in the new letters are plainly almost painfully in love and fired up with a vertiginous erotic energy, just as Abelard describes his own relationship in his autobiography and Heloise confirms in her later letters. If these letters were written by a couple other than Abelard and Heloise they contain the most amazing string of coincidences.

The world we see in the newly discovered letters is consistent with what is known from the later letters except that we now see a brief period in much more detail. Within this narrow window is a sequence of extravagant declarations, occasional tiffs, arguments, and disagreements about the nature of love, and we eventually sense the effects of stress and the pain of separation. Even beyond the facts of the case, as Mews continued to read and to study the new letters he experienced a feeling that was to be shared by others who read them: scholars who know medieval Latin as well as they know their mother tongue agree that the style is unmistakably that of the couple. Particularly in the case of Heloise, it is almost like recognizing the voice of someone you know: modes of expression, references, areas of interest all indicate that this is the same woman who wrote the three well-established letters.

How could this very personal collection of letters have come into the hands of Johannes de Vepria? There was a plausible explanation. Johannes was a monk from Clairvaux, a monastery very close to the Paraclete convent where Heloise had been abbess. The two houses are known to have maintained close relations over the years. It seems quite credible that the bibliophile monk from Clairvaux should have been allowed to go through the Paraclete archive, where Heloise would have stored her collections of letters. Even if he himself had no inkling of the authorship of the letters (which seems, on balance, unlikely), an attentive reader such as de Vepria could not fail to realize that he had stumbled on something of great interest.

In 1999 Mews published the letters in Latin with an English translation, along with a scholarly account of Abelard's life. He chose the confident title *The Lost Love Letters of Abelard and Heloise*. Mews has now been joined in his confidence by other scholars. Although, in the nature of academic discourse, decades will go by as theory and countertheory are advanced about what the "letters of two lovers" really represent, the consensus at the moment is with Mews.* It is a paradox born of the convincing nature of the new let- ters that they do not substantively affect the main points of the story. If they had introduced whole, previously unsuspected episodes that were corroborated nowhere else then one would be much less inclined to believe in them (the one possible exception to this I discuss in its place in this book). The result is that if at some time in the future the newly discovered early letters turn out, by coincidence or conspir- acy, not to be what they seem it will make almost no difference to the outline of the story told in this book.† What would be lost, however, would be the mass of detail that gives insight – sometimes poignant and sometimes even funny – into one of the most famous affairs in history, an all-consuming love between two exceptional people.

In the totality of letters, early and late, we meet Abelard and Heloise as people: we know about their most intimate terms of endearment; we even know about the passion of their lovemaking, of frantic, stolen moments in churches, of inventive sessions and erotic role-play. Even the early letters are so unfettered by what we might imagine to be the conventions of their age that it is quite common for anyone reading them for the first time to think that they must be fakes. Today, unshocked by their sexual candor and with fewer preconceptions about the age in which they lived, we have a chance to appreciate not only their story but their single-minded attempt to find peace in the face of adversity. Their letters have given us privileged access not only to their inner world but also to a

---

* This is not to say, of course, that basically genuine letters might not have been subedited or changed since writing – not least by one of the authors themselves.

†On the general question of evidence and rigor, this book is not a scholarly work of aca- demic history, but neither is it fiction. I have indicated the evidence for the assertions made in it whenever possible. Where I have speculated, or am reporting somebody else's specu- lation, I have said so. What is absent here that would be present in an academic work is the analytical consideration of every counterargument and opposing theory. In many cases, where the controversy is in itself interesting, I have outlined it. In a minority of cases I have chosen what I consider to be the most likely theory and stuck to it in the interest of comprehensible narrative.

stage of human civilization that many now see as the first step toward the modern world. There has never been a better time to meet them.

Author's note
In this book I refer to the recently rediscovered Johannes de Vepria letters as the "Early Letters" because they were written earlier in the story of Abelard and Heloise. The more established letters, which were written about twelve years after the start of the affair, I refer to as appropriate to the context: "Autobiography," "Heloise, First Letter," "Abelard, First Letter" etc.

ONE

"Darling"

1132

Not long ago, my beloved, by chance someone brought me
the letter of consolation you had sent to a friend.
Heloise, First Letter

 ELOISE (we do not know her second name, or
even whether she had one) begins the series of
love letters through which she has gathered admirers and devotees for over twenty generations with a
line that at first sight is remarkable only for its
ordinariness.

The circumstances seem straightforward enough: she is confirming that she has read a letter that the recipient had previously sent to
someone else. Only the words "my beloved" – *delectissime* in Latin –
indicate that anything more passionate than acquaintance may be
involved in the relationship between the two correspondents. Even
that is muted: a schoolmaster might translate it as "oh most beloved
one" but it is more likely to be something nearly equivalent to the conventional "darling" that well-established couples use in public. Later
on her preferred form of address will be "my only one."

The unseen folds of emotion and history that surround this opening line can be unpacked only slowly and carefully but the facts
behind it can be easily stated. The writer is the 31-year-old abbess in
charge of a convent called the Paraclete, near the town of Troyes in
the Champagne region of northeastern France. The year is 1132, the

early Middle Ages – thirty-six years after the first crusade, fifteen years before the second. The person whom she addresses as "darling" is her husband, Peter Abelard. He is a famous man, by common consent the brightest philosopher of his generation. He was once the master of the prestigious cathedral school in Paris, and has continued ever since to make his mark on the ideas of the age. She has not had any close contact with him now for fifteen years. The letter to which she refers is really more of an autobiography, Abelard's concise (20,000 words) and almost naively frank account of the first part of his life.

In this autobiographical letter, which he has apparently addressed to a third party without any reference to her, Heloise has just read his account of their meeting and falling in love, which also includes a full account of their lovemaking and far-ranging sexual experimentation. She has also read of their hasty marriage, the birth of their son, and the subsequent story of jealousy and horrific revenge that led to Abelard's castration, to the couple taking holy orders and ultimately to Heloise finding herself where she is as she writes her reply.

If, in the summer of 1132, the Abbess Heloise had been asked to read aloud the first sentence of her letter, what might we have detected in the tone of voice of this intelligent and perceptive woman? Love? Pain? Desire? Fury at being ignored for so long and then finding her intimate story related to an unnamed stranger? Her reply to Abelard eventually communicates all those feelings eloquently, always in the stylish Latin that has endeared her to scholars through succeeding centuries. But it is very unlikely that she read the letter aloud to anyone in the convent, because it soon becomes clear that the content is so personal and so potentially shocking that it could never have been revealed to the nuns in her charge.

As she sat in whatever place of privacy she was able to find in the little convent of the Paraclete, the Abbess Heloise could probably not even have risked letting her emotion show. She took her job seriously; she had built the community up from nothing, braving physical deprivation and political conspiracy. To achieve and sustain that success the person in charge must maintain her authority. For the abbess's devout subordinates to have known what was in the letter and heard about her erotic fantasies, let alone her doubts about her vocation, would have been dangerously undermining.

Heloise begins her reply to Abelard – as one must always do with writers, especially if one is married to them – by congratulating him on the quality of the work she has just read. Abelard had started his letter by offering his own story as a consolation to his unnamed correspondent, promising that, "in comparison with my trials you will see that your own are nothing, or only slight, and you will find them easier to bear." She assures him that this strategy has undoubtedly worked:

> *You did indeed carry out your promise that you made your friend at the beginning that he would think his own troubles insignificant in comparison with your own ... No one, I think, could read it dry eyed; my own sorrows are renewed by the detail in which you have told it.* (Heloise, First Letter)

The catalogue of misfortunes in Abelard's autobiography, which Heloise calls "the unending suffering which you, my only love, continue to endure," is certainly relentless. Heloise says that it must have been effective, and even today we cannot help but agree: no matter how miserable the original recipient might have been it is scarcely conceivable that, having read it, he or anyone would have wanted to swap places with Abelard.

We never do find out who this third person was, or the nature of his misfortunes that necessitated hearing all of Abelard's in order to feel better. At the end of the letter he is referred to as "dearly beloved brother in Christ, close friend and long-standing companion." Abelard says that he is "following up the words of consolation that I gave you in person" with his own story, so we can imagine this letter is the culmination of a series of discussions.

Some people have suggested that the recipient did not really exist, that he is just a literary device introduced by Abelard to help the narrative drive of his book. This seems very unlikely: first, Abelard's story needs no literary device to make it work, and second, it would be out of character for the couple to communicate by using any sort of pretense. In all their other correspondence they quite plainly pride themselves on their openness and directness. It seems much more probable that the monk was real and that the letter was addressed to him. Far from using a conscious conceit in a letter intended for Heloise, Abelard just seems to have badly miscalculated the hurt that she might suffer on reading this third-party correspondence. (Did she just happen to be sent it or did he send it to her himself? We have no idea.) If this is the case, it is by no means the only time that Abelard, for all his intelligence, failed completely to anticipate the emotional consequences of his actions.

It is always slightly disturbing to hear oneself being referred to in the third person, even in a quite innocent context. To find the episode of a life by which all other things are measured retold to a stranger for the purpose of spiritual consolation is bound to produce a strong reaction. For Heloise it revivified all the pain of separation:

> *The detailed account you gave of these misfortunes may have been intended for his comfort but it greatly increased my feeling of desolation; in your desire to heal his wounds you have dealt me fresh wounds of grief as well as re-opening the old.* (Heloise, First Letter)

But nothing can obliterate the pleasure of hearing from him again – "thank God that at least there is a way of restoring your presence to me that no malice can prevent." The abbess knows, as she has known for the past fifteen years, that she is still completely in love with Abelard:

> *You know, beloved, as the whole world knows, how much I have lost in you, how at one wretched stroke of fortune that supreme act of flagrant treachery robbed me of my very self in robbing me of you.* (Heloise, First Letter)

The conversation, in the shape of an exchange of letters that will develop out of the reply she is writing, will center on Heloise's loss and her desire to rid herself of her pain.

～

Abelard's account of the love affair is efficiently told and well structured, but it concentrates on facts rather than feelings. The relationship with Heloise constitutes only one self-contained episode within his broader story. His main purpose is to recount the series of misfortunes and setbacks that he has suffered, mostly motivated, in his opinion, by the jealousy of others. His narrative goes beyond the end of the affair and the couple's separation to concentrate on the vehement condemnation that his philosophical ideas attracted from theologians of the day. In his autobiography he leaves Heloise in the convent, as he seems to have done in life. His account is commendably factual but it also has an instructive purpose: it is intended to demonstrate to his monastic friend how his own lust and pride brought misfortune upon him. He ends the episode with a picture of Heloise now at peace, her wisdom and her love now diverted toward God – she has become a model of chastity and piety:

> *And such favor in the eyes of all did God bestow on that sister of mine who was in charge of the other nuns, that bishops loved her as a daughter, abbots as a sister, the laity as a mother; while all alike admired her piety and wisdom, and her unequalled gentleness and patience in every situation.* (Abelard, Autobiography)

This account gives the impression, if not of a happy ending then certainly of a satisfactory closure to the Heloise story: Abelard has been punished for his lust and pride; Heloise is now settled and doing good. It is possible that Abelard himself believed that this was the case. She had indeed been very successful in running the Paraclete.

The convent had not only survived but expanded, gaining papal approval and setting up a number of daughter houses. It would become the center of one of the most important women's orders in Europe.

That was an achievement: monasticism in the early twelfth century was competitive. It was in a sense the defining activity of the age – in the same way that, say, manufacturing and marketing are primary occupations of the early twenty-first century, religious observation then occupied the same kind of position. It was religion practiced on an industrial scale. Networks of monasteries and convents covered Europe. Different orders of monks and nuns competed with each other for prestige and patronage. It was religion practiced on a grand scale.

Orders varied in details of style and approach, but at root they all had the same purpose. In our secular age several accounts of the true purpose of monasteries are current: to preserve learning, to reorganize society, to oppress the people, to educate the people, to act as a job-creation agency for disinherited sons and unmarried daughters, to distill fine liquors, or to save civilization. While all of these are arguably by-products of monasticism, its true purpose, as perceived at the time of Abelard, was much simpler. Monasteries existed in order to practice religion. They celebrated the glory of the Creator and of the world around them, which was sometimes rather charmingly described as God's work of art. Through the cycle of prayer and meditation that was their daily routine, they maintained, as it were, a perpetual dialogue between heaven and earth.

Being in charge of a convent would have tested all of Heloise's personal qualities. The abbess's function combined, among other things, chief executive, priest, and role model. Above all she had to maintain the constant smooth running of the house. The nuns submitted themselves to a set of rules (of varying strictness, according to the order) that regulated their life absolutely. In particular, the rules set out a cycle of observances – Matins, Prime, Terce, Sext, Nones, Vespers, Compline, and Vigils – religious ceremonies that took place at fixed times, marking out the unchanging pattern of the monastic day. While the monks or nuns might be involved at other times in anything from brewing beer to translating Arabic texts, the main purpose of the monastery was to maintain that regular cycle of devotions known as the *officium,* or "offices." It was a grueling regime: Matins started while it was still dark and led up to sunrise; services continued at regular intervals throughout the day until Compline, which followed the evening meal; Vigils were the nightly prayers that finished after midnight, leaving sometimes as little as three hours before Matins. In the winter there was a little more time to sleep after Vigils, but rising was more unpleasant in the cold. It is no wonder that, in the song, Frère Jacques is discovered oversleeping and has to be roused in order to make him get back to work and "sonner les matines" – ring the bell for the office of Matins.

As well as running the convent itself, Heloise was responsible for managing the house's main means of support: income from the surrounding lands that had been pledged to the convent. It is a measure of Heloise's success that by the time of her death she had taken the convent from a state of poverty such that the sisters had to forage their own food to such financial security that, according to a papal document of 1147, it controlled a large part of the valley of the river Ardusson in which it stood.

We do not have any details of Heloise's dealings with the local landowners whom she persuaded to give up portions of their wealth either by the promise of prestige in this world or of salvation in the next. The records of a similar convent, however, do survive. In the abbey of Fontevraud, in the county of Anjou, the duties of the abbess included constant negotiation with local benefactors. It was necessary not only to persuade them to be generous in the first place but also to ensure that they remained generous. The idea of land-ownership at that time appears to have been rather flexible in rural France; occasional visits to court were necessary to clarify matters. One woman in Fontevraud, for example, asserted in court that, although she had indeed given a piece of land to the convent, she still reserved the right to use the land and to spend the monies it generated. The abbess made a personal appearance before the judge to make the opposite case and won. The Fontevraud record gives a revealing picture of a society still with a barely concealed undercurrent of lawlessness and violence. This is the roll-call of the local characters with whom the Abbess of Fontevraud corresponded: "Jerorius Fat-Lips," "Ogerius Sword-Rattler," "Peter Booty-Seizer," "Geoffrey Bad Monk," and "Raginald Who Folds Up Peasants"[1] — and they are just the ones who *did* give funds to the convent.

Heloise had doubtless been obliged to deal with a similar cast of characters and had triumphed. This is a significant achievement for someone who, we learn in Abelard's autobiography, had been known in Paris as an intellectual, renowned for her love of classical literature. Heloise had been obliged to develop what we might today call her management skills at a time when management was a new invention. It had become necessary to invent it largely because of the growth of monasticism itself. Monastic orders were expanding internationally to become large organizations with great wealth and power in their own right. They were in the process of inventing methods of organization suitable for large and potentially unwieldy entities. They were the first multinational corporations — monasteries developed systems of decision-making, delegation, and voting that would be recognizable in today's boardrooms. It can even be argued that they developed the principles of representative democracy that form the basis of government in today's democratic states.*

By the end of her life the place that Heloise had established for herself in this world where temporal power and religion met was

---

* The word *democracy* comes from ancient Greece, it is true, but Athenian democracy, as many people pointed out at the time, was really a sort of formalized mob rule. The entire population of the city turned out to vote on a single question. The next day, if they wanted to, they could turn out and vote on the same question quite differently. It was unstable and largely unworkable, based apparently on an almost paranoid fear of granting anybody executive power for more than a day at a time. The type of democracy with which we are familiar, where a delegate or representative is sent to take part and use a vote in a governing body, was developed in twelfth-century monasteries.

such that she could correspond as an equal with the most powerful clerics of the age. In addition to her other qualities she seems to have had the kind of intelligent charm that instills confidence among those in authority. Abelard was certainly right in one aspect of his assessment – she was indeed able to make bishops love her and abbots regard her as a sister.

It may seem surprising that a woman was able to gain a position of such status in the Middle Ages. Intuitively one might feel that, because we know that women in the past were oppressed and exclud-ed from power, the further back in time we look the more disenfran-chised women must have been. But in fact we can never rely on our intuitions about this age – the truth is more complex.

In medieval society, religion, custom, and received wisdom did indeed combine to make women appear inferior and even unaccept-able at many levels. Heloise herself acknowledges this when she later seeks advice from Abelard on how to run a convent on the grounds that women are weak and need help from men. But, for all her protes-tations of obedience to Abelard, she frequently – especially in the newly discovered early letters – expresses confidence that she is capa-ble of being his equal in matters of ideas and philosophy. There were ways in which a woman could wield power and influence even in a predominantly patriarchal society. One of them was to be an abbess. Heloise was not alone: all abbesses had not only authority within the convent but also the right – granted them by the original rule for Western monks, the rule of St. Benedict – to leave their cloisters at will and take part in whatever worldly affairs were necessary for their house. Abbesses (though not Heloise) often also had aristocratic con-nections, in which case their influence was all the greater.

Wives and mothers of kings, even more than female members of the aristocracy, had power and money that was under their own con-trol. Women in these circles commonly commissioned palaces and great works of art. Famously, for example, Blanche of Castile funded the great rose window in the transept of the cathedral of

Notre-Dame-de-Chartres. There are other examples of women who achieved fame by their intellectual abilities throughout the Middle Ages. The collected works of Hildegard of Bingen, Christine of Pisan, Julian of Norwich, Hadewijch of Antwerp, Mechthild of Magdeburg, Christina of Markyate, and Marguerite Porete would provide an impressive compendium of thought and letters spanning a 300-year period. There are also many images of women sculptors and painters, indicating quite a widespread acceptance of women in the arts. For a woman to be able to live her life independently and make her own decisions may well have been exceptional but was by no means impossible.

Another woman of the Middle Ages who might claim to have generated as much interest in modern times as Heloise, Hildegard of Bingen, was as it happens almost an exact contemporary of hers. She was an artist of enormous energy, also an abbess. Her convent was on the banks of the Rhine about 200 miles to the east of the Paraclete. The haunting music she wrote, together with strange, mystical Latin lyrics, can now be found on CD in music stores throughout the world. Her bizarre visionary paintings combine with her music to give a clear impression of a woman with an intense and highly individual intelligence. Hildegard not only ran her convent, commanding the absolute loyalty of her nuns, but was in a strong enough position to conduct a long-running dispute with the head of her order. It was a row that was to lead to her spending a long period cruelly banned from singing, but she won it in the end.

There is no evidence of the two women ever having met, or even having known of each other. It is by no means certain that, had they met, they would have got on. Heloise, champion of a newly discovered clear-sighted rationalism, is not likely to have been impressed with the woman whose typically medieval prefiguration of new-age mysticism has won her a substantial cult following in California. What the two women did have in common was that they were both the bosses of substantial institutions. Hildegard's convent had a feature that Heloise's did not: an accompanying monastery, populated by monks. These twin institutions operated in tandem, presumably with the monks helping with the manual work while the nuns con-centrated on singing and painting. "Dual-gender" monasteries like this were not uncommon. While much of the detail of their day-to-day running remains unknown, research has shown one thing: in every recorded case the abbess of the convent had precedence over the abbot of the monastery. The woman was always in charge.

When, in the autobiographical letter that she has just read, Abelard left Heloise at peace in the convent he was not necessarily abandoning her to a freakish form of incarceration. She was well on the way to becoming a successful, independent woman. Abelard might have argued that the convent was the natural culmination of the career of a gifted woman. What could be a more fitting end to her story than for her to spend the rest of her life participating in the most important project of the Middle Ages?

This version of Heloise's life would have sounded plausible to a medieval mind, even if it does not to a modern one. But if Abelard really believed that it was the whole truth it can only have been because his subsequent troubles had been so terrible that they had obliterated any memory of the true nature of Heloise's love. The let-ters she had written to him every day during the affair in Paris tell him repeatedly that her love is undying and indestructible. Lovers fre-quently profess things sincerely that later events will alter, but this was Heloise, Abelard's student who had spent hours with him dis-cussing the truth in between lovemaking. Did Abelard really believe that she would have been able to abandon everything that she said? Now she had to remind him again that he was the centre of her life: "You alone have the power to make me sad, to bring me happiness or comfort."

Abelard had been with her when she became a nun; he must have remembered that she did so not as the result of a conversion or of a change of heart, but because he told her to. Again Heloise reminds him:

At every stage of my life up to now, as God knows, I have feared to offend you rather than God, and tried to please you more than him. It was your command, not love of God, that made me take the veil. (Heloise, First Letter)

The Abbess of the Paraclete is telling Abelard that since the end of their affair her life has been a pretence. Irrespective of any external measures of success and piety, inside she is a bad nun. She took vows giving herself completely to God but, ever since their first meeting, everything she has done has been motivated by the love of Abelard. There is nothing – no vow, no incentive – that could have diverted her loyalty or distracted her from him. Heloise is completely Abelard's:

God is my witness that if Augustus, emperor of the whole world, thought fit to honor me with marriage and conferred all the earth on me for ever it would be sweeter and more honorable to me to be, not his empress, but your whore. (Heloise, First Letter)

Heloise's apparent eagerness to be Abelard's whore is quoted, properly attributed to the abbess, in that French classic of erotic submissiveness, *The Story of O.* This is not by any means the only time we find her in submissive mood: in the same letter we hear, "it was not my own pleasure and wishes I sought to gratify, as you well know, but yours." Heloise may well have derived deep satisfaction from giving herself over totally to the physical pleasure of her lover, but she never loses track of her moral and ethical thinking. It is characteristic of her that she says that to be Abelard's whore would be both "sweeter" and "more honorable" than to be an empress. Typically, in the middle of an erotic thought she is considering what is morally correct behavior. Heloise has thought deeply about all aspects of her life – in this she is the equal if not the superior of her philosopher husband – and, for her, the idea of moral rightness and the idea of their love are so deeply mixed that they cannot be separated.

Neither is she able to separate the physical nature of their love from the spiritual. Some people find, in the sexual abstinence of monasticism, relief and inner peace at being freed at last, as they see it, from the fetters of sexual desire. For the serious and reflective Abbess Heloise there seems to have been no such option. The physical delight of her affair is so intermingled with its spiritual counterpart, which is in turn mixed with ideas of religious bliss, that she can never bring herself to repudiate them:

> *In my case the pleasures of lovers that we shared have been too sweet — they can never displease me, and can scarcely be banished from my thoughts.* (Heloise, Second Letter)

Her mind is quite incapable of placing an effective barrier around her sexual self; it will reappear, unbidden, at the most inappropriate moments:

> *Even during the celebration of the Mass, when our prayers should be purest, lewd visions of the pleasures we shared take such a hold upon my unhappy soul that my thoughts are on their wantonness instead of on my prayers. Everything we did, and also the times and places, are stamped on my heart along with your image, so that I live through it all again with you.* (Heloise, Second Letter)

This is another much quoted passage: there is not a book that mentions Heloise with any seriousness that does not cite this confession. Nowhere else in medieval writing, or for a long time afterward, does anyone say anything of such shocking honesty. References to sex are not in short supply in medieval literature and art. It is not hard to find innuendo and lewdness, even blasphemous and disgusting images and ideas. But Heloise's simple confession that she thinks about sex during church services is none of these. It is not a teasing or intentionally shocking reference to sex; it is the result of her ability to see and understand her own mental processes with a disturbing clarity and to report them with honesty. This gift can be both a blessing and a curse, so it is perhaps not surprising that to this day such simple revelations are so rare.

Heloise is able to see her own feelings toward the physical pleasures she shared with Abelard with such clarity that she can never deny them. To allow herself to say she regretted them, or, even worse, to try to persuade herself to believe that she did when she didn't, would be not just hypocritical, it would be a betrayal of the philosophy, the search for truth, that she shared with Abelard.

> *I know I should be groaning over the sins I have committed, but I can only sigh for what I have lost. Everything we did and also the times and the places are stamped on my heart along with your image.* (Heloise, Second Letter)

She cannot take a way out of her dilemma that would be typical of the age and publicly repudiate what she has done as sinful. The erotic element of her love has also endured through fifteen years of separation and hardship. It is as real and as important to her as the spiritual love that she regards as part of the divine. Her love remains what it has always been: a passionate but balanced mixture of the cerebral and the physical.

A twenty-first-century Westerner, mentally putting herself in Heloise's situation, might be tempted to find another way to resolve the inner conflict. She might feel that it was medieval society that was at fault, that its emphasis on religion was an intolerable fettering of the human spirit. She might feel that her erotic yearnings were of prime importance and that she would be justified in rejecting both the religion of the Middle Ages and the society that supported it. Such thoughts, however, are not possible for the abbess. Neither she nor the rebellious logical philosopher whom she loved could entertain for a moment the idea that the tenets of their religion could be wrong. This is not the story of a woman who considered herself repressed by an authoritarian church. Heloise was, like those all around her, a believer. The struggle that we see in her is not against the prevailing beliefs of her world; it is rather her personal attempt to fit all aspects of her life into a single framework of understanding. Heloise is not betraying her religious ideas by acknowledging her sexual feelings. On the contrary, it is entirely consistent with her general program of self-knowledge, which for her and for Abelard was a necessary condition of religious understanding.

Some historians have in the past tried to reinterpret the letters as the story of a transformation: an instructive tale of the young Heloise, preoccupied with erotic thoughts, who becomes eventually the sensible abbess. But there is no evidence in the letters for a transformation; Heloise herself insists on the contrary. The authoritative abbess who sits quietly in a corner, writing at a desk as perhaps she always does at this time of day, is perfectly consistent with the picture she is painting of herself in her letter, her body arching and luxuriating in imagined pleasure, as erotic memories invade her dreams:

Even in sleep I know no respite. Sometimes my thoughts are betrayed in the movement of my body, or they break out in an unguarded word. (Heloise, Second Letter)

The coexistence of these two images gives Heloise an attractiveness that has survived for centuries. The complexity of psychology that Heloise herself expresses has proved much more powerful than the simplicity of Abelard's version of her as the perfect nun at the height of her career. The dialogue that Heloise is beginning as she writes her first letter continues to show an insight into her own and others' emotions that has fascinated and delighted readers throughout history.

Her ability as a writer is clear even in translations of her letters. In the autobiography Abelard tells a comprehensible story, leaving little that is unexplained, but when, in later letters, he is replying to Heloise he starts to justify his arguments with what to us seems a bewildering and unnecessary barrage of quotations and references. To modern eyes this makes him seem prosaic and repetitive. Quotation is part of medieval style – the Latin language was learnt through a series of quotations and, with most authors, the habit stuck – but Heloise, although she does quote, does so more sparingly and with greater effect. Abelard sometimes reads like a slightly pedantic academic; Heloise manages to keep her train of thought fluid and clear. She is such a good writer and what she says has such a ring of truth that her letters transcend whatever aspects of style time may have rendered incomprehensible. That is why on the strength of only three letters her writing has become famous. Very few authors can equal that achievement.

One of the oldest surviving copies of the letters was once in the library of Petrarch, the great Italian humanist who lived over 200 years after Heloise. Petrarch is sometimes credited with having single-handedly created the idea of the Renaissance, the new age of classical learning that was, in his opinion, sweeping away the darkness of the Middle Ages. As the champion of what he saw as a new phase of civilization he was at pains to point to the deficiencies, real or imagined, of the outgoing age. The name "Middle Ages" does a disservice to all those who lived their lives during what, depending on definition, can be a period of as long as 1,000 years. Abelard and Heloise saw the age in which they lived as almost bewilderingly modern, a time when new ideas and new things were changing the world at a dizzying speed. They were at the beginning of something, not the middle.

But even Petrarch has to make an exception to his negative view of the Middle Ages when he comes into contact with Heloise. In the margin of his copy of the book he has written excited comments. We find him cheering her on: "Totally charming and most elegant!" (*Amicissime et eleganter!*), he exclaims at one point for no particular reason. When Heloise writes to Abelard to reassure him that he was indeed the first and only man to have her, a marginal note gushes, "You, Heloise, act with the utmost sweetness and gentleness in everything!" In the same passage she confesses that it was Abelard's ability as a songwriter that first attracted her. Petrarch cannot resist a (to modern sensibilities) patronizing, but well-meant "Just like a woman!" (*Muliebriter!*). He is besotted. Petrarch has seen Heloise's full range: she is by turns intelligent, sexy, stylish, and faithful. This is a combination that has always made scholars fall for her.

Historians now speak of the "twelfth-century renaissance" and "twelfth-century humanism." These phrases are an admission that — contrary to Petrarch's opinion — various ideas and attitudes were becoming current that were once thought to have existed only much later. Many scholars now consider that in Abelard's lifetime the spirit of the age underwent a transformation; the medieval worldview was readjusted to a more human scale. It showed itself first in the way people thought about religion. In earlier ages God had been an all-powerful and capricious agent of the supernatural, visiting retribution on humanity — sometimes on whole cities and nations at one go. But now religion was starting to be seen as a personal experience: when Abelard writes about good and evil, for example, they are not defined in terms of damnation for wrongdoing but as the correct and incorrect responses to the love that God spontaneously gives to humanity.

Medieval theologians were starting to talk about the relationship between human beings and God as a kind of friendship. As a consequence, personal interactions, particularly friendship, became of great interest. Friendship was hailed as a good thing both within marriage (acceptable but always second best to celibacy) and inside the monastery. Those who write about monasticism often underplay the camaraderie that must have been one of its major appeals to both sexes. At its best, being part of a monastery must have been like being a member of a club. Shared hardship in a joint enterprise can draw people together into a wonderfully cohesive unit — actors who work in the same production, crews who race the same ship, even soldiers who serve in the same unit can all attest to this phenomenon. The monk Aelred of Rievaulx, writing just after Abelard's death, was so taken by the special strength of comradeship in the monastery that he declared that "friendship is wisdom" and even said "God is friendship."[2]

Heloise grew up in a world of developing awareness of the individual. It is the foundation of her love of Abelard. Her specific, individual love cannot be overwhelmed by her social and religious responsibilities as head of a convent. It has not died. She writes about it in the present tense: "I have finally denied myself every pleasure in obedience to your will, I am yours," she affirms in her letter, and again, "now, even more, I am yours."

Her love will continue and remain constant with or without sexual gratification, with or without contact. The letter she is writing is not prompted by a longing for the past: although she tells Abelard that all the times and places are fresh in her mind, she never makes an attempt to rekindle the feeling by recalling special moments. The purpose of her letter is not to look back; it is a request for action:

> It is a small thing I ask of you and one you could so easily grant
> ... I beg you to restore your presence to me in the way you can —
> by writing me some word of comfort ... I beg you think of what
> you owe me, give ear to my pleas. (Heloise, First Letter)

The final pages of the letter constitute an extended plea. The Latin for "I beg," *obsecro,* is repeated again and again — it is a word that had been used since the Romans to beseech gods and emperors for favors. Although sometimes her words seem to be requesting no more than a reply — "whatever you write will bring us no small relief in the mere proof that you have us in mind" — it is clear from the context that she is asking for something more than just a few lines on any subject. She wants Abelard to acknowledge the special mixture of friendship and love that they had created together in Paris fifteen years before.

She knows that she will have to cajole and implore him to respond to her request. One letter will not be enough; if he is to give her what she wants it will only be after a protracted dialogue. But she makes a start by marshaling her arguments. She finds several ways to remind Abelard of what she regards as his duty to reopen the philosophical friendship. First, she makes appeal to the fact that it was actually he who founded the Paraclete — Heloise only took it over later, after he had moved on. She points out that he has an obligation not just to her but to all the nuns of the community. He has made a start but more is required:

> *You have done your duty as to friends . . . but it is a greater debt that binds you in obligation to us who can properly be called not friends so much as dearest friends, not comrades but daughters, or any other conceivable name more tender and holy.* (Heloise, First Letter)

Heloise has reminded him that she became a nun in the first place as an act of submission to him. Her submission, however, goes only so far. Now she uses it as a negotiating point; Abelard is in her debt:

> *I have finally denied myself every pleasure in obedience to your will, kept nothing for myself except to prove that now, even more, I am yours. And so, in the name of God to whom you have dedicated yourself, I beg you to restore your presence to me in the way that you can — by writing some word of comfort, so that at least I may find increased strength and readiness to serve God.* (Heloise, First Letter)

She even tries to taunt him with the suggestion that the whole affair might have been merely physical on his part. The evidence of the letters — both newly discovered and established — is that this was very definitely not the case. Heloise has probably judged the psychology of the individual correctly. Abelard is quite likely to be goaded by an accusation of shallowness:

Why, after our entry into religion, which was your decision alone, have I been so neglected and forgotten by you that I have neither a word from you when you are here to give me strength nor the consolation of a letter in absence? Tell me, I say, if you can — or I will tell you what I think and indeed the world suspects. It was desire not affection that bound you to me — the flame of lust rather than love. (Heloise, First Letter)

Her argument mostly rests, however, on the idea that their love is such that it creates a duty — she frequently calls it a debt — for Abelard. The spiritual duty of love is for her much more binding than the temporal duty of marriage:

You are bound to me by an obligation that is all the greater for the further close tie of marriage sacrament uniting us, and are the deeper in my debt because of the love that I have always borne for you, as everyone knows, a love that is beyond all bounds. (Heloise, First Letter)

Heloise is determined that she will not abandon the love that is beyond all bounds. Her letter is full of complaint but it is also full of a hope for an improved future, rediscovered love. She is not ending a story with a satisfying closure as Abelard wanted; she is beginning, or rather restarting, something. She ends the letter with a final "*obsecro*" and, with a skilled writer's feeling for rhythm, she creates an effect with a startlingly brief farewell:

I beg you, think now what you owe me, give ear to my pleas, and I will finish a long letter with a brief ending: farewell my only love. (Heloise, First Letter)

What the English renders as "farewell my only love" is even crisper in Latin: "*vale unice,*" a neat, assonant phrase. Perhaps it is not the first time she has used it. She may be recalling other farewells, made when their affair was a wonderful secret, familiar phrases whispered in haste before Abelard tiptoed back to his own room.

The letter is finished. It is evening now; the bell sounds for Vespers. The abbess must once again take her love, her emotions, and the story that led her to this moment, close them up inside herself and assume her role as leader of a convent. She folds the letter, ties it up and seals it. Perhaps she slips it inside her habit like a secret, perhaps it goes with a pile of other letters where there will be no risk of special treatment drawing to it unwelcome attention. Eventually it will be handed to a trusted layperson (who will be properly motivated by the promise of cash on delivery) and begin its long journey to Brittany where Abelard is living out an agonizing period of exile.

As the bell sounds she leaves her quiet place and makes her way to the chapel with the dignity appropriate to an abbess, descending by the stairs that connect the dormitory to the chapel for the convenience of the sisters attending night prayers. Outwardly she follows the service. Inwardly she reviews her situation: the minor irritations of the day, the responsibilities of her office, memories of sexual delight, memories of love. Her analytical mind turns them over, trying to perceive in them the elusive unity that all of us seek in the story of our own life. She goes over the story again, assessing right and wrong, selfishness and generosity, loyalty and betrayal, recalling above all the wild man of medieval logic whom she met in Paris so long ago.

TWO

"At last I came to Paris"

> I began to travel about in several provinces disputing, like a true peripatetic
> philosopher, wherever I had heard keen interest in the art of dialectic. At last I
> came to Paris, where dialectic has been particularly flourishing.
> *Abelard, Autobiography*

ETER ABELARD, the man who was to become Heloise's only love, arrived in Paris from his native Brittany in the year 1100, at the dawn of a century that was to see change and innovation in every aspect of existence. He was 21 years old; he would not meet Heloise for over a decade. In the autobiographical letter he devotes only a single paragraph to his place of birth, education and early travels before he gets to the moment when he arrived – "at last" – in Paris. It is from that moment that he himself counts the real beginning of his career as a philosopher and therefore of his life.

The description he gives of himself at this stage does not lack confidence. He was, he says, quick-witted, good-looking, and amusing – "preeminent in grace of youth and form." Heloise, when she met him several years later, did not disagree – "What perfection of mind or body did not adorn your youth? . . . What woman did not envy me my place in your bed?"[1] He was also well born and, although as we shall see he was not keen to talk about them, he seems to have had some rather impressive contacts. He had come to Paris to indulge the first great love of his life – logic.

At logic Abelard was a natural. He was like a prizefighter, a master of the cut and thrust, inference and counterinference, of philosophical debate. In stand-up fights and in considered analysis, his skill at exposing the weak points in his opponents' arguments was without equal. It was all done with the supreme confidence of one who knows beyond doubt that the cold clear instrument of logic will always lay bare the truth. Not only did he have faith that the truth was attainable, he knew with unerring certainty that he was the man to find it. After only a few successes at sparring with his rivals he would, as he confesses in the autobiography, think himself the only philosopher in the world. When, a little later, Heloise became his adoring student she would back him in that belief — "You are clear-er than glass, stronger than steel," she tells him. She eggs him on in his bouts with the intellectuals of Paris: "You are a teacher of char-acter, a teacher of virtue, to whom French pigheadedness rightly yields." She correctly perceives in him the makings of a far-reaching greatness — "Although it may be in the future, I already see the moun-taintops bowing down before you." She begins one letter to him: "To my shining light, the city set on a hill, may he fight in order to con-quer, run in order to win."[2]

The confidence of the lovers was justified in at least one respect. Even at the end, nobody — neither the enemies who crowded round him when he was weak nor the powerful people who protected him who were gone, not even his archenemy, Bernard of Clairvaux, who wilfully misinterpreted his every word and tried to spread it about that he was some kind of deranged sorcerer — not one of them ever asserted that Abelard was not in one respect exactly what he claimed to be: the greatest logician of the age.

He had all the strengths of a great logical thinker: a gift for abstraction, tenacious clarity of mind, the nerve to take his reasoning into areas others considered unsafe. He also had one weakness char-acteristic of an abstract thinker: the tendency, at crucial moments in his life, to fail completely to understand the psychology of those around him. In those moments — when his logical insight told him he was right — he could see the truth of the situation like a plain fact, something that was just obvious, which needed no discussion. Those who disagreed appeared, in the heat of mental combat, not even to be worthy of consideration. By failing to see the truth of the argument, either from stupidity or some evil intent, it was as if they had excluded themselves from the human race. Inflamed by the desperation of one who sees the truth being wilfully denied by wicked people, he would react with rage — one contemporary account describes him as a rhinoceros. Even when not locked in verbal struggle with an opponent, Peter Abelard could exhibit that disastrous inattention to the feelings of others that is often read as hostility, even cruelty, and reacted to with mistrust and aggression. He had a gift for making enemies. There must have been ill-suppressed joy in many a theologian's cell when eventually, twenty years later, his most daring new ideas were officially declared erroneous. It was only with the insight of maturity that he was able to confess to Heloise toward the end of his life that "logic has made me hated in the world."[3]

Abelard always played to win. The quiet and scholarly search for truth is described by him in his autobiography as if it were a competitive sport, or even mortal combat. When describing the decision to choose philosophy as a career he uses the language of the jousting field rather than the lecture room:

> I preferred the weapons of dialectic to all the other teachings of philosophy, and armed with these I chose the conflicts of disputation rather than the trophies of war. (Abelard, Autobiography)

He himself ascribed his combative nature to the soil of Brittany, where he was born, but it seems more likely to be due to family rather than location. He was a nobleman and his family were therefore in the business of land-ownership and warfare. The young Abelard, however, renounced the inheritance to which he was entitled as the eldest son in favor of life as a scholar. In order to experience the thrill of philosophical combat he had given up not only physical combat as a knight in war but what could also have been a very comfortable existence.

His family were land-owning noblemen living in the small town of le Pallet in Brittany, then an independent duchy. He is at pains to point out that it is just on the edge of Brittany, at the gateway to the more sophisticated duchy of Anjou in the western Loire valley. Today le Pallet is perhaps best pinpointed as the center of the Sèvre-et-Maine wine-growing area to the southeast of Nantes, where Muscadet is produced. Historians of wine date the first planting of vines in the area to the beginning of the eleventh century, so it can be reasonably hazarded that muscadet-producing vineyards were among the possessions of Abelard's family. Le Pallet's 2,500 inhabitants are becoming increasingly aware of their most famous son: a recently erected road sign proclaims "le Pallet, Cité d'Abélard." There is no museum commemorating Abelard in his home town but the local (very interesting and informative) wine museum has recently opened a room dedicated to him. On the hill at the edge of the town the foundations of what was once a medieval castle can still be discerned. The only structure still standing is farther down the slope: a ruined chapel, claimed, quite plausibly, to date from the eleventh century. It seems reasonable to imagine therefore that Abelard himself might have prayed there; it is now designated by the town's guide book as la chapelle d'Abélard. The surrounding countryside is flat and, standing on the hill, it is not hard to imagine the isolated agrarian community that surrounded the castle in Abelard's day. It was probably relatively prosperous, undevastated by major wars, but still part of a world where political authority was structured by ancient feudal allegiances and backed up by force of arms.

Abelard's father, whose name according to a contemporary writer was Berengar, was not himself a Breton but came from the neighboring county of Poitou. Berengar seems to have married the daughter of the lord of le Pallet. So far as can be deduced from Abelard's own account and from the records of the Paraclete, they had five children: one daughter, Dionisia (Denise), and four sons, whom the Latin text names as Dagobertus, Porcarius, Rudaltus, and Petrus (Peter "Abelard"), who was the eldest.

The lord of le Pallet, of whose household Berengar was a member, would have had not only property and wealth but also military responsibility. In times of war he would have to raise an army from among the peasants on his estates. The family was apparently on quite close social terms with the Duke of Brittany, and later in his life Abelard made a special journey to visit him when he was ill. It does seem that Peter came over as someone high up the social scale: during his career in Paris people would sometimes call him "Palatinus," a pun meaning both "man from le Palet" and also "man from the palace," presumably because his relatively grand origins were conspicuous in academic circles.

As eldest son Peter stood to inherit both his father Berengar's feudal title and the associated property and income, but Berengar had probably inadvertently offered his son something that was then very rare – the ability to decide his own future:

> *My father had acquired some knowledge of letters before he was a soldier, and later on his passion for learning was such that he intended all his sons to have instruction in letters before they were trained to arms.* (Abelard, Autobiography)

It was perhaps because of his origins in Anjou, to the east of Brittany, which prided itself on its cultured courts frequented by poets and troubadours, that Berengar had educated his boys (but not his daughter). It was crucial to Abelard's choice of career that he was able to read Latin from an early age. Without that he would have been unable to read anything – reading at that time meant reading Latin. There were no books in French and, although there were songs and poems, attempts to write them down show a huge amount of uncertainty and variation. Latin, on the other hand, was a well-established language that united all people in Europe who could read. In the Middle Ages Western Europeans actually referred to themselves as "the Latins" to distinguish themselves from their Christian neighbors in Byzantium, who spoke Greek.

Everyday conversation was, however, almost never in Latin, the exceptions being in religious institutions and the student area of Paris. At home Abelard's family would have spoken what was called at the time a "vulgar tongue," meaning a language used by the common people. Presumably it was French in their case, as the father came from outside Brittany. Abelard does not seem to have spoken Breton: he is at pains to point out rather dismissively that, when later in his career he was exiled to the monastery of St. Gildas de Rhuys in northern Brittany, he could not understand a word of the local monks' dialect. In fact Abelard does not seem to have liked Brittany very much. He not only tells us with pride that he didn't speak their language but in one of his lectures he even seems to be getting a cheap laugh out of a pun referring to Bretons as "brutes."

Had Abelard wished to stay on and inherit his father's position he would have been obliged to remain on the estate in order to learn the skills of feudal husbandry and make himself available for occasional military service. He would not have been able to attend the schools in Paris or to have access to libraries. There was probably very little time taken for the decision; the call of logic was too strong – "I renounced the glory of a soldier's life and made over my inheritance and rights of the eldest son to my brothers."[4] As eldest son he could in fact have gone back to claim his inheritance at any time until, much later in life, he became a monk and therefore was forbidden material posses-sions.

Having turned his back on life as a Breton aristocrat, Abelard traveled through the towns of Anjou, studying at cathedral schools along the way. In his own account he is in such a hurry to get on with the story that he does not give any detail, but we do know from another source that he spent some time in the town of Loches in the valley of the Loire learning philosophy and studying at the feet of Roscelin, one of the big names of the generation before him. When he had proved to his own satisfaction, and from Roscelin's account to others' distress, that he was destined for success on the battlefield of logical debate he felt he was ready for Paris.

Abelard had other qualities, not always found in a logician: under the right circumstances he seems to have had a talent for enter‑ tainment. Heloise may have admired his intellectual abilities but she also says specifically that the thing that first attracted her to him was his ability to write popular songs:

> *You had also two special gifts that would win the heart of any*
> *woman — your gift for composing verse and song . . . The beauty*
> *of your tunes ensured that even the uneducated did not forget you.*
> (Heloise, First Letter)

He had probably first learned to write songs while he was travel‑ ing along the Loire valley in Poitou and Anjou, the country of the troubadours. Nobody writes popular songs independently of an existing culture of performance and composition, so he must have mixed with performers who worked in the courts of noblemen and in the taverns, quite possibly even performing himself. That Heloise tells us it is the *tunes* that were remembered by the uneducated implies that the *words* were written in Latin — the ordinary people could only hum along. Unfortunately, none of Abelard's popular songs has sur‑ vived; many of his hymns, however, do exist and in them he shows himself to be an able lyricist.

He seems to have had the ability to entertain his students as well. All the accounts of his teaching (including, of course, his own) agree that his lectures were very popular. One account remarks that students came from far‑off Germany and even braved the perils of the sea‑crossing from England to hear him. Another account men‑ tions how amusing and even funny he was. The ability to amuse stu‑ dents when lecturing is not necessarily at odds with the picture of Abelard as the irascible and combative dialectician who managed to alienate almost every one of his contemporaries. He might well have reacted with rage to an opposing philosopher but with warmth to an audience of young minds who had come with the express purpose of hearing his thoughts. Humor too can have different effects, depend/ ing on the audience: what is amusing and witty to a class of students might well seem flip and supercilious to an old/established church/ man.

His name also has an element of show business in it. "Abelard" is not a name he was given at his baptism; he conferred it on himself as a sort of act of self/invention. It is a stage name, the sort of thing normally adopted by troubadours, not philosophers. It is not known why he chose this particular name. It has been suggested that it is a pun on the word "lard" because there is some indication that he was physically quite large. This is not necessarily at odds with his descrip/ tion of himself as handsome. Bodily size, in a culture where food is less plentiful, can look like an indicator of that great determinant of male attractiveness, material wealth. Whatever the reason, Abelard the performer chose his own name.*

At the time of writing, in the Nantes telephone directory (the modern city closest to his home town), there are thirteen people listed with the surname Abelard. It is puzzling how the name could have survived. In the twelfth century inherited surnames were only just beginning to be used and many of them were indeed derived from nicknames. It is, however, quite hard to see how "Abelard" could have ended up being used by descendants of Abelard. He and

---

* Nobody was quite sure how to spell it, though. The man whom Heloise calls "my only one" appears in manuscripts, public records, songs, and poems with his name spelled in a wide variety of ways. The very helpful and informative German Web site www.abaelard.de lists them: Abaalardus, Abaalarz, Abalardus, Abalard, Abarlardus, Abaelardus, Abaëlardus, aBaGelardus, Abagelardus, Abaelar, Abaelart, Abaialardus, Abbajalarius, Abaielardus, Abaielart, Abaillardus, Abailar, Abaielard, Abailardus, Abailart, Abailard, Abaillard, Abaiolardus, Abaiulardus, Abaulardus, Abaulard, Abaulart, Abaylardus, Abayelard, Abbaalardus, Abbaelardus, Abelardus, Abélard, Abelard, Abälard, Abeilard, Abéilard, Abellardus, Abellard, Abeillard, Aboilard, Abulart, Abulard, Abylardus, Adbaiolardus, Alardus, Allebart, Baalardus, Balard, Baalaurdus, Baelardus, Bailardus, Baillard, Baiolardus, Baiulardus, Baialardus, Balaardus, Baylardus, Bealaardus, Belardus, Beillard, Biolardus, Esveillard, Esbaillart, Espaillart, Habaelardus, Habelardus.

Heloise were indeed destined to have a son who himself became a monk and although, as is clear from this story, that does not necessarily mean that he had no offspring, it would be unlikely that any children he did have would have adopted the nickname of their clerical grandfather. Perhaps the Abelards of Brittany are in fact descended from some later admirer of Peter of le Pallet.

The confident and good-looking young man was plainly cut out for city life, especially in a city like Paris. But in 1100 he was just a little early. Only during his time there did Paris become what could really be called a city. When he arrived it was not obvious that it was even the major town in France. Orléans, to the south, was slightly larger and was regarded at the time as at least of equal importance. Louis VI, for example, chose, in 1108, to be crowned there rather than in Paris. By the end of Abelard's life, however, several factors had combined to make Paris not only a city but the capital of France.

What would have struck Abelard as a newcomer on his first day in Paris was the large number of ruined buildings to be found there. During the 700 years or so since the end of the Roman empire the city had fared rather badly. In Roman times it had been called Lutetia, which, appropriately enough for a city with its center on an island, is said to mean "midwater dwelling."* During Roman times, it was a wealthy trading town with all the typical Roman amenities: aqueducts, roads, a theater, a bathhouse. Lutetia wasn't a Lyons, or even a Londinium, but it was a substantial town whose central area spread over the left bank of the Seine to the south, covering the area between the river and what is now the Sorbonne.

In the period of turmoil known as the Dark Ages that followed the end of the Roman empire, Paris had been obliged to become more and more a defensive settlement. It pulled in its extremities and huddled for safety on the island in the river Seine, known today as the Ile de la Cité. Its nature began to change. No longer were there bath-

---

* The name Paris derives from the name of the Celtic tribe, the Parigii, who lived there in Roman times.

houses and theaters. Paris, like all early medieval cities, comprised a collection of walled monasteries and fortified houses. Each of these was capable of autonomous life, owning land and serfs, farming, and bringing the harvest back within the keep. Trading with other institutions and other cities did occur, but it was minimal compared to the home-produced sustenance that the monks and the soldiers enjoyed in their respective institutions. Defensive walls were the defining feature of the units that made up the city, and the inhabitants were ready at all times to shelter inside them in the event of trouble. And trouble was frequent enough: Normans and Vikings had in the past used the river Seine as a convenient artery along which to launch raids, snatching goods and people that could be exchanged for ready currency further down the line. The island in the river was the most defensible area and as a result, even in Abelard's time, not only did it have its own houses and monasteries but the outlying ones on the banks each maintained a smaller house on the island so that in an emergency everybody could withdraw into a final, extra-secure enclosure.

Many of the ruins that greeted Abelard in 1100 – on the island itself and on the banks of the Seine – dated from 885, when things did indeed get very bad. A concerted raid by Vikings had destroyed most of the area settlement and dealt it a psychological as well as a physical blow from which it had not yet recovered. There were churches on the southern banks that remained damaged from that raid that were not rebuilt until after Abelard's death. Even the royal palace on the island was still in ruins, although it was restored during his lifetime. On the site of the current Notre-Dame-de-Paris, or rather just behind it, was the ruin of a much bigger Romanesque cathedral of St. Stephen. It was never rebuilt, just swept away as the influence of Notre-Dame increased – partly because of its famous cathedral school that Abelard was about to join. Also to the south of the island the ruins of Roman opulence still survived: the theaters, one of which is today commemorated in the name of the Rue des Arènes, and the baths, which are still there and still a ruin, now adapted to house the Musée de Cluny, the beautiful Parisian museum of the Middle Ages.

This area just south of the island, across the bridge that was known, then as now, as the Petit Pont, was charming, as areas with ruins often are. The banks of the river at the time were much more like the Loire, with sandbanks and beaches rather than the built-up stone *quais* that line the Seine today. One writer, Geoffrey of St. Victor, described them as a nice place for a swim; another, Guy of Bazoches, said that people liked to gather there and discuss issues of the day.[5]

This area, the left bank, 200 years later would become what it is even to this day: the intellectual center of Paris. It would become known as the Latin Quarter because the students there were obliged to speak Latin even during their evenings out in the taverns. In Abelard's lifetime it would, however, remain rural: an unspoiled area where vines stretched up the gentle slope away from the city, containing nothing more than a few barns and a wine press.

The king of France at the time was Louis VI, a young man of about Abelard's age, known even during his lifetime as Louis the Fat. Louis is generally credited with being one of the kings who put France on the road to stable nationhood. What people in Abelard's time meant by France was the area stretching from just north of Paris to just south of Orléans – approximately the present Ile de France. Surrounding dukedoms – Anjou, Poitou, Beauce, and Abelard's own Brittany – owed allegiance to the king in theory, but quite how this was expressed was variable. The situation was further complicated by the political fallout of the Norman invasion of England in 1066. The Duke of Normandy was now also the king of England; Brittany was not sure whether to ally itself with France (French-speaking southern Brittany, where Abelard came from, tended to side with France; the north had more flexible loyalties). The situation in Anjou was even more complicated: in theory the duchy owed allegiance to the king of France but in fact the count of Anjou was the son-in-law of the king of England, so his loyalty was moderated by other considerations.

In addition to the autonomous political units that surrounded his relatively small kingdom, the French king had to play out a political game with the various barons and other nobles who had territories within the kingdom. They each owned land, commanded the people who lived there, and could therefore raise armies. Louis took a firm line with his barons. One chronicler has a story of him dispatching a nobleman who had raised an army against him with the words "chess isn't the only game where you are not allowed to take the king."[6]

It was to be a squabble with just such a baron that would cause Louis to take the measures that would set Paris on the road to becoming a true city. Eleven years after Abelard's arrival, while the king was away from Paris fighting a long campaign against Henry I of England, one of the many fractious lords, the comte de Meulan, who, thanks to the sharing out of power occasioned by the recent Norman invasion of England was also the earl of Leicester, decided to take a chance and capture Paris. The land on which the king was fighting at the time actually belonged to Meulan, so there was a rather shaky quid pro quo justification for the incursion. At any rate, he probably didn't find the operation too difficult to plan as he himself owned a castle in Paris, just across the river from Louis's palace.

The chronicler tells us that he took possession of the city in the year 1111 and destroyed the wooden bridges by fire in order to consolidate his position. At the time Abelard was teaching at a monastery on a hill to the south of Paris – on the site of the present Sorbonne – so presumably he had a perfect view when the Petit Pont went up in flames. The events that followed are referred to only tantalizingly briefly by the chronicler, but what seems to have happened is that the people of Paris did something for which in succeeding centuries they were to become justly famous. They took the political process into their own hands and made it impossible for Meulan to continue his occupation. Manifestations of popular feeling were not so uncommon in the Middle Ages as one might think: it does not seem to have taken much to provoke a serious bout of questioning of authority among the people about whom medieval history, in the normal run of things, has nothing to say. In fact it is unlikely that Meulan could have held Paris even with the consent of the people. The king was in the end more powerful. All societies, especially medieval ones, tend to support the status quo and he would have found eventually that the church as well as the rulers of surrounding territories would have made life untenable for the perpetrator of so gross an act of usurpation.

In the wake of Meulan's withdrawal Louis VI reoccupied his palace and started a program of fortification and modernization of the city. He rebuilt the palace and added a fine modern tower with a fortified garden walk linking it to the old building. He also founded a couple of monasteries but, more important, he learned from the experience of the torching of the bridges and rebuilt them in stone. The bridge to the north, the Grand Pont, he rebuilt in a slightly different place. Previously it had led onto land belonging to one of the noblemen who had been causing him trouble. He now rebuilt it a little to the west so that it led onto royal land where he could build a defensive emplacement, a small castle, or *châtelet*. Today the site is commemorated by a square of that name and a Métro station that is one of the major junctions of the Paris underground railway system.

The presence of the *châtelet* on the bank to the north of the island provided a very reassuring emergency refuge. For this reason it was in this area that the city of Paris first began to grow. As Heloise and Abelard were beginning their affair Paris was expanding along the road out of the *châtelet* that led toward the great and ancient monastery of St.-Denis that was to be of great significance in Abelard's life. The monastery was seen by the king as an advanced defense against attack from the north. It was therefore given preferential treatment and grew in wealth and prestige, another reason why it was the road that is still called the rue St.-Denis that became the commercial thoroughfare of the new Paris.

It is trade that makes cities increase their size. In addition to creating a secure zone to the north of the island, Louis introduced a number of measures to stimulate trade. He removed the tax on bakers but imposed a tax on goods being transported by boat through the city. The local guild of river boatmen and allied trades, the *Marchands de l'eau,* were given exclusive rights to all waterborne commerce with in Paris. This had the effect, at a stroke, of encouraging the build up of the urban infrastructure and of eliminating competition from merchants from the downstream city of Rouen, who were no longer allowed to sail into the center of Paris and undercut local traders. A new annual royal fair was inaugurated near the rue St. Denis. It was opened with an official blessing by Gilbert, the Bishop of Paris, armed with a fragment of the true cross sent from Jerusalem specially for the occasion. Such was the proliferation of buildings in the new Paris that by the 1140s merchants were having to join forces to buy the land on which they held their market, the place de la Grève, in order to save it from being built over with new housing. As the general wealth increased, the industry that makes its profits by handling money itself began to emerge. Money changers started to cluster on the new stone Grand Pont, forming the beginning of the banking system that is a necessary condition of healthy trade. Very soon the bridge became known as the pont au Change, which remains its name today.

Presumably among the shops along the rue St. Denis could be found the taverns in which Abelard's popular songs, which so attracted Heloise to him and brought him fame "even amongst the unlearned," were first sung. Nowadays the street is lined at night with rather intimidating prostitutes. On an evening stroll along its dingier end it is hard not to imagine that in Abelard's day in the same place their twelfth century sisters would have already started to trade on the ancient connection between sex and money. Prostitutes are, after all, an urban phenomenon – in a rural setting it is hard to find the client base to support it as a full time occupation. The growing population of Paris, with its new disposable income, encouraged a proliferation of prostitutes, as did the warriors returning from the crusades with memories of action in the bordellos of Byzantium.

Predictably, this was of concern to many contemporary commenta-tors. There was a debate about whether the ladies of the night should even be allowed to go to church or give alms. In the end the argument that while in church they at least were not on the streets triumphed. One commentator frankly admitted that there were too many of them to think about banning them and – to the credit of medieval moralizers – pimps tended to attract more disapprobation than pros-titutes themselves.

The changes that Louis instigated in Paris were of great impor-tance, but they were really a response to wider changes that were shaping the Europe of the twelfth century. Over the previous 200 years the general pattern of weather had changed for the better, allowing farmers to gather bigger harvests for the same amount of effort. Improved techniques of metallurgy, which were to provide sculptors with the better chisels they needed to produce the beautiful statuary in the new Gothic style, could also be used to make sharper and more efficient ploughshares. When the ploughs were pulled by horses instead of oxen, as was increasingly the case, more land could be farmed by the same number of people, producing more food per head of population.

The immediate effect of a food surplus on a society is to make it feel more secure, a feeling enhanced by the fact that, although warfare was still a commonplace of European life and would remain so for 900 years, the type of conflict had at least been contained. People were no longer subjected to such frequent excoriating raids as they had been in the Dark Ages. Neither was there yet the all-out grueling warfare among nations that characterized, for instance, the fourteenth and so many centuries after. While Abelard had been in the Loire valley the first crusade had been mobilized; the second would take place shortly after his death. Some historians believe that this actual-ly made Europe more peaceful. Any young man who had decided, unlike Abelard, to pursue a military career could seek excitement and glory in the Middle East without disrupting the peaceful pros-perity of his homeland. Europe had effectively found a way of exporting a large fraction of its aggression to the general benefit of those at home.

Historical records from almost all cultures show that more food and relative social stability result in an increase in population; people feel confident enough to marry earlier and are more assured that they will be able to feed children when they arrive. Earlier marriages produce more children, who in the next generation will in their turn produce more, and so on. By 1100 this process had been under way for some time. The population had greatly increased with the result that there were people to spare who, so long as they themselves could be provided with food, could work on things other than agriculture. Sculptors, builders, architects, musicians, poets, and philosophers all have to eat, as did the students who paid to hear Abelard's lectures, and the other academics who worried about whether or not he was a heretic. They could exist only because twelfth-century France was rich enough to produce surplus food on a reliable basis.

More people doing new things constitute a changing society – the world of Abelard and Heloise was one of rapid change and newness. This in itself was a new development that was reflected in language: it was around this time that writers began for the first time to use the word "modern" – or its Latin equivalent derived from the words *modus* (manner) and *hodiernus* (of today) – in its current sense of something that is up to the minute in the context of a changing world. The new word had applications in many areas. In music, for example, a great innovation happened in the Paris of Abelard: Leoninus, the master of music in the cathedral of Notre-Dame, developed multipart harmony, an idea that has remained at the center of western music ever since. To have heard it for the first time, having heard previously nothing but plain chant and simple melody, must have enriched the world of the hearer beyond imagining.

At the same time the visual arts were stimulated by a proliferation of new churches (built to service the increased population), all of which needed to be fitted out with the instructive decoration that was at the heart of popular religion. Visual representation blossomed:

first came the fantastic and inventive Romanesque sculpture that can still be seen on the portals of French churches in Vézelay, Autun, and Moissac. As works of art they appear primitive at first sight but in fact are frequently masterpieces of graphical innovation, conjuring up a world of the imagination that flips, in a very modern way, between comedy and horror. Later came the Gothic style of art and architecture, elegant and, to its first viewers, exhilaratingly modern. The first Gothic building was the renovated abbey of St. Denis built toward the end of Abelard's career.

Cities felt the effects of change most: not since the Roman empire had there been such significant urban populations with spare money in their pockets. Commentators at the time foresaw that this state of affairs would undermine the old loyalties of feudalism. Serfs had almost no cash; they had no need of it because they were tied to the land that provided their food. But the people in the cities were quite different. They were no longer restricted to the single country inn that doled out a mug of ale to one lone traveler a week. They had streets full of taverns that vied with each other for business. Not for them the arranged marriage with the only available girl in the village. They saw new people every day. These new possibilities meant that patterns of marriage, like patterns of loyalty, began to shift and widen. This new state of affairs was beginning to change the existing social order irreversibly.

Each person who plays a part in the story of Abelard's life – friend or foe, clever or simple – is motivated to some extent by the need to cope with these changes. Some of them were struggling to maintain the status quo. Some railed against the changes, thinking they were going back to the basics of some previous age when in fact they were advocating radical reforms. Others, like Abelard, saw in the changing world an opportunity to move forward and solve at last the long-standing puzzles of the past.

The existence of so many groups, each reacting to change in different ways, inevitably led to conflict. While the cities with their spare cash and increased mobility generated freedom and flexibility for their populations, many clerics embraced the idea of change because it promised an opportunity to renew and purify the church. An increased emphasis on celibacy and a reassertion of the power of bishops and clergy were both part of a new reforming clerical move-ment that had by that time become a significant political force.

The chronicler Guibert of Nogent, writing while Abelard was in Paris, makes an impassioned complaint about modern young women speaking out of turn and discussing matters of love in open conversation. Heloise certainly seems to fit into this pattern, although no doubt at a more elevated intellectual level than most. Guibert settles into a lengthy complaint about modern styles of dress, a favorite theme of those who criticize the young of any generation. These same young women who talk so freely, he tells us, select their clothes in order to excite desire: tight dresses, wide sleeves, shoes from Cordoba with long curling beaks.[7] Shoes with excessively pointed toes were a major issue throughout the Middle Ages. Three centuries later they were still being complained of and indeed banned by sumptuary laws designed to curb the ostentations of the nobility.

That Guibert fingers Cordoba as the origin of this fashion is sig-nificant. As one of the major cities of Muslim Spain it was a likely source of heresy and contamination. Attitudes to the Islamic world were also complicated by a nagging feeling that it was actually more civilized, more cultured, and had a much better handle on such qual-ities as good manners. In a situation like this two apparently opposite anxieties can be combined by accusing the other culture of being a source of decadent and effete contamination. Muslim Spain was, according to some, too civilized for its own good. Another French chronicler, Orderic Vitalis, goes so far as to name the guilty man who introduced the new shoes to France. He blames Fulk, the count of Anjou – an area known for troubadours and effete habits including, again according to Orderic, long hair for men.[8] It was also, as it hap-pened, the area in which Abelard gained his philosophical training.

Cities respond, almost like an organism, to new ideas and new people. It is hard not to imagine that the Paris of Abelard had begun to develop at least a little of its characteristic elegance and excitement – the beginnings of the "buzz" that it retains to this day. Heloise herself was a well-brought-up girl, the niece of a cathedral canon from one of the higher strata of society, so perhaps we should not try to visualise her stepping out across the pont au Change in a clingy dress with six-inch toes on her shoes. Plainly, however, that is what some girls did, and Paris became a better city because of it.

At this time new, fashionable ways of behaving, even of moving, were being invented. Genteel comportment – a correct way of doing things that marked out the civilized from the uncivilized person – began to be sought after. It started in the monasteries. Devout and respectful deportment was felt to be an important step in a monk's religious training; treatises were written on the subject. When ineptly practiced, a monk trying to follow somebody else's rules as to how to move his hands and body must have produced a stilted, even comical effect – Abelard himself attacks one of his philosophical opponents for overblown gesturing. But in the right person who had a genuine feeling of inner peace it is not hard to see that graceful movement would contribute to the feeling of contemplative calm that we associate with a monastery and that is so powerfully evoked to this day by medieval plainsong.

Increased interest in good writing style – the literary equivalent of the new, civilized way of behaving – is the reason for the survival of the newly discovered love letters of Heloise and Abelard. In their daily exchanges of secret notes the couple experimented with a kind of verbal equivalent of good deportment. They invented poetical phrases for each other, and for their feelings. They worked out clever tricks with language and with ideas, all the time trying to display the mark of civilized writing: good classical Latin. Johannes de Vepria, the copyist who is responsible for the survival of the early letters, made his collection in order to demonstrate this good style. Slightly annoyingly, therefore, he extracts examples of fine writing from the letters, often the opening and closing formulas, ignoring the meat in between. This frequently leaves the modern reader lacking information that is vital to the understanding of the letter, and, no doubt, much else that would be of incomparable interest. He does, however, redeem himself in the eyes of historians by including more and more text as he becomes increasingly absorbed in the story. The beginnings and the ends of the recently discovered letters do indeed follow conventional patterns but sometimes, especially for a gifted writer, the constraints of convention can be an aid to creativity rather than a hindrance. Even the briefest of Heloise's notes from the newly discovered letters are both elegant and original:

> *To one flowing with milk and honey, the whiteness of milk and the sweetness of honey, I send the flood of delight and the increase of joy . . .*

> *I give you the most precious thing I have — myself, firm in faith and love, steady in desire, never changeable.* (Heloise, Early Letters, 102)

Conventional behavior and stylized language would, in the hands of those less gifted than Heloise, turn into the formalized mode of conducting an amorous relationship known as courtly love. To us courtly love is mannered and artificial — masking feelings rather than expressing them, rarefying the dialogue of love to such an extent that it loses its necessary link with the physical realities of a sexual relationship. Heloise, however, is evidently more than equal to the challenge of maintaining that link:

> *For I often come with parched throat longing to be refreshed by the nectar of your delightful mouth and to drink thirstily the riches scattered in your heart. What need is there for more words? With God as my witness I declare that there is no one in this world breathing life-giving air whom I desire to love more than you . . .* (Heloise, Early Letters, 23)

Heloise was probably only ten years old when Abelard first came to Paris — it was to be fifteen years before she met him. As she grew she would no doubt have felt keenly the changes that were happening around her. In the world of the new Paris that she was to inhabit with Abelard it would be she who struggled to fit together the different aspects of her experience: the new learning she was discovering in ancient texts, the promise of joy and peace that religion offered, the transporting pleasure of her lover, the promise of a deep spiritual friendship. From the first time we hear from her she is trying to form that relationship, which combined intelligence, elegance, love, and friendship. That would be a fitting achievement for an age that was beginning to appreciate the civilized behavior of the individual over that of the brutal masses. It was what she was to beg Abelard for in the letters she was to write following their separation. It was what she would struggle for all her life.

When he was first in Paris, however, Abelard was not looking for friendship. He had come to pick a fight. Not only was Paris the center of new ideas and new learning, it was also the home of William of Champeaux, the current master of the school of Notre-Dame. In the combative terms that Abelard favored for describing his own career William might be described as the reigning champion whom he had come to challenge.

THREE

"By doubting we come to inquiry, by inquiry we come to truth"

I joined William of Champeaux, who at the time was the
supreme master of the subject both in reputation and fact.

Abelard, Autobiography

HE MASTER of the cathedral school of Notre-
Dame-de-Paris was William of Champeaux. He
was an established philosopher and an important
figure among that small group of people who had
real power in France. He lived where the powerful
people lived: as one of the canons, he had his own house within the
cathedral precincts on the Ile de la Cité. Cathedral canons were a
kind of halfway cleric, known as minor clergy. They had some of the
special status of priests and monks, but they were not bound to the
same extent by strict vows. Unlike regular monks, for example, they
were allowed to earn an income and have possessions of their own.
The question of whether they were obliged to follow monkish rules
of chastity was one of the hot issues of the day. A series of papal
decrees reiterating the need for celibacy among the minor clergy indicates that, whatever the rules were, they continued to be systematical-
ly broken throughout the period. An attempt in the previous century
to enforce absolutely a ban on concubines for canons led to riots in
Paris, Rouen, and Poitiers. William, however, was on the side of

those who were attempting to impose celibacy. He was known, in fact, to be a leading figure in the radical reform movement that was sweeping Europe, intent on eradicating laxity and immorality in church and state.

William was destined to rise even higher through the circles of the powerful. He would become archdeacon, wielding so much influ‑ence that people would count him as a close adviser to the king. To the 21‑year‑old Abelard as he arrived in Paris, however, he was of interest only by virtue of his position as master of the school. That was the job that Abelard wanted; he was soon to feel that it was his right, if he didn't already. An encounter with William, therefore, was the real purpose of his visit. Abelard did not as a rule lavish praise on other philosophers; his intellectual rivals usually turn out to be fools or heretics or both. In the case of William, however, he made an exception and admitted that he was good at his job, calling him "an outstanding teacher of logic." Despite, or perhaps because of, this, the philosophical disputes he had with William would turn out to be combats of the utmost seriousness.

Abelard joined the cathedral school as soon as he arrived and straight away started to attend William's lectures. It never took Abelard long to fall out with a fellow thinker and sure enough, in his autobiography, the sentence that follows the one that begins "at last I came to Paris" already finds him becoming unpopular:

> I stayed in William's school for a time, but though he welcomed me at first, he soon took a violent dislike to me because I set out to refute some of his arguments. On several occasions I proved myself his superior in debate. Those who were considered lead‑ers among my fellow students were also annoyed, the more so as they looked on me as the most recent and the youngest pupil . . .
> (Abelard, Autobiography)

Abelard had started as he was to go on: amassing enemies often to the point where he found himself with only one friend to support him in

a sea of hostility. Looking back as he wrote the autobiography he had the insight at least to recognize the pattern of his professional career, "this was the beginning of the misfortunes that have dogged me to this day." He attributes this conflict, as he does almost all the hostility he ever encounters, to jealousy, "as my reputation grew, so other men's jealousy was aroused." There might well be some truth in his claims; jealousy is not an unknown emotion in academic or even clerical circles. On the other hand, to ascribe all criticism of oneself to the jealousy of others is a temptingly soft option when perhaps a little searching might reveal a more credible mix of causes.

The subject over which Abelard and William had their disputations was called by medieval philosophers *dialectica*. It was philosophy as a kind of combination of word-game, search for truth, and competitive sport. It was carried out to a large extent in the classroom in front of students. There was a distinction between two kinds of class in medieval schools: the first, *lectio,* was an old-fashioned lecture in the modern sense where a learned person did his best to redress the balance of ignorance and knowledge in favor of the students. The second was *disputatio,* a form of teaching in which students were encouraged to debate with the lecturer using their own reasoning abilities to puzzle out difficult problems for themselves. It was at this that Abelard was to excel, not only when he himself was the questioner, out-arguing and, not infrequently, humiliating his lecturers, but also as the teacher encouraging and guiding his students. John of Salisbury, the English scholar who attended his classes much later in his career, said that Abelard "dedicated himself to explaining things, instructing and stimulating his students through elementary points rather than behaving like a grave philosopher."[1] To be able to explain complex things in an elementary way is the privilege of those who are really confident in their understanding of their subject. He plainly inspired his classes and they responded by being faithful audiences, following him wherever the events of his life might take him.

But *dialectica* was more than a diverting academic exercise. For Abelard it was a project that, if properly handled, could lead to the

discovery of all-embracing truth. It could potentially make sense of the complex ideas of man, the soul, and God. This is the program that Abelard summed up in one of his most famous phrases, "by doubting we come to inquiry, by inquiry we come to truth."[2] When it had been completed the result would be full understanding of life and the world. It was typical of the optimism of his age and even more typical of Abelard that he believed himself capable of achieving this goal.

Dialectica was a popular subject because of, rather than in spite of, its abstractness. The best comparison today is with Stephen Hawking's *A Brief History of Time,* hard to understand but a best-seller none the less because of its apparent promise to give the reader an insight into fundamental truth. The last sentence of Hawking's book actually expresses its scientific theme in theological terms. When the work of fundamental physics is done, he promises, "we will see into the mind of God." Abelard would have understood that goal perfectly.

Although the subjects are obviously different, the similarities between fundamental physics and *dialectica* are striking and illuminating. Both subjects are obscure, often to the point of complete incomprehensibility, requiring the finest minds to study for years in order to master them. Both subjects tend to bring out an intense competitiveness in those who practice them. Both are acknowledged by their practitioners to have very little prospect of producing any practical benefits, yet *dialectica* occupied the greatest minds of Abelard's generation and fundamental physics not only occupies today's minds but absorbs millions of dollars of funding for its experiments. Both subjects are or were new: a hundred years ago it was widely believed that there was no more physics to do and that all the fundamental questions were answered; likewise, a hundred years before Abelard you would have been hard put to find a *dialectica* class anywhere.

The key similarity, however, is that both disciplines promise a solution to a long-standing puzzle, a solution that has not been offered before and the existence of which is itself part of the newness of the subject. In the case of physics it is the equation that will pro-

vide an explanation of how all material things interact and yet will be so short it can be written on a T-shirt. Were Abelard to have achieved his ultimate goal, his solution would have marked the same heroic achievement of the mind that Stephen Hawking imagines at the end of his book. What the two subjects have in common is ultimately not their content but the fact that both are responses to the same desire. Their popularity demonstrates that this desire is not restricted to academics or scientists – there is a level at which everybody would like to know the secrets of the universe.

Abelard's starting point in his investigation was not the tiny constituents of matter but the shades of meaning that exist between language and the things it describes. Puzzles about language and truth occupy philosophers to this day; some of them are the same ones that Abelard studied. They remain some of the hardest of all things to think about: even an idea that starts straightforwardly can suddenly open up into a vertiginous abyss of contradiction and confusion.

Begin, for instance, with a simple idea: "Abelard has three brothers; they are all human." Dagobertus is human, and Porcarius is human, and Radulphus is human. Still sounds simple, but consider the idea "human." Does each of the brothers have his own humanity, like a coat as it were, or do they all have a share in some general thing called humanity? It would seem a little wasteful to be obliged to create a separate idea of humanity for each member of the human race, so we should perhaps admit that there is a general thing called humanity. On the other hand, it is a rather peculiar thing. Both men and women participate in it, for instance. Does that mean that when we talk about humanity we are talking about something that is both male and female, or something that is both left-handed and right-handed, both tall and short, and so on? Perhaps "humanity" is not a thing at all. Perhaps it is just a word. If that is the case, then what am I saying when I say, for example, "humanity is rational"? Am I talking about nothing? How can I talk about things that don't exist? Does talking about them bring them into existence in some way? Are these questions really about things at all? Perhaps the whole discussion is just about words. A word is just a sound wave, a vibration in the air, how can it carry meaning? Is the meaning it carries a thing or just a convention? But when I say something like "Heloise is in Paris," that isn't just about words — Paris and Heloise are real things. Maybe some words are about words and some are about things. But how do we know which is which? And so on . . .

The more you concentrate on these questions the more they slip away. What seems to be a clear picture can suddenly fragment and become incomprehensible. Often you are uncertain whether you are thinking about real things at all or just things you have made up. It is like staring into a shifting, kaleidoscopic pattern in an infinity of mirrors.

Abelard could look into that pattern and see through the confusion better than most. He could hold it still and see how it fitted together. He can never have really stopped thinking about philosophy — there is no other way to do it if you wish to make progress. When the conversation became dull, in quiet moments, when he was walking back from his classes, the arguments must have run over and over in his head as he searched for a clearer picture, feeling for the right way of looking at it that would make it all click into place. When he was with Heloise the letters they exchanged on a daily basis are filled with references to the jargon of *dialectica*. They play with philosophical ideas: "if a physical thing can be divided you are the best part of me," says Abelard. Heloise describes herself as the "indivisible part of your soul," and calls him "special by virtue of the experience of reality itself."[3]

Dialectica was not in itself controversial. It was too hard to understand to invite much condemnation. So long as Abelard stuck to wondering whether words were real or not he was unlikely to find himself in conflict with the basic tenets of the church. Conflict with religion was not what Abelard wanted. His ultimate aim was a spiritual one — it was his intention to apply the logical tools of *dialectica* to sort out ambiguities and contradictions in religious thinking.

To use logic on religion, however, to practice what he called *theologia* (a word derived from Greek meaning something like "God logic" that he seems to have coined himself) was enough to anger people. But to Abelard it was an essential part of religion. Understanding was all-important: he believed it was a sin to say a prayer that one did not understand. The idea of chanting a mantra, or the ritual recitation of certain phrases as part of religion, would have been horrific to him. The understanding that *dialectica* offered wasn't just about knowledge, it was a question of good versus evil.

His altercations with William were to force Abelard into the first of the frequent changes of location that would characterize his professional life. He stayed at the school in the cathedral for only about a year.* He then decided, because of his growing unpopularity with William, to open his own school:

> *It ended by my setting my heart on founding a school of my own, young as I was and estimating my capacities too highly for my years.* (Abelard, Autobiography)

William, he tells us, did his best to prevent this:

> *My master suspected my intentions and . . . before I could leave he secretly used every means he could to thwart my plans and keep me from the place I had chosen. But among the powers in the land he had several enemies, and these men helped me to obtain my desire. I also won considerable support simply through his unconcealed jealousy.* (Abelard, Autobiography)

Abelard did open his own philosophy school. It was in the town of Melun, to the southeast of Paris at the northern tip of the forest of Fontainebleau. Melun was a favorite royal residence. It was there that

---

* Abelard is hopelessly imprecise about dates and times in his writing, so much so that he is discussed in learned papers about how medieval perceptions of the temporal might have differed from our own. It is quite possible that people were less concerned about time in the Middle Ages, but it is as likely that he was, like many logical thinkers, just a bit vague about specifics.

Philip I, then still king, had been born and where his son Louis VI would set up his court while Paris was temporarily under the control of the Count of Meulan.

Abelard's admission that he was "estimating [his] capacities too highly" in thinking that he could run his own school at the age of 21 was uncharacteristically modest and, as it turned out, misplaced on this occasion. The school was a success. Students flocked to him, wanting to hear the brilliant and witty lecturer, to experience the thrill of seeing a young philosopher of such promise.

Abelard's success demonstrates that at this period a state of affairs is quite unusual in the history of ideas obtained: it was possible to make a living as a freelance philosopher. Most philosophers since the Greeks have been either subsidized or rich in the first place: Plato was an aristocrat, Socrates had a day job, Aristotle was on a retainer from Philip of Macedon, and the vast majority of philosophers since Abelard's day have picked up a salary from some academic institution. That Abelard was able to survive by fulfilling the ultimate theatrical criterion of attracting an audience is an indication not just of his abilities but also of the particular conditions that prevailed in the society – a perception among students that learning would lead to advancement in the church, disposable income in the appropriate section of society, and perhaps even a general sense of confidence that progress was possible even in the arcane world of philosophy.

It was the potential of teaching as a method of making a living that was to give rise, less than forty years later, to the foundation of the first universities. Rather than being institutions set up with the noble purpose of perpetuating learning, universities started as bodies that granted a license to teach. They passed knowledge on to their students, it is true, but their authority derived from what in other circumstances would be called a union closed shop: only those who had the university's license (called a degree) had the right to teach for a living. In 1150, shortly after Abelard's death, the first university received its charter in Bologna in Italy, followed soon after by ones in France and eventually in England. Had teachers not been able to make money in the first place, degrees would not have been in demand and universities – one of two major medieval institutions that survive virtually intact to this day* – would not have developed in the form that they did.

Students loved to be spectators at the public displays of erudition and mental athleticism that took place whenever Abelard showed up in William's audience. The conversation of very intelligent people is thrilling. According to Abelard he continued to get the better of these confrontations with satisfying results:

> *Thus my school had its start and my reputation for dialectic began to spread, with the result that the fame of my old fellow-students and even that of the master himself gradually declined and came to an end.* (Abelard, Autobiography)

Since William and his cronies appeared to be in retreat, Abelard, using the thinking from the military career he had chosen not to pursue, decided to push home his advantage. He was emboldened to move nearer to Paris, and to William:

> *Consequently my self-confidence rose still higher, and I made haste to transfer my school to Corbeil, a town nearer Paris, where I could embarrass him with more frequent confrontations.*
> (Abelard, Autobiography)

This explanation for the relocation from Melun to Corbeil doesn't seem quite to make sense, however. Like all moves it must have involved some work. He would have had to make new arrangements for rooms both to sleep in and to teach in. He would have had to make sure that all his students were informed of his new location and that all future students knew where to find him – a lot to do for a man

---

* The other one is Parliament.

who was dedicated to full-time philosophical inquiry. Was it worth it? How much closer to Paris was he actually moving?

Both Melun and Corbeil are now part of the motorway-veined urban sprawl to the southeast of Paris. The French authorities make life easy for medieval historians by continuing to measure all distances from Paris from a point in front of the cathedral of Notre-Dame, only a few hundred meters from the spot where William used to teach. Melun is, according to the Michelin map, 45km from this point. Corbeil, on the other hand, is 35km. Abelard had moved only 10km (6 miles) closer to William. This is not really a significant difference, especially when you consider that both towns are on the river Seine, which was, in the age of difficult muddy roads, by far the most convenient means for Abelard to get into town. When Abelard wanted to go to Notre-Dame for another bout with William the difference in journey time from Corbeil, as opposed to Melun, cannot have been more than an hour. Was it really worth all the effort of moving just for that?

There was another reason for the move to Corbeil. Abelard himself hints at it when he says that he was helped in his original move to Melun by "enemies of William among the powers that be." Further investigation indicates that Abelard is understating more than a little the amount of help he received from those powers. As we trace the story of his life we find other evidence for the fact of which this remark is a passing acknowledgement: Abelard had aligned himself with not just the enemies of William but with a whole political faction. One person in particular seems to have done his best to help Abelard throughout his career: Stephen de Garlande, an adept politician and, as it happens, long-standing enemy of William. Stephen's political fortunes mirror perfectly the periods of success and failure of Abelard's career. The lives of the two men seem almost to oscillate together, perfectly in phase, like two corks bobbing on the same wave. It is this link that provides a more credible explanation for the relocation of Abelard's school.

The powerful elite that controlled France comprised only a few people. Those who had influence and power were often related to and certainly all knew each other. This little group — centered around the king — squabbled incessantly as its members jostled for position. Alliances were forged and broken; obligations repaid and scores settled. France of the early 1100s resembled nothing so much as a small but volatile company where occasional boardroom coups take place in an atmosphere of toadying and back-stabbing that pervades all other activities, obliging employees to keep a running tally in their heads of who is in and who is out: who can be safely vilified behind their back and who must be unquestioningly praised.

Stephen de Garlande seems to have been particularly good at this infighting. He had the gift of combining charm, chutzpah, and mendacity to get himself to the top in the first place and to return there after a succession of setbacks. He never showed the slightest interest in philosophy. His support for Abelard was apparently given purely on the principle that anyone who embarrassed and annoyed William of Champeaux was to be encouraged.

The Garlandes were a large family. Stephen had three brothers and, between the four of them, they at one time or another held nearly every significant post in France: Chancellor (administrative head, equivalent in power to a Cabinet member), Seneschal (head of the royal household combined with commander of the armed forces), assorted bishoprics, archdeaconships, deanships, and various other lucrative government posts with names like Seigneur de la Bouteillerie. They originated as landowners to the east of France but they also had property in Paris. In particular, they owned those pleasant vineyards to the south of the Ile de la Cité that surrounded the Roman ruins and led up the hill to where the current Sorbonne stands. Stephen's brother William is recorded as having generously donated two barrels of wine from that area for the benefit of the lepers of Paris.

The Garlande boys, with Stephen at their head, had come to prominence a decade earlier when they had supported Philip I in the row over his second wife, Bertrada de Montfort. Bertrada had previously been married to the Count of Anjou, Fulk V, but when Philip met her he had developed such a passion that he just took her back to

Paris and married her, despite vociferous church opposition. Fulk of Anjou was the very man who had been named by the chronicler Guibert of Nogent as having been responsible for importing the effete fashion of pointed shoes into France. If shoes from Anjou could be seen as carriers of virulent social corruption it is easily imag/ ined that a woman would be considered even more dangerous. Sure enough, Bertrada was demonized by the persistent rumor that she was a sorceress. Abbot Suger of St./Denis, in his account of the events, was in no doubt about the potency of her Angevin female wiles. He called her "a virago ... seductive and clever in that amaz/ ing artifice of women by which they boldly trample on their hus/ bands after tormenting them with abuse."[4] No doubt she also spoke well of the abbot.

Ivo, bishop of Chartres, led the campaign against the marriage. He was a very influential man who had written a comprehensive trea/ tise on law and sexual morals. The work was so voluminous, in fact, that town burghers used to complain that their community was unable to afford to have it copied. Eventually (long after his death) to become Saint Ivo by virtue of his piety and zeal, he was effectively the spokesman for the movement for the reform of the church. Ivo refused to officiate at the wedding and became so outspoken about the affair that Philip had him locked up and tried for treason.

The Garlandes, on the other hand, showed themselves to be sup/ porters of the king's (bigamous) marriage and reaped the benefits for years to come. Within twelve months Bertrada's brother, William, was bishop of Paris. He appointed Stephen de Garlande an archdea/ con – a largely nonclerical post that involved responsibility for the col/ lections of tax and therefore presented significant opportunities for financial advancement. Stephen was also later appointed to the unde/ niably clerical post of bishop of Beauvais. Again there was strong opposition from the influential Bishop Ivo of Chartres, by then out of prison. Ivo summed Stephen up as "not even subdeacon material, illiterate, a woman chaser and publicly condemned adulterer."[5] We do not know what, if anything, was his evidence for these accusations.

It may be that he was saying no more than that Stephen was not really a cleric at heart, something that few people would have denied. In an age when only the clergy were literate, nonclergy who opposed them often had their reputations besmirched without being able to answer back in a way that shows up on the historical record.

Ivo was backed in his opposition to Stephen's appointment by his onetime pupil, the ambitious young cleric William of Champeaux. Stephen didn't forget that. A decade later he was still happy to take the opportunity to befriend any enemy of William. It made perfect sense, therefore, that Abelard should find himself supported by Stephen and by those who opposed the reformers.

Abelard seems to have pretended — probably to himself as much as to posterity — that his life was less politically circumscribed than in fact it was. That is because, other things being equal, he would not have chosen for things to be that way. As a logician he would have much preferred that decisions in the world really were made on the basis of the truth as determined by informed debate. Which is, of course, why he was himself demonstrably useless at any kind of political infighting. He ended as the loser in any interaction he ever had with authority because he believed in the power of logical argument. He acted as if all he needed to do was to state the truth as he understood it (usually in a rather aggressive way) and everyone would agree. This strategy never worked because, then as now, human beings make their decisions on the basis of prejudice and self-interest quite as much as logic. Only those who understand this regrettable reality and accept it will succeed in politics. They will be able to overwhelm pure logic with a froth of spin and distortion that can hide the truth indefinitely, while those who put their faith in reason are left complaining how unfair it all is.

Abelard was committed to logic but he was not immune from self-interest. The support of a patron was, it is true, unclean, corrupt, and illogical but on this occasion it was doing no more than helping Abelard himself and therefore giving assistance to the cause of truth. In fact he really had no choice: if he wanted to make a career in philosophy he needed to become involved in the power struggles of the day. Without a patron he would not have had his own school and would quickly have been driven out of the world of philosophy entirely. Without Stephen de Garlande we would never have heard of Peter Abelard.

The disputes in which Abelard had become embroiled were about much more than the king's new trophy wife, or even who became bishop of where. They reflected the struggle between two different, competing ruling systems in medieval society. All civilizations have at their head an elite that makes decisions and enforces them through a network of power. Revolutionaries have tried to build societies without such a power structure but, so far, they have never quite worked out: a new set of rulers always seems to emerge as soon as the old one is sent packing. While it may be impossible to have no system of power within a society, history shows that it is perfectly possible to have two. This was the situation in France.

On the one hand there was the secular state, presided over by the king, who collected revenues and enforced his own legal system through the feudal hierarchy. The church, on the other, constituted a largely separate system with its own revenues and its own government. It even had its own legal system that dealt not only with ecclesiastical crimes such as heresy, but also with crimes ranging from pilfering to murder. Which legal system you were tried by depended on where you had committed the crime and who you were. The decisions of the church's law (known as canon law) were technically outside even the jurisdiction of the king.

The two power groups coexisted because they needed each other. The king needed the church because it had, by definition, complete and unopposed possession of the moral high ground. It gave ultimate legitimacy to the temporal power of the nobles, and, equally important, had a virtual monopoly on literacy: all historical precedents and treaties, for example, had to be drawn up and endorsed by clerics. The church in its turn needed the king because ultimate military power resided with him. This situation of dual government persisted in Europe until the great upheavals of the Reformation 400 years later. Until then neither side could gain absolute control over the other, with the result that they were obliged to cooperate – this was a recipe not for peaceful coexistence but for constant conflict.

The changes that characterized the beginning of the twelfth century made both sides very active. They were each aware of an opportunity to increase their stake in the new civilization that was emerging. King Philip I and, later, his son Louis VI were working to consolidate a centralized political power and to turn France into what we would today call a nation. They, especially Louis, were busy strengthening the military infrastructure and making sure that the noblemen who surrounded the monarchy functioned more like a hierarchical political structure and less like a fractious rabble.

The church had in its turn become suffused with the reforming zeal that animated Ivo of Chartres and William of Champeaux. The reformers wanted the church and the monastic orders to return to strict observance of its rules and principles. They wished to root out corruption and laxity and concomitantly to strengthen canon law as an effective counterbalance to the king's law (it is not a coincidence that Ivo's major work was a book about law).

Insistence on the chastity of the clergy was, of course, part of the agenda of the reform movement. Strangely, there is little in the Bible that can be interpreted as indicating that priests ought not to marry. St. Paul, it is true, makes it clear that marriage is second best to celibacy but superior to fornication. Christ himself, on the other hand, does not forbid his disciples to marry. Many were married, including St. Peter, who founded the church in Rome and who is recorded as having a mother-in-law. In other words, the first pope was married. All of which might prompt one to wonder whether there was some other reason why in the Middle Ages the church suddenly found celibacy so important.

The historian Harold Perkin suggests that stricter adherence to celibacy may have been a method of shielding the hierarchy of the church from interference by the feudal state.[6] If priests were allowed to marry and have legitimate children, goes the argument, it is in the nature of things that bishops, canons, and deacons would ensure that their own children took up their posts after them. The jobs would become, in effect, hereditary; key jobs would stay in certain families. The secular nobility would then be able to insinuate itself into families possessing clerical power by, for instance, marrying their sons to the daughters of bishops or, if all else failed, by using whatever means available to ensure that it was their own families that obtained clerical power in the first place. The two systems of government would merge, amounting effectively to the end of church power. It was in the interest of the clergy therefore that the method by which clerical power was passed on should follow a different pattern from the one in which aristocratic power was transmitted, just to ensure that the two were never able to mesh together.

It was the aim of the reformers to ensure that clerical power remained forever separate from the state. They were vigorously opposed, therefore, to any interference by the king in the election of bishops. This is the reason for the row over the appointment of Stephen de Garlande as bishop of Beauvais. He was the king's candidate who was maneuvered into power ahead of the reformers' choice, a man named Galo.

With the king's authority behind him, Stephen would have had no trouble in making sure that Abelard was allowed to set up his own school in the royal city of Melun. For Stephen it was probably one of many little schemes for needling William of Champeaux and the reformers, but for Abelard it was the making of his career. Everything had turned out very well – he was 23 years old with his own philosophy school. But political fortunes can go down as well as up.

In November 1104 Fulco, the bishop of Paris (whose appointment Stephen de Garlande had supported) died unexpectedly. In a surprise move the chapter appointed as a replacement Galo, the man who had been passed over as bishop of Beauvais when Stephen was appointed. Galo had been a pupil of Ivo of Chartres and was a supporter of the reformers. Stephen de Garlande should have been

able to prevent this appointment by the simple expedient of intimidating his fellow canons. (It was not unknown for senior clergy to
be attacked physically. In succeeding years, for example, one Thomas,
prior of St.-Victor, would meet a very mysterious end at the foot of
the walls of Stephen's own castle at Gournay-sur-Marne.) But on
this occasion Stephen found it difficult to act. A nobleman called
Guy de Rochefort had just returned from the crusaders' occupation
of Jerusalem. A powerful member of the old aristocracy, he took
the position of royal favorite and acted as a rallying point for the enemies of the Garlandes. Stephen had to accept the new bishop and
with it the loss of his own prestige. Guy moved quickly to consolidate his power. His sister Luciane became betrothed to the king's
son, Prince Louis, and he himself was appointed Seneschal, the key
post that included among other things commander-in-chief of the
king's army. Abelard's patron had fallen out of favor with the king.

Since Melun was a royal city, as soon as that happened it was
time for Abelard, and presumably any other people who suddenly
now found themselves on the losing side, to make other arrangements. Even if nobody thought it was worth actually going so far as
to kill Stephen's tame philosopher, life for Abelard could be made
difficult enough. Access to key people could suddenly be withheld;
perhaps the building in which he taught would become unavailable.
Abelard's position could easily have become impossible. This is the
real reason for his move to Corbeil, not that it was slightly nearer
Paris. Corbeil was a good choice: it was, in a sense, the opposite of
a royal city. It had a quasi-independent status as a separate fief. The
smooth daily running of a school there would not be dependent on
royal approval.

But there was more to come. The marriage of the old king to
Bertrada continued to be a thorn in the side of the reformers. Now
that they were in the ascendant they were able to put pressure on the
king. Eventually the new bishop, Galo, prevailed on him to make a
public denunciation of the "sin of carnal and illicit union" of his
marriage to the hated Bertrada.* This act was an official negation of

the reason for the Garlandes' success and a complete reversal for Stephen and his followers. The lowest point for Abelard must have come when, in 1104, William of Champeaux was made an archdeacon of Paris. He decided to go back to Brittany:

> I was not [at Corbeil] long before I fell ill through overwork and was obliged to return home. For some time I remained absent from France, sorely missed by those eager for instruction in dialectic. (Abelard, Autobiography)

There is no way of knowing whether Abelard is telling the whole truth when he says that the reason for his return to Brittany was illness. It is certainly not impossible that he was exhausted. In the previous four years he had set up two philosophy schools, taken on one of the greatest thinkers of the time, and become a pawn in a vicious political struggle. He might well have needed a rest. On the other hand his patron had suffered a total defeat. Even if he wasn't ill at all the situation would probably have called for a retreat in at least one sense. It is perfectly possible, of course, that both explanations are true and that Abelard was both ill and obliged to return home for political reasons – defeat and illness often appear in tandem.

He was to spend about four years with his family, away from Paris. In Brittany he would be without books and without philosophical sparring partners whose conversation is often essential to the enquiring mind. We do not know how he spent his time. There does not seem to be any record of writing from this period. Perhaps he was not even intending to continue his work.

---

* The dissolution of the marriage seems to have been gradual. The couple continued to live together for a while – even making an official joint visit to the wronged husband back in Anjou – until Bertrada eventually retired to the Angevin convent of Fontevrault, where the likes of "Jerorius FatLips" and "Raginald Who Folds Up Peasants" were her neighbors and benefactors. In her letters Bertrada continued to style herself "Queen of the French" until her death.

His journey to Brittany would have lasted at least five days. First he had to travel south as far as Orléans and then by boat down the slow, broad Loire. As he traveled down the river he passed great towns such as Blois, Tours, Saumur, and Angers, each one of them with a newly built castle lowering over the river. Abelard would have had time to reflect, as he looked at them, that in the real world victory is given not to those who think logically and love the truth, but to those who have might on their side.

FOUR

Master of the schools

I Galo by the grace of God Bishop of Paris and William of Champeaux, archdeacon, finding such great scandal and plague unbearable, from the precept of Pope Pascal II, from the advice of our King Philip and his son Louis, from the encouragement also of our canons, have eliminated these infamous and incorrigible people from the aforesaid convent.

Bishop Galo of Paris, Charter concerning the Convent of St.-Eloi

T THIS TIME Heloise was growing up in Paris. Not very much is known about her origins. The autobiography introduces her as living in the household of her uncle on her mother's side, Fulbert, a canon of the cathedral of Notre-Dame. Prior to that, we are told, she was educated at the convent of Argenteuil, a short way downstream from Paris. The fact that her uncle is a canon places her, like everybody who appears in the historical record of this period, somewhere in the upper strata of society.

We know that her mother's name was Hersint (Hersendis) from the only surviving record dating from Heloise's time at the convent of the Paraclete. It is called a "Necrology," a list of benefactors and friends of the convent together with the day of the year on which a mass must be said for them.

There is no mention at all of her father in any document, a fact that, as the genealogist Brenda Cook points out, might well indi-cate some massive scandal behind her parentage.[1] This would have to be more serious than a birth outside wedlock — illegitimate children were commonly acknowledged by their fathers and not infrequently included in the family and allowed inheritances. There is a tradition that her mother was an abbess. If Heloise was the daughter of a nun it would probably be enough of a scandal to explain the lack of information about the father. Fathering a child by a nun broke far more taboos than the one that simply discouraged fornication, and might well have warranted complete silence. Traditions are, of course, unreliable: in this case the story is told by only a single French writer, Turlot, in the year 1812. It could be that the story is just false and that Turlot made an honest mistake, or even a deliberate fabrication, but there is also a slim possibility that it is true. He might be recounting a tradition that dates from before the destruction of Heloise's convent and its library after the French Revolution, in 1789. It is possible that the last abbess knew things that were recorded only in the lost library. Perhaps she passed them on by word of mouth. There is only a 32-year gap between Turlot's book and the destruction of the Paraclete. It is not inconceivable that the abbess gave otherwise unrecorded information either directly to Turlot or to an intermediary.[2]

This idea is given a little circumstantial support by the fact that we do know of a major Parisian scandal involving nuns that happened at the appropriate time. In 1107, while Abelard was still in Brittany, the convent of St.-Eloi on the Ile de la Cité was disbanded because of alleged gross sexual impropriety. The newly appointed reforming bishop, Galo, assisted by William of Champeaux in his capacity as archdeacon, is forthright in his condemnation in the preamble to the charter that abolished the house:

> *We want it to be known to all that the convent of St.-Eloi of*
> *Paris was anciently assigned to an order of nuns; but neverthe-*
> *less by diabolic instinct that weaker sex fell to such great misery*
> *of turpitude that arrogantly adhering to open secularism, their*
> *vows of chastity broken, the message of the Rule of St. Benedict*

thoroughly rejected, they made the temple of God a cavern of fornication and did not hear the voice of our admonition and correction at all. (Bishop Galo of Paris, Charter concerning the Convent of St.-Eloi)

"Diabolic instinct [of the] weaker sex" does sound like the language of prejudice, and of course there is no way of knowing whether the accusations are true, but it is clear from this document that Galo and William believed they were talking about some long-term habitual impropriety, not a single indiscretion. They are proud to have acted against the convent with the utmost severity. In their words, they have "eliminated these infamous and incorrigible people from the aforesaid convent, for the foulness of their lives and have altogether driven them away."

Cook suggests that Heloise's mother, Hersint, may have been among the nuns of St.-Eloi and that the pattern of scandalous behavior may have gone back long enough to have included her becoming pregnant with Heloise. The little girl would have grown up in the convent – a fact that would no doubt have added to the aura of scandal that surrounded the nuns.

The disgraced nuns were still nuns and therefore still had to reside in convents. In all probability they would have been distributed to various houses around Paris, which would explain why Heloise found herself, as Abelard describes in the autobiography, continuing her education at the convent of Argenteuil before coming to live with her uncle Fulbert.

The convent of St.-Eloi itself, together with its not inconsiderable land holdings to the east of Paris, was handed over to the nearby abbey of St.-Pierre des Fosses. Many of the convent buildings were demolished. This provided space – conveniently enough – for Louis VI to build the road that led toward the newly built, stone pont au Change and the area to the north of the river where the new city was growing.

The dissolution of this ancient convent (it had been founded, reputedly, in 630 by St. Eloi himself) would have been a major scandal about which all Parisians would have had an opinion. Among the powerful and influential, Heloise's origins would have been known and the identity of her father (a priest, a canon?) no doubt speculated about, though not, crucially for history, in writing.

Whether Heloise and her mother really were involved in these events will never be known, but the story does have one final, satisfying irony. The charter abolishing St. Eloi is the first recorded act by Abelard's enemy William of Champeaux in his capacity as archdeacon. It is also, as it happens, the last. The winds of fortune were about to turn and William would soon be out of office.

Guy de Rochefort, the man who had ousted Stephen de Garlande from power, had evidently overreached himself. The king began to withdraw his support. It started when, as part of a complicated move to curry favor with the pope, Prince Louis was persuaded to divorce Guy's sister, Luciane. This was soon followed by an unambiguous sign of the weakening of Rochefort power: the king appointed a Garlande, Stephen's brother Anseau, as Seneschal, the key post of commander of the armed forces. Guy, who seems to have lacked Stephen's diplomatic skills, responded to these insults by launching an armed rebellion, the first act of which was the abduction of Anseau de Garlande. Stephen, naturally enough, came to the aid of both king and brother. Guy's uprising was defeated and the Garlande family was once again in favor.

With Guy de Rochefort disgraced, William of Champeaux resigned as archdeacon and ceased to hold the post of master of the school. Stephen de Garlande, swept forward on a wave of royal favor, not only became archdeacon in his place but was also made dean of the abbey of Ste. Geneviève. This abbey stood just outside Paris, on the hill to the south of the island that is now the site of the Sorbonne. It was also conveniently sited adjacent to the Garlande vineyards, which ran up the slopes of the hill. More important for the abbey as an institution, though, it was outside the limits of the jurisdiction of the cathedral canons and therefore answerable to only the king.

Abelard was now able to return from Brittany. He was to discover that not only had William resigned but he had apparently made a radical change of lifestyle:

A few years later, when I had long since recovered my health, my teacher William, archdeacon of Paris, changed his former status and joined the Canons Regular, with the intention, it was said, of gaining promotion to a higher prelacy through the reputation of increased piety. (Abelard, Autobiography)

By becoming a canon regular William was making a bold public statement. He was joining one of the monastic orders favored by the reforming movement, thus confirming irrevocably his position in opposition to the Garlandes and, by association, Abelard. The canons regular lived strictly according to the rule of St. Benedict. They were committed to poverty and austerity. Unlike the canons of the cathedral (or for that matter the canons of Stephen's own abbey of Ste./Geneviève) they were not allowed to run their own private households or take payment for their teaching.

This visible act of piety plainly impressed contemporaries. A woman called Hildebert of Lavardin wrote to William: "Before you merely gathered knowledge from philosophers; you did not bring forth in yourself beauty of conduct. But now you begin to draw out from it the pattern of good behavior like honey from the comb." A letter from an unknown German student has survived in which – in the middle of a very familiar-sounding plea for money – he praises William, once almost an adviser to the king, for now going to live in miserable surroundings and serving God.[3]

There is no hint in these reactions of the cynicism that Abelard shows when he accuses William of making the move because he wanted to gain a "higher prelacy." History does bear Abelard out: William did indeed become bishop of Châlons in 1113. For the moment, though, William continued to teach – something else about which Abelard makes snide remarks. It did mean, however, that Abelard would have the chance of the decisive philosophical show-down with William that would confirm his philosophical creden-tials once and for all:

> *I returned to him to hear his lectures of rhetoric, and in the course of our philosophic disputes I produced a sequence of clear logical arguments to make him amend, or rather abandon, his previous attitudes to universals.* (Abelard, Autobiography)

The battleground for the pair's dialectical showdown was a philosophical puzzle known as the problem of universals. Univer-sals are those general properties that can be applied to classes of objects and tell you something about their nature: "white," "red," "intelligent," "human." They are called universals to distinguish them from features such as "has a red coat" or "lives in Paris," which are known as particulars. Universals are important because they underlie thought itself. Any search for pattern and understand-ing in our world must involve universals. They are what allow us to perceive the differences and the similarities between objects and states of affairs. Without them we could describe our experiences only as a catalogue of unrelated facts.

William took the view that universals were things in their own right; in other words that there was an abstract entity, "white," for example, which existed in a peculiar way (to use the jargon, it "sub-sisted") and in which all objects that are white had a share. There is, after all, only one "white" – it would not only be ridiculous but defeat the idea of white if every white object had its own version of that property.

Abelard rejected the idea of an abstract entity. To him the concept white was no more than a word. Its meaning was universal but there was no world of abstract properties "out there" to which the objects in the world were mysteriously connected.* He attacked William's claim at the point in his argument where he said that there was only one "thing," white. True, Abelard agreed, the white of a white cat does not have any difference from the white in a white wall or, for that matter, a white cloud. However, Abelard pointed out that a lack of difference does not imply that they are all one thing; it certainly does not imply a mysterious "subsistent entity" in which all white objects participate. That would be going too far. William was unable to provide answers to Abelard's arguments and was forced to revise his position:

> *He had maintained that in the common existence of universals, the whole species was essentially the same in each of its individuals, and among these there was no essential difference, but only variety due to multiplicity of accidents. Now he modified his view to say that it was the same not in essence but in nondifference.* (Abelard, Autobiography)

The real arguments, when developed fully and pursued vigorously, are mind-stretching and subtle but they are not pointless abstractions. Abelard and William were not arguing about how many angels could walk on the head of a pin†; they were wrestling with questions about concepts that are of lasting importance and are still

---

* William's view is called Realism because he believes that universals are real. Abelard's opposing view, that universals are not entities in themselves, is called Nominalism. The word *nominalist* actually seems to have been ascribed first to those who followed Abelard.
† The angels on the pin story is a very old misconception. It was first used by thinkers of the Renaissance about the philosophers of the Middle Ages, whom they considered to have been wasting their time on trivia. There are two effective replies to this libel: (1) nobody has ever been able to find any record of any medieval philosophers ever discussing any such thing, and (2) if they had discussed it, it might have been a fruitful area of investigation. Physicists to this day wonder about the ultimate nature of space and speculate about what is the smallest volume that could exist — not so very far from the angels on the pin.

(in a slightly different form) current. Among modern philosophers, there is still not an agreed-upon answer to the question that they were disputing. Abelard would be able, without too much adjustment, to resume the debate today in the philosophy department of any of the great universities of the world.*

It is an achievement to make a professional philosopher publicly retract a dearly held view. In the world of philosophy there are many ways of dodging an argument, launching a counterattack, or even just agreeing to differ. That Abelard had been able to box William in so completely that he had to admit he was wrong impressed all those who followed the combative world of *dialectica*. Even William's supporters started to transfer their allegiance to Abelard:

> *The strongest supporters of Master William who had hitherto been my most violent attackers now flocked to join my school . . . William's lectures fell into such contempt that he was scarcely accepted on any other points of dialectic.* (Abelard, Autobiography)

The fight with William over universals is important not only as a sign of Abelard's growing status and skill but as a step in the development of his own ideas. Abelard's books on logic – written over a decade after the fight – still use the question he debated with William as the starting point for the subject. In Abelard's books William's ideas are expounded and demolished but William himself is darkly referred to as simply "Master W."

Abelard was now undisputed champion of *dialectica*. It would surely be appropriate for him to become master of the school of Notre-Dame-de-Paris. William had been succeeded as master by

---

* The philosopher Christopher Martin has characterised Abelard's position in modern terms as that of a "transferable trope anti-realist" (see Paul Spade, *Survey of Medieval Philosophy* (Bloomington: Indiana University, 1985). Philosophy has not become any less jargon-filled in 900 years.

somebody whose name we do not know but who was plainly impressed with Abelard:

> *Even William's successor as head of the school offered me his chair so that he could join the others as my pupil, in the place where his master and mine had won fame.* (Abelard, Autobiography)

The offer of the current master to step down in Abelard's favor angered William. Despite having been forced out of the job himself and being associated with the disgraced Guy de Rochefort, he was evidently still not without power. He managed to block Abelard's appointment as master. Abelard had once again to set up his own school. He chose – or perhaps he didn't need to choose because it was offered to him – to locate it in the abbey of Ste. Geneviève, which was now under the deanship of Stephen de Garlande.

Abelard began, in his own phrase, to lay siege to his usurper. From Ste. Geneviève, his new home on the hill outside the city, he could see William's own school, recently set up in the abbey of St. Victor on the banks of the river, slightly to the east. Both houses were small, relatively new, foundations. These two walled communities, facing each other across the vines of the Ste. Geneviève hill, must have seemed symbolic of the two embattled men themselves. They represented not only the opposing views of two philosophers, Abelard the nominalist and William the realist, but also the opposition between the factions who championed them.

In St. Victor the canons all lived together like bona fide monks, eating communally in silence while the Gospel was read to them, following the rule of St. Benedict with a diligence that was the aim of all reformers. In Ste. Geneviève, however, the canons had been given a special dispensation to live as the canons of Notre Dame lived, running their own households (although the charter explicitly forbade them to include women) and still having the right to receive money for their teaching.

Abelard remained at Ste. Geneviève for three years, teaching students as well as keeping up a constant battle with William, who does not seem to have been quite so willing to lie down and die as Abelard tries to claim in his account of their fight. We do not know the details of the disputes that took place in this period but we do have one account of what seems to have been a sort of academic commando raid made on Ste. Geneviève by one of William's students. One Goswin, later to be made St. Goswin as a reward for his piety, is said by his biographer to have deliberately engineered a fight with Abelard on a dialectical matter. He found Abelard, in this account, making a mockery of faith with his oversophisticated reasoning and scornful humor. When Abelard was challenged by Goswin on a specific point he flew into a rage and told him to be silent. Other students, however, protested that the young Goswin should be heard. The account then claims that Goswin was able to outwit the furious Abelard and force him, rather as Abelard had forced William, into a position where he contradicted himself. Unfortunately the biographer was not able to give the details of the subject matter of the dispute so it is impossible to know quite how effectively, if at all, Goswin got the better of Abelard, who might very well have given quite a different account of the incident.

Neither do we know just what brought this period of what was probably quite creative conflict to a close. Abelard tells us that he was once again called back to Brittany:

> *Meanwhile my dearest mother, Lucie, begged me to return to Brittany, for after my father Berengar's entry into the monastic life she was preparing to do the same.* (Abelard, Autobiography)

It was not uncommon for high-ranking people in the Middle Ages to take holy orders as a kind of retirement strategy. One historian estimates that as many as a third of female recruits to convents were, in fact, married women in retirement. There is some possibility that Abelard's father might have accompanied the Duke of Brittany himself and several other followers into a monastery. This practice had several attractions for retirees: guaranteed companionship and support for the rest of their lives coupled with what was probably the best medical attention available. They would also have the consolation of concentrated religious contemplation at a time in life when the mundane round of getting and spending frequently begins to appear more and more pointless.

The practice also had a practical and legal benefit in that it provided an opportunity for property to be handed over calmly to the next generation at a time when all parties were living. For Abelard in particular, as well as filial duty and a quite natural desire to attend a significant family occasion, it might have been important for him to be there in person to confirm that he really had relinquished his claim on the eldest son's birthright.

Knowing, however, that in the autobiography Abelard often hides the political background to his moves one cannot help wondering if there was some other event – perhaps a temporary wobble in Stephen's hold on the favor of the king – that might have made a trip to Brittany prudent. It is also possible that things were not going so well for him and his followers in the dialectical arena. He closes his account of the episode with a quotation that turns out to have a slightly ambiguous message: "'If you demand the issue of this fight / I was not vanquished by my enemy'[4] . . . the facts cry out and tell the outcome."

Whatever the facts might cry out, those who recognized the quotation would have known that it came from an account by the Roman poet Ovid of an episode in the Trojan War. The Greek hero Ajax is recalling a fight with the Trojan, Hector. "At least I didn't lose," he says. In fact, in the story the two combatants were eventually pulled apart by the heralds because they were so evenly matched that neither could gain the upper hand. In legend Ajax is a notorious braggart, here seen putting the best possible spin on an episode of ambivalent outcome. Is that what Abelard is telling us he is doing in his account of his three years at Ste.Geneviève?

1. Abelard from a fourteenth-century manuscript of the letters. In his time artists did not make portraits so we have very little information as to what the couple looked like. This drawing is presumably the idea of the copyist, having studied the letters.

2. Heloise represented in a late-nineteenth-century engraving by Alphonse François. (Musée d'Art et d'Archéologie de Cluny)

3. The first page of Johannes de Vepria's manuscript of the "new letters." The letters "m" and "v," for mulier *(woman) and* vir *(man), alternate down the left-hand margin. The title* Ex epistulis duorum amantium *(From the letters of two lovers) can be seen in its contracted Latin form. The first line of the letter, from Heloise, is* Amori suo precordiali omnibus aromatibus dulcius redolenti, corde et corpore sua . . . , *"To her sweet love, more sweetly scented than any spice, from she who is his in heart and body . . ."* (Médiathèque de l'agglomération Troyenne—photo P. Jacquinot)

4. *A copy of Abelard's autobiography dating from about a century after his death from the Municipal Library of Troyes. The first sentence is* Sepe humanos affectus aut provocant aut mittigant amplius exempla quam verba *(Often human beings are stirred or soothed more by example than by words). By the third paragraph he has covered the introduction and his early life and begins the story proper with the words* Perveni tandem Parisius *(At last I came to Paris). (Médiathèque de l'agglomération Troyenne—photo P. Jacquinot)*

5. *Le Pallet where Abelard was born. Local tradition refers to the remains of the medieval castle on the hill above the town as "Berengar's Tower." Berengar was Abelard's father; he married the daughter of the lord of le Pallet but it is not known whether he inherited the title. Whether or not he was the son of a lord, it is certain that Abelard was at the center of le Pallet's first family.*

6. *Nothing is known of the origins of the little chapel that stands on the hill above le Pallet. Its style suggests that it is of the right date for it to have been seen and possibly used by the young Abelard.*

7. *As the city of Paris grew life became more recognizably urban. Critics were swift to condemn what they saw as the decadent lifestyle of the young. Excessively pointed shoes in particular were singled out as a dangerously effete style, foisted on the upright citizens of Paris by Bertrada of Anjou.*

8. *A lustful woman is taunted by a demon while snakes attack her body. This sculpture from the church of Moissac was made during Abelard's lifetime and is a powerful graphical representation of the disgust, which itself bordered on the sensual, with which some (but not all) medieval thinkers regarded sexual pleasure.*

9. *Abelard and Heloise from a thirteenth-century manuscript. They are depicted deep in conversation, using the exaggerated hand gestures that are believed to have been developed to enable monks to communicate during meals when conversation was banned.*

10. *A group of medieval astronomers. In the center one of them measures the elevation of a heavenly body with an astrolabe. Using the markings on the instrument he can then calculate the time of day. It is a handheld model of the universe, which is a physical manifestation of their understanding of the heavens.*

11. *Heloise holds Abelard's severed genitals (historians, however, are mostly of the opinion that only his testicles were removed) as depicted on a carved column capital in a late-medieval building (the Conciergerie) that stands on the site of Louis VI's new palace, only a few hundred meters from the place where the castration took place.*

12. *The castration of a knight illustrated in a thirteenth-century law book. The perpetrators are using a cord and a knife, a method that has been favored for the castration of farm animals for centuries. (Bibliothèque nationale de France)*

13. *The Royal Abbey of St.-Denis, where Abelard first took holy orders, from a nineteenth-century engraving. This building was to become the last resting place of many French monarchs. Its significance in the history of France derives from its position on the northern approaches to Paris and from the fact that powerful abbots kept it in the forefront of political life.*

Abelard's duties were completed quite quickly in Brittany, but when they were done he did not return to the abbey of Ste. Geneviève. Surprisingly he went instead to Laon, about 150km northeast of Paris. There he joined the school of Anselm of Laon, who had been William's teacher. Abelard does not give a reason for his failure to return to his own school, apart from saying that he went to Laon "with the special purpose of studying theology." He may well have made a conscious decision to study theology, but it is not at all clear why he chose to enroll in a school whose master he so clearly despised.

In contrast to his attitude toward William, Abelard shows no respect for this old man who "owed his reputation more to long practice than to intelligence or memory." Abelard demonstrates his facility for pithy and telling insults:

> *Anyone who knocked on his door to seek an answer to some question left more uncertain than he came ... He had a remarkable command of words but their meaning was worthless and devoid of all sense.* (Abelard, Autobiography)

Abelard shows himself at his most creative when being rude. He even manages, when talking about Anselm, to produce a precursor of the modern phrase "the lights are on but there's no one home":

> *The fire he kindled filled his house with smoke but did not light it up; he was a tree in full leaf that could be seen from afar but on closer inspection proved to be barren.* (Abelard, Autobiography)

When it became obvious to Abelard that Anselm was totally devoid of intellectual merit he started skipping his classes entirely and, egged on by some other students, began to give his own lectures on the interpretation of the scriptures. The application of *dialectica* to the divinely revealed texts that were at the foundations of religion was a new departure for Abelard but, according to him, his first efforts – commentaries on the book of Ezekiel – were acclaimed by the students. Perhaps Abelard had hoped to be able to usurp Anselm's position and take over his school (it is hard to see any other reason why he might go there if he considered the old man so disastrous a teacher), but it was not to be. Anselm was so furious that Abelard had dared to lecture on theology that he forbade him ever to do so again. Abelard was obliged to leave. The autobiography gives the impression that he not only rather relished the disapprobation of Anselm but felt that it had done his reputation some good; as he says, "through persecution my fame increased."

Among the students at the Laon school two names are singled out in the autobiography as being devoted followers of Anselm and therefore enemies of Abelard: Alberic of Reims and Lotulf of Lombardy, "whose hostility to me was intensified by the good opinion they had of themselves." The two of them were to go on to have illustrious careers of their own. They later ran a school together in Reims and Alberic eventually became archbishop of Bourges. They never forgot Abelard: at the foot of almost every edict and declaration condemning Abelard can be found the signatures of Alberic and Lotulf.

The number of Abelard's enemies was also increasing in the town of Châlons-sur-Marne, some 320km to the east. William had now taken up residence as the newly appointed bishop of Châlons. It was his duty to preside over the ceremony at which those who wished to become monks took their final vows. Among the novices joining the new reformist order of the Cistercians whom he met in his first year in office was a rather intense young man with slightly staring eyes who, it was easy to see, would make an impression wherever he went. This young man, Bernard of Clairvaux, was in fact destined to have more effect on history than any other individual of the century. He would turn the Cistercians into the most famous order in Christendom; he would dictate the aesthetic style of a generation and denounce the unrighteous of a continent; he would become the adviser of kings and popes. He would also manage to persuade the people of France wholeheartedly to support the launch of the second crusade. He would be known to history as St. Bernard.* William was to become friendly with him; several letters between them have survived. The new bishop would doubtless have told the eager young man about the new city of Paris that he had not yet visited and about the work that reformers had yet to do there to purify Christendom for the new century. He would have mentioned in particular one man – intelligent but fundamentally wrongheaded, full of irreverent flippancy and given to the potentially disastrous mis-application of logic. Bernard, like Alberic and Lotulf, would not forget the name Abelard.

With William out of Paris and safely occupied as a bishop, Abelard himself was able to return there and at last take up the post that he had believed, ever since he came to the city, was his by right: master of the school of Notre-Dame-de-Paris. He is also careful to point out that the move to Paris followed directly after Anselm's ban on his theology lectures:

> *A few days after this I returned to Paris, to the school that had long ago been intended for and offered to me, and from which I had been expelled at the start . . . The numbers in the school increased enormously as the students gathered there eager for instruction.* (Abelard, Autobiography)

Abelard was a celebrity. His lectures on both theology and dialec-tics were crowd pullers. Heloise recollects exactly the same period and concurs that he had achieved the status of a star:

---

* It is probably important to state here that, for all his achievements, St. Bernard of Clair-vaux did *not* have a breed of dog named after him. That honor belongs to St. Bernard of Aosta, who lived and preached some fifty years earlier, earning a reputation for giving help to travelers as they crossed the Alps.

What king or philosopher could match your fame? What district, town, or village did not long to see you? When you appeared in public, who did not hurry to catch a glimpse of you, or crane his neck and strain his eyes to follow your departure?
(Heloise, First Letter)

The autobiographical letter that Abelard wrote was intended to show to his friend the monk that Abelard's own pride led to his downfall. He describes himself at this triumphant moment as "puffed up with pride," thinking himself "the only philosopher in the world, with nothing to fear from anyone." It is not hard to imagine that this degree of success probably made him close to insufferable as a person. Few modern readers, however, would agree with Abelard's stated view that the misfortunes that followed were no more than just retribution for his worldly vanity. What is certain is that after a decade of trouble, skirmish, and setback, Providence had finally put him in a position of perfect readiness for the episode of his life that would indeed bring him the lasting fame that he had always sought.

FIVE

"Need I say more?"

There was in Paris an "adolescentula" named Heloise,
the niece of Fulbert, one of the canons.

Abelard, Autobiography

BELARD BEGINS the description of his love affair with Heloise with a simple statement, like a good storyteller. The beautiful Latin word that he uses to describe her has given some people a mistaken idea about her age. The word *adolescentula* – a little adolescent – makes us imagine a young girl, a teenager. It is a beautifully evocative word that brings to mind Vladimir Nabokov's famous musing about how pronouncing the name Lolita obliges the tongue to move successively to three different positions on the roof of the mouth. The word is, however, deceptive: a reading of medieval Latin texts shows that it can refer to anybody up to the age of thirty, the explanation being that, up until that age one is still growing – *adolescens.* In fact Abelard, also in the autobiography, describes himself as *adolescentulus* when he was teaching at Corbeil, a time when we know that he was at least 22 years old. The best estimates of Heloise's age when she met Abelard – both from the internal evidence of her writing and from the subsequent story – put her in her early twenties. She had clearly had time for study in depth:

... she was the niece of Fulbert, one of the canons, and so much loved by him that he had done everything in his power to advance her education in letters. In looks she did not rank lowest, but in the extent of her learning she stood supreme.
(Abelard, Autobiography)

Heloise was already an educated woman. In the early letters Abelard calls her "the only disciple of philosophy among all the young women of our age" (there might, however, be an element of flattery in that remark: in the same sentence he also calls her "the only attrac-tive woman" and "the only gracious woman").[1]

Not only had she learnt Latin, presumably while with the nuns at Argenteuil and, before that, at St.-Eloi (if indeed that is where she was), but it is obvious from her writings that she had absorbed in depth the literature of ancient Rome. She fills her letters with refer-ences to it. Ideas about life she takes from the great speech writer Cicero and ideas about love from Ovid. Classical literature provides her with a rich set of references, a vocabulary with which she can pre-cisely and powerfully express her feelings. Her erudition can be set against the claim that it was only during the Renaissance, 300 years later, that classical literature was suddenly "rediscovered" and the light of learning flooded into the darkness of the Middle Ages. This picture of the Middle Ages, which is still quite widespread, as the unenlightened run-up to the Renaissance is made nonsense not just by Heloise but by a whole host of writers in the twelfth century. The light of learning did burn particularly brightly in Heloise, it is true: her classical references are much more varied and consistent, for example, than those of Abelard. In times of stress it is the background of liter-ature that comes back to her to help her articulate her anguish.

She had also already learned how to write in her own distinctive style. One scholar who has analyzed the rhythmic patterns of her let-ters, the particular cadences she uses to bring her sentences to an effec-tive end, detects in her prose an Italian influence different from the north European style of those around her. Had she been instructed by an Italian teacher? Perhaps she had picked up and developed the style for herself. From the first of the new letters, patterns of meaning, rhyme, and rhythm mark her as a natural wordsmith. Her prose is always halfway to poetry; it is a unique and characteristic talent. Abelard is even of the opinion that she has outdone her models:

> *You who discuss the rules of friendship so subtly that you seem to have not only read Cicero but to have taught him about it.*
> (Abelard, Early Letters, 50)

From the quality of the first of the early letters it is clear that by the time she met Abelard she was already a practiced writer. A study of the letters of both lovers seems to indicate that it is Abelard who picks up stylistic tricks from her, not the other way round. Abelard acknowledges her talent:

> *A gift for letters is so rare in women that it added greatly to her charm and had won for her renown throughout the realm.*
> (Abelard, Autobiography)

That she was already famous in her own right is confirmed by Peter the Venerable, the abbot of the great monastery of Cluny who was to become her friend near the end of her life. Writing to her thirty years later, he says that although he did not meet her he knew her from her reputation as a scholar when she lived in Paris and he had "not quite passed the bounds of youth."[2]

Heloise lived in the house of her uncle, a canon and therefore a powerful man, in the cathedral precinct in the center of Paris, only a few hundred meters from the royal palace. It had been nearly four years since the temporary capture of Paris and destruction of its bridges by the count of Meulan. Louis VI's program of improvement was well under way. The city was developing all around her: new buildings to the north, new ideas in the cloisters, new music in the churches and the taverns.

It was natural that she would want to take her place in this new world, even to make her own mark. As soon as Abelard arrived she must have been aware of him, the new, good-looking young master of the school. They were both living in the cathedral precinct, the home of no more than a couple of hundred people. It was like being in the same school or college. In addition, Abelard was a hard person to miss: he was tall and boisterous, always to be heard discussing the latest ideas with students and scholars. He even wrote popular songs. He was the personification of everything that was new and intriguing in the year 1115 — the new world made flesh.

There was a moment in 1115 (or possibly the following year) when, for Heloise, Abelard became like a god. Where previously she had had many motives for the things she did, now there would be just one. Whatever she did, whatever she said, and whatever she thought would from that moment on be part of her love for Abelard. Her deepest thoughts on philosophy and religion would relate to her love for him. It would from that moment on be paramount: she would never quite be able to transform it into a love of God, even though Abelard was one day to beg her to do so. She would never again feel the need for inner warmth and comfort without thinking of Abelard. He would be "the sweetest protector of my soul, planted at the root of my love."[3]

> At every stage of my life up to now, as God knows, I have feared to offend you rather than God, and tried to please you more than him. (Heloise, Second Letter)

Her love was all-consuming, but it did not rob her of her own free will or dim her intelligence. She would never be slow to argue with Abelard, sometimes with devastating force. She would try to guide him, even to manipulate him, but beyond all that would remain her immutable, unconditional love. She would come to see it as a kind of debt that she gladly accepted. In one of her rhyming Latin phrases she was eager "to repay you and in all ways obey you" (*tibi rependere et in omnibus obedire*). That debt, a kind of imperative to continuous giving, was the basis of her idea of friendship and of love. And, as she herself said, "the greatest thing that love does is to form perfect friendship."[4] It is Heloise's unwavering love that has made the story of the couple endure long after the politics, philosophy, and theology of their time have ceased to have any significance.

The state of being in love is a very familiar one to us, not least from personal experience, but also from songs, poems, and stories. Centuries of writing about and celebrating the condition of romantic love have made it seem almost a cliché, something best handled now with the protective gear of postmodernist irony. In the twelfth century, however, there was no vast body of literature about romantic love. Although, presumably, people were falling in love with the same frequency as they do now, discourse about love was to some extent a new phenomenon. Young girls who discussed it openly had shocked the social commentator Guibert of Nogent. Those who attempted to reform monasticism talked with fresh enthusiasm about the intense friendship and close comradeship of the cloister, surely a cousin of romantic love. It was as if human beings were gaining a new level of self-awareness, and if Heloise had a natural talent for anything, it was self-awareness. We know about Heloise's emotional experience because she is able to describe it in great detail; there is no shortage of words for love and its attendant emotions in medieval Latin. The process of developing a language of love was, however, by no means complete in her lifetime – vocabulary sometimes lags behind feelings. There is one important lacuna: in the Latin of the twelfth century there is no precise phrase for what had happened to Heloise, no phrase for the cataclysmic experience of "falling in love":

> *Throughout all Latinity, no phrase has yet been found that speaks clearly about how intent on you is my spirit, for God is my witness that I love you with a sublime and exceptional love. And so there is not nor ever will be any event or circumstance,*

except only death, that will separate me from your love. (Heloise, Early Letters, 53)

When we first meet Heloise, writing in the early letters, her love for Abelard is already at its maximum intensity. We do not know precisely how the affair began. The only clue Heloise gives us in one of the later letters is to say that it was Abelard's songwriting that first attracted her, but she does not tell us when this happened. It is tempting to surmise that she was attracted to him as soon as she was aware of him, talking and singing as he made his way around the cloister. Abelard, on the other hand, does give us an account of the beginning of the affair from his point of view, one in which it is he who takes the initiative.

Abelard was at the peak of his confidence. He was master of the school of Notre-Dame at the age of 36; he had defeated his adversary William of Champeaux; his supporter Stephen de Garlande was in power. He thought he was not just the only philosopher in the world but the only lover too, judging by his description of events. Remember that he has already introduced Heloise in a slightly dismissive way, describing her beauty with faint praise: "in looks she did not rank lowest." He goes on in this vein but, having weighed up the situation, decides magnanimously to give her the benefit of the doubt:

> *I considered all the usual attractions for a lover and decided she was the one to bring to my bed, confident that I should have an easy success; for at that time I had youth and exceptional good looks as well as my great reputation to recommend me, and feared no rebuff from any woman I might choose to honor with my love.*
> (Abelard, Autobiography)

"Choose to honor with my love"! This sounds like the kind of language that only occurs when men talk to their friends. Which of course is exactly what is going on: he is writing a letter of consolation to a monk who is also a close friend with whom he has had many long talks, as he tells us at the end of the autobiography. Abelard's account has about it the ring of a pub conversation. It is talk from the fictional lads' world in which all women are up for it and all men are completely irresistible, especially after a few drinks. Nobody in real life is that confident with the opposite sex, especially not Abelard, who previously has told us that, before meeting Heloise, he had had no experience of the company of women.* It can just about be argued that Abelard's apparent arrogance is a literary device designed to demonstrate to his monk friend the flaws in his personality that were to lead to his downfall through the agency of divine justice. Even if this is so it has to be admitted that he has a disturbingly accurate talent for portraying his own arrogance.

The self-image of cynical seducer does not seem to survive long with Abelard. The newly discovered letters tell a different story. "Did not rank lowest in looks" is replaced with "How fertile with delight is your breast, how you shine with pure beauty, body so full of moisture, that indescribable scent of yours."[5] We find him soon sending her poems full of affection. Without her, he says, light (*lux*) becomes night (*nox*) and with her *nox* becomes *lux* – "*Te sine lux mihi nox, tecum nox splendida lux est.*" Far from being the helpless plaything of an irresistible stud, Heloise has womanly power; she can transform night into day.

Abelard quickly comes to need the daily routine of letter writing:

> For even if I could write to you continuously so that I did nothing else, I would undoubtedly still have enough material: namely your integrity and your merits, which for me are so many that I could not count them all. (Abelard, Early Letters, 14)

---

* A letter to him from prior Fulk of Deuil does tell a slightly different story, it is true, suggesting that Abelard at this period consorted with prostitutes and had even squandered all his money on them. Abelard, however, does say specifically that he had had no experience of prostitutes. Even if he were lying, though, what experience he had would almost certainly date only from his return to Paris and therefore hardly be enough to have developed the kind of devastating suavity he is claiming for himself.

Not only is he brimming with tender feelings but he also shows all the insecurity that is such a common symptom of true love. We find him desperate for a letter from her — "Write anything, even a couple of words if you can,"[6] he begs. At times Heloise even seems slightly casual about the exchange, as if confident that she has the upper hand. She ends one short letter with "I would write more things to you but a few words instruct a wise man." This sounds suspiciously like an excuse, a variation on "must dash now to get this in the mail." Abelard is plainly disappointed that she has not written more but puts a brave face on it: "Indeed your words are few but I have made them many by rereading them."[7] He is under her thumb.

The apparent conflict between Abelard's account of his attitude toward love in the autobiography and the lover we meet in the new letters might at first sight seem like a reason to doubt the authenticity of the latter. Some historians have in the past indeed tried to construct an account of the affair where Abelard is telling no more or less than the truth in the autobiography. He never mentions love, goes the argument, so he never felt love. Abelard, in this account, really is a cynical seducer with no tender feelings, seeking only sexual gratification and the further inflation of his already swollen ego. Heloise was duped.

Anyone who chooses to accept this version of the affair might have a strong reason to doubt that the early letters were written by Abelard and Heloise. Other evidence, however, both from the later letters and from subsequent events, makes this premise very hard to accept. In the exchange of letters that follows the autobiography it is plain that Heloise has had many indications of love from Abelard. Remembering the days before their marriage, he says, "I desired to keep you whom I loved beyond measure for myself alone." It is hard to believe that someone with such insight into her own feelings could be easily taken in by insincere protestations of love. In later letters Abelard, without dwelling so much as Heloise on the erotic, responds to her with obvious tenderness. He does not take the opportunity of telling her that the whole relationship was based on lust. He accepts that it was love and merely tries to persuade her, as a nun, to redirect her love in more appropriate directions. Apart from the letters, we also know that Abelard wrote songs in celebration of their love. Even men seldom write verses about casual, loveless relationships.

Abelard may have believed at the beginning of the affair that he was a skillful and heartless seducer acting purely out of carnal desire. He may have resurrected that self-regarding and frankly infantile version of himself later on to reassure himself, or to ease the pain of his loss. It may even be that the misfortunes of his friend the monk also involved romantic love, making it tactless to dwell on that aspect of things in a letter of consolation. Whatever the reason for Abelard's tone in the autobiography we have all the evidence we need (with or without the new letters) to say that Abelard very soon loved Heloise. Whether that love was as intense, or even of the same quality as that of Heloise, or whether anything could be, is another question.

Abelard is very precise in his account of how the affair started. Acting as the cunning seducer, he went to Heloise's Uncle Fulbert, a fellow canon of the cathedral and therefore a man well known to him whom he could now approach as an equal. He suggested that he should become Fulbert's lodger:

> *I came to an arrangement with her uncle, with the help of some of his friends, whereby he should take me into his house, which was very near my school, for whatever sum he liked to ask. As a pretext I said that my household cares were hindering my studies and the expense was more than I could afford. Fulbert dearly loved money, and was moreover ambitious to further his niece's education in letters, two weaknesses that made it easy for me to obtain his consent and obtain my desire.* (Abelard, Autobiography)

Abelard's confidence that he was capable of reading and manipulating Fulbert's desires would later prove disastrously misplaced, but on this occasion it worked. He moved in and the philosophy lessons started. During one of them somebody, presumably Abelard, made a move. If we follow his story we can imagine the completely unsus-pecting Heloise being shocked – shocked to discover what had been going through Abelard's mind. If we prefer to see the mature and intelligent Heloise, who herself had every reason to be attracted to Abelard from the moment he walked into the cloister, sitting beside a man who by his own confession had no experience with women, then we might imagine that the affair took longer to get started. Per-haps lesson after lesson went by with Heloise waiting, hanging on his every word, gazing intently into his eyes, astonished at how slow Abelard was to realize what was being offered, until finally she man-aged to maneuver him into pouncing.

We will never know. Abelard summarizes the whole first move – whoever made it and whoever planned it – with the simple phrase "*Quid plura?*" (Need I say more?). The next thing he gives us, how-ever, is a description of their sessions together that is both charming and credible:

> . . . *and so with our lessons as a pretext we abandoned ourselves entirely to love. Her studies allowed us to withdraw in private, as love desired, with our books open before us, more words of love than of our reading passed between us, and more kissing than teaching. My hands strayed more often over the curves of her body than to the pages; love drew our eyes to look on each other more than reading kept them on our texts.* (Abelard, Autobiography)

This scene is emblematic of the love of Abelard and Heloise: the couple together in a private study, surrounded by books, talking, touching, and kissing. The closeness of their conversation combin-ing with the wordless bond of shared laughter and thrill of intimate caresses to cocoon them in their own world – a universe of two. These moments of joy and security were to become a sort of creation myth for their affair: the golden age upon which they would always look back, longing to return.

Heloise remembers and loves the specifics of their meetings. When love is lost or lovers are separated it is these precise details of time and place that take on an achingly poignant significance:

> *Everything we did, all those times and those places are stamped on my heart along with your image, so that I live through it again and again with you.* (Heloise, Second Letter)

It was a time of incomparable bliss that Heloise could never bring herself to regret:

> *The lovers' pleasures that we enjoyed together were so sweet to me that they can never displease me . . . I ought to deplore what we did but I sigh only for what we have lost.* (Heloise, Second Letter)

We have, in the new letters, the great good fortune to have been given unique coverage of the golden age of Abelard and Heloise from the inside. Abelard, writing after the event, of course, tells us in one of his less insensitive asides that the potential for written correspondence was part of the appeal of a relationship with Heloise:

> *Knowing the girl's knowledge and love of letters I thought she would be all the more ready to consent, and that even when we were separated we could enjoy each other's presence by exchange of written messages in which we could speak more openly than in person, and so need never lack the pleasures of conversation.* (Abelard, Autobiography)

It was these "written messages," so plainly referred to by Abelard, that Johannes de Vepria was to copy and edit 350 years later. The lovers originally wrote the messages on wax tablets, parchment being far too precious for everyday use. Two wooden frames were hinged together so that they looked like two pages of a book on to each of which a thin layer of wax had been melted. The message was scored on the wax with a pointed stylus and then given to a servant (who definitely did not read Latin) to take to the addressee. When the recipient had read the message it could be erased by warming the wax and smoothing it over. A reply could then be made, sometimes even conveyed by the delivering messenger if the servant had been asked to wait. It was the perfect cover: it would be quite natural for teacher and pupil to exchange exercises, essays, comments, and so forth. So long as no Latin reader saw the letters their relationship would remain secret and could be carried on right under Uncle Fulbert's nose.

At one moment Abelard even complains about having to return the tablets to Heloise so quickly:

> *If I may be permitted to keep your writing tablets a while longer, sweetest, I would write many things, just as many things would come to mind.* (Abelard, Early Letters, 14)

How, one might ask, did such communications, as ephemeral as mobile phone text messages, come to be recorded in a form that has lasted 900 years? The beginning of the story is undoubtedly Heloise herself. She presumably wrote a draft of her message on a roll of parchment before sending the wax tablet. When she received the reply she copied it underneath and then drafted her own reply underneath that. This process would produce a continuous record of the correspondence that was to continue on a daily basis for up to two years. It seems likely that de Vepria was actually looking at this roll because he sometimes seems to have had a little difficulty in knowing where one message ended and another began, which is quite understandable if he was confronted by a continuous record of the correspondence in one handwriting.

To keep a record of her letters is far from, as some have suggested, a conscious act of self-aggrandisement – keeping an eye out for the literary potential of her own emotions. It is an expression of love itself.

The most natural thing in the world to do with love letters is to keep them, read them, and reread them, to go back to them for reassurance when doubts begin to crowd in, to want to hold the thoughts that they express forever. It is part of being in love. Heloise would have kept her copies of the letters for all her life, perhaps to come across them years later in her personal library almost by accident when tidying her papers, to look at them again and be lost for an hour. Abelard tells her that this is what used to happen to him, even on a first reading:

> *Every time I begin to read your letters I am flooded with so much delight inside that I am often forced to go back over the letter I have read because the extent of my happiness takes my attention away* . . . (Abelard, Early Letters, 110)

Heloise's record of her correspondence would have been in the library at her convent when she died; it would have remained there to be discovered and copied by Johannes, the curious monk from Cîteaux who was researching his textbook on letter writing. He took his copy away and the original would have in all likelihood stayed where it was until the library of the Paraclete was destroyed during the upheavals that followed the French Revolution in 1789.

What first caught the attention of Johannes de Vepria was the openings to the letters, the salutations as they are called. Classical authors such as Cicero had a special formula for beginning a letter. Their salutations were rendered punchy and telegraphic by the special property of the Latin language, which allows it to do without prepositions such as "by," "to," and "from" simply by modifying the ending of words. In this way three words – for example *Petro Jacobus salutem* – would suffice to open a letter in a way that would have to be unpacked in English as:

Petro – [To] Peter
Jacobus – James
salutem – [sends] a greeting

"James says hi to Peter" is a simple enough phrase and classical open-ings also tended to be simple. The twelfth century, however, with its new celebration of personal relationships, had developed a fashion for complicated variations on this theme, and few carried it out to such dazzling extent as Abelard and Heloise:

> [To] *one shining wonderfully with the light of wisdom through the signs of his nobility, spreading out in the likeness of the radiant lily and the blooming rose, flourishing with the youthful flower of his whole body.*
>
> . . .
>
> *His most faithful one of all*
> [sends] *half my soul and my whole self in complete faith.*
>
> (Heloise, Early Letters, 53, 11)

Abelard is not far behind her in style:

> [To] *a singular joy and only solace of a weary mind.*
> . . .
>
> *That person whose life without you is death*
> [sends] *what more than himself insofar as he is able in body and soul.*
>
> (Abelard, Early Letters. 2)

Nor is flamboyance the only option: Heloise sometimes uses the compressed, telegraphic style of Latin with a rhythmic elegance that is evident even before one works out what it means. For example, "*Amanti amans amoris viriditatem*":

> Amanti – [To] *one who is loving*
> amans – *One who is loving*
> amoris viriditatem – [sends] *a green branch of love.*
>
> (Heloise, Early Letters, 48)

Because of the way the language works, the first three words of the letter are essentially the same – in a sense she begins her letter "Love, Love, Love," but this is modulated so that it becomes "To a lover from a lover – I send love's fresh green branch."

Because the letters have been condensed to show off the best examples of style, vital pieces of information have sometimes been left out. What remains is a kind of telegraphic record that, if taken all in one go, takes on the feel of a collection of text messages sent by teenage lovers – a slightly cloying, if always beautifully written, stream of terms of endearment. To give a selection, taken more or less at random: "his most brilliant light who is used to shining in the darkness" . . . "the spice of perfect quality and finest fragrance, multiplied a hundredfold with the seed of sweetness" . . . "his beautiful one whom neither mind nor tongue is capable of praising enough" . . . "one flowing with milk and honey" . . . "one more shiny than silver, more brilliant than any precious stone, the greatest comfort of weary spirits" . . . "the insatiable sweetness of love, surpassing every delight in pleasantness" . . . "the untainted joy, solid hope, and home of all things joyful."

Although the excisions made in the letters by Johannes de Vepria make for some difficulties of interpretation, and some downright puzzles, much of the correspondence can be linked to the circumstances of Abelard and Heloise and many of the details provide insights into the day-to-day progress of the relationship. The strain of running a secret affair, for example, shows occasionally in the shape of what must surely have been regular crises. We find Heloise warning Abelard not to make a rash decision. Why? Has there been a bad experience recently?

> *Farewell, remember that thoughtful delay is better than imprudent haste. Choose a suitable time for our meeting and let me know.* (Heloise, Early Letters, 34)

Picturesque but trivial details are included by Johannes on the grounds of style. Abelard recovers from a winter illness, and one cannot help but feel that Heloise is sending him her love laced with some affectionate irony as she looks forward to revisiting their habitual pleasures:

> *Know indeed that the midday sun has risen for you, that the chorus of birds is rejoicing over your health . . . And look too how, now that this slight snow has melted, all things flourish again, the seasons will smile on them and by the grace of God there will be for us a not unfamiliar joy.* (Heloise, Early Letters, 32)

There is at least one tiff. Something has gone wrong, Heloise has asked for forgiveness and Abelard is as magnanimous as he is precise in his thinking:

> *I would have forgiven you readily, most beloved, even if you had committed some serious act against me, because too hard would he be whom your speech so tender and amiable could not soften. But truly you have no need of forgiveness, because you have not wronged me in any way.* (Abelard, Early Letters, 35)

In a later letter the situation seems to have been reversed. Heloise is apparently giving Abelard the silent treatment in response to some misdeed. He protests how much he is suffering:

> *Have mercy on your beloved, wasting away and almost fading away unless you come quickly to help me . . .*
> *. . . ask the messenger what I did after I wrote this letter: there and then I threw myself on to the bed out of impatience.*
> (Abelard, Early Letters, 37)

In other words: "Just ask the messenger to tell you about the totally spontaneous act of desperate passion to which your behavior will drive me in a minute or so when I have finished this letter"! It is hard to work out whether this is an intentional joke or whether in his distraction he has somehow lost track of quite what a written account of an event is. Did he perhaps throw himself on the bed and then get the idea of making the remark, ask for the tablets back, and add the instruction to ask the messenger as an afterthought? Whatever the truth, it is not the cleverest thing that Abelard ever wrote.

Heloise may have found the letter appealing, however, because not long afterward it becomes obvious she has relented: "do not delay in coming; the quicker you come, the quicker you will find cause for joy."[8] This sounds to modern ears like a promise of sex and it probably is, but the new letters in general present a slightly ambiguous picture of the physical activity of the lovers. The question of when exactly they consummated their love awaits more assiduous scholarship. Whatever the precise nature of their relationship at any moment – guesses about other people's sexual activity are notoriously liable to error – it is impossible not to sense the eroticism of the letters. It is evident early on with Abelard's reference to "your body so full of moisture, that indescribable scent of yours." Heloise is able to match this with "To one who is sweeter from day to day, is loved now as much as possible and is always loved more than anything, her only one."[9] Although elsewhere she makes a remark about a wise man being able to control his passions, eventually she compliments him on his abilities as a lover, calling him "in truth very skilled in love."[10]

What is clear is that both Abelard and Heloise liked sex. That may seem an obvious remark, but in fact not only is there a wide spectrum of interest in the physical gratification of love in the population at any one time, we also tend to make assumptions about people's interest based on other aspects of their lives. To this day people find it quite surprising that an intellectual and devoutly religious woman can also have been so outspokenly keen on the physical act. In the past that surprise has frequently manifested itself as disbelief. There have been a number of theories dismissing the erotic Heloise as an invention of Abelard or some other right-minded person in order to make a moral point. All these conspiracy theories fail, however, through the complexity of the mechanism that needs to be posited in order to make them work. The sensual, brilliant, and devout Heloise is just more credible than her moralizing rivals.

Abelard, in the guise of telling his monk friend how deep he was mired in the cesspit of carnal lust, manages to give a robust account of the lovers' developing sex life:

> *Our desires left no stage of lovemaking untried, and if love could devise something new, we welcomed it. We entered on each joy the more eagerly because of our previous inexperience and were all the less easily sated.* (Abelard, Autobiography)

He is later to tell us how exhausted he was from nightly love-making, from which we can presumably conclude that the couple were able routinely to sneak into each other's rooms. Abelard goes on in his excitement to give, by way of illustration, some more specific details of the sessions behind closed doors:

> *In order that there might be no suspicion, there were, indeed, sometimes blows, but love gave them, not anger; they were the marks, not of wrath, but of a tenderness sweeter than the most fragrant balm.* (Abelard, Autobiography)

This is not the first time that chastisement is mentioned. A little earlier Abelard has gleefully told his monk friend that, when he took up his job as her tutor, Fulbert had expressly given him permission to punish Heloise:

> *He gave me complete charge over the girl . . . and if I found her idle I was to punish her severely. I was amazed at his simplicity — if he had entrusted a tender lamb to a ravening wolf it would not have surprised me more. In handing me over to punish as*

well as to teach what else was he doing but giving me complete
freedom to realize my desires . . . ?

Corporal punishment was part of medieval education, it is true,
but in the context of making children learn the repetitive rules of
Latin grammar. Heloise was in her early twenties and her Latin was
already exemplary. The kind of teaching that Abelard was doing
with her involved reading philosophical texts and commenting on
them, not drumming grammatical paradigms into a resistant young
mind. Did Uncle Fulbert really say of this woman, whom he loved
so dearly, and who would soon be addressing Abelard as "an equal
to an equal," "please teach my niece philosophy, Abelard, my dear
fellow, and feel free to smack her backside whenever you feel like it"?
It doesn't quite seem credible; nevertheless, that is the impression
Abelard gives. He is so gleeful in his description – she was like a
lamb and he was a wolf – that it sounds much more like an exagger
ation born of sheer fascination with the idea. In his mind it was an
integral part of the erotic content of their affair, so integral that he
feels the need to mention it twice, both times in the context of physi
cal love.

There does not seem to be any implication here that Abelard
coerced Heloise into having sex with him by threatening her with
violence. Abelard, when describing it, talks about "our joy," and
Heloise herself makes it plain time and again that her physical
involvement with him was both voluntary and enthusiastic. It is
plain even from Abelard's early, laddish description of the affair that
he wants what most people want when they find somebody else
attractive: that the other person should reciprocate the desire.

Later, when she was writing to him as abbess of the Paraclete,
Heloise had every opportunity to deny that sex gave her pleasure or to
claim that she was forced into it. It would be the most natural thing
in that world for her suddenly to say that the power of prayer had
enabled her to rid herself of her shameful desires and that she now
repudiated her sinful behavior. Abelard gives her the opportunity to

do so, but she resolutely refuses. Her reward is to be loved for 900 years.

The "marks of tenderness" that Abelard gave to Heloise "to allay suspicion" when they were pretending to be teacher and pupil somehow enhanced the relationship. Since there is no evidence of later complaint or recrimination it seems not unreasonable that the enhancement was mutual. It was part of the intimate world that the lovers had created for themselves. Playing out the charade probably reinforced for them the sensation that they were sharing a special experience, united in secret against a common foe. This was not punishment in the sense of retribution, but part of the sensuous round of kissing, talking, and touching that Abelard describes. They were locked into a special world of their own making, a world in which physical sensation, emotions, and ideas were explored together as the couple became almost overwhelmed by their own relationship.

In this heightened atmosphere it is possible that the "blows given by love" played a special psychological role in the lovers' lives. For Abelard there may have been pleasure in apparently controlling another human being. Did that charade relieve for him the perceived humiliations of a world that had, in his estimation, not really appreciated him? Abelard certainly had difficulty controlling or even influencing other people by the means of more conventional human interaction. If this was the case then it must have given only a fleeting relief. Outside the bedroom Heloise shows herself quite capable of arguing with her teacher: in among the language of the obedient wife is the (twice used) assertive opening "from an equal to an equal." Even at the distance of nine centuries it seems fairly clear that if one were looking for a person to dominate effectively and completely then Heloise would be a very unlikely candidate.

For Heloise, perhaps, the act of submitting to blows – giving herself symbolically to the man whom she adored – served not only as an expression of her love but also as a relief from whatever worries and torments might be distracting her. Pain is a sensation that is immediate and direct, hard to argue with. It can drive out deep anxiety of the soul and actually facilitate the enjoyment of physical pleasure.

Heloise does, despite her demonstrable independence of spirit, repeatedly use the language of submission and obedience in her letters. On two occasions in the outside world, both of great significance, she would demonstrate in deed as well as in word an absolute obedience to Abelard, even against her stated wishes. If these events really were some kind of extension of their erotic play one can only wish that Heloise had reconsidered – both acts of obedience were to have disastrous results.

The erotic intensity that was increasingly absorbing the couple in their own sensations did not put a stop to the discussion of ideas. During the affair Abelard really was teaching Heloise; they generated a friendship that blended philosophy with sensuality and love. As they become closer and closer Abelard admits that she is a constant spiritual companion:

> *You are inside my breast forever . . . you are with me until I fall asleep, while I sleep you never leave me and when I wake I see you before even the light of day . . .* (Abelard, Early Letters, 22)

He credits her with a special kind of philosophical closeness: "To others I address my words, to you my intention."[11]

The distinction between intention and words is of the greatest significance to Abelard. To the philosopher words were treacherous, capable of having a life of their own entirely independent of truth. They could distort and deceive. He was a nominalist, someone who believes that words are not necessarily an accurate guide to the way things really are. Words, in the nominalist view, could as it were be decoupled from reality to give an entirely false picture of the world, reducing them to what an earlier medieval philosopher had called *flatus vocis,* "vocal flatulence," something empty and unpleasant. Abelard's philosophical vision led him to try to go beyond words to look straight at the way things were. He goes on in the same letter to tell Heloise that he may tend to be inept with words because his thoughts are on the reality beyond them: "I may stumble over words because my thoughts are far from them."[12]

In the same way, when thinking about the rightness or wrongness of an action he was aware that what people did, and indeed what they said, was not a reliable guide to whether they were good or bad. It is possible to do something for entirely good reasons that turns out to create nothing but misery, and contrariwise to do something out of self-ishness that appears to others to be the most altruistic act imaginable. Intention was to Abelard the truth of the soul to which actions were an unreliable guide. What we intend is, to Abelard, what decides the value of our action; it is the part of ourselves that we cannot fake.

When he tells Heloise that to her he is expressing not words but intention he is making the most profound expression that he can of their emotional closeness. He is saying that he is so close to her that he is able to bypass the deceitfulness of words and share with her the truth of his soul, the part that cannot be false:

> *Now that our love has grown so strong that it shines forth by itself there is little need of words because we are overflowing with what is real.* (Abelard, Early Letters, 54)

By investing all the moral value of an action in the intention of the doer Abelard finds himself with a slightly eccentric view of the idea of sin. There are many things that might make someone consider an act evil: it might be considered against the will of God, it might have horrific consequences, it might be done by somebody who is in the grip of rage or of some other distortion of the mind. Abelard in his ethical writing is quite specific about rejecting all of these possibili-ties. For him evil originates, by definition, from "consent to that which we believe to be wrong."[13] He makes sin something to do with consent — a thing of the mind, not an action at all. If we are unable to consent, therefore, we cannot sin.

Intentionalism (as this particular ethical view is called) leads him to attach great importance to individuals and their thoughts. This is reflected in the title of his book about moral philosophy: Know Thy-self – significantly not "Know the Commandments" or even "Know What Is Good." An ethical concern with intention is not only very much in keeping with the emerging humanism of the twelfth century but is also very congenial to modern sensibilities – it is a morality that is slow to apportion blame. A newborn baby, for instance, cannot consent to anything, therefore it cannot sin. This is at odds with the orthodox Christian view that all people are born sinful because humanity itself entails "original sin." Abelard's argument leads him to question this – a newborn baby who dies without having been baptized cannot have sinned and therefore will not go to hell, runs the potential argument. He does not blame any person who is driven to a desperate act by strong emotions akin to madness, because if the person was truly mad they were incapable of rational consent to the action.

There is every reason to believe such ideas were discussed by Abelard and Heloise during the eighteen months or so that their affair went undetected. In the few philosophical writings that date from before the affair he does not write about them, but he does afterward. So does Heloise: intentionalism is the guiding principle behind her complaint to Abelard about being in a convent. She knows that her true feelings are not in accord with her situation. While this is the case, no show of piety and no amount of good behavior will ever make her life morally worthwhile.

Typically for the man who followed logic at the expense of any other consideration, Abelard managed to push his definition of sin to such an extent that it upset people. Determined to show how far he could travel by logic alone, he pronounces in his treatise on ethics that even those who crucified Christ did not sin in their action if they believed that they were doing the will of God. The logic is impeccably applied and the effect to modern ears is wholly laudable – once again Abelard comes across as a compassionate man. To some of his contemporaries he was apparently saying that what was believed to be the most awful crime in the history of the world was not a sin. This conclusion was buried in the detail of philosophical argument and he does couch the remark as a hypothetical question, "If someone asks whether the persecutors of Christ sinned . . . we cannot say they sinned from this."[14] Years later, however, its effect, when taken out of context by those who were not philosophers, was to be very damaging for Abelard.

While philosophy remains the first concern of Abelard, it is Heloise who provides the understanding of love. She often takes charge of the conversation, describing herself as "the foundation of a secure and faithful love,"[15] even calling Abelard a beginner, and ending one long letter by declaring that she has now given an account of how their love should be maintained. In the words of Constant Mews, the scholar who first argued the case for the authenticity of the new letters, it is Abelard who in matters of love is "tagging along behind, trying to pick it up and only just managing it."[16]

It is Heloise who by contrast senses the completeness and the scope of their love affair:

> *Surely I have discovered in you the greatest and most outstanding good of all.* (Heloise, Early Letters, 49)

For her, ideas of good and truth intertwine with the intense longing, respect, and need for another person. They come together into that grand, wide-reaching feeling of everlasting peace that sometimes comes to lovers on a starry night:

> *Since it is established that this is eternal, it is for me the proof beyond doubt that you will remain in my love for eternity.*
> (Heloise, Early Letters, 49)

The heavens, of all the things we ever see the closest to eternal, were plainly of interest to the couple. Abelard calls her "my brightest star whose rays I have recently enjoyed."[17] She calls him "my dear-est light and solstice" and calls herself "she whom no sun but you warms by day nor moon at night."[18] Abelard observes that he feels like the moon deprived of the sun's light:

> *Physicists say often that the moon does not shine without the sun, and that when deprived of this light, it is robbed of all ben-efit of heat and brightness and presents to humans a dark ashen sphere.* (Abelard, Early Letters, 22)

Perhaps they had walked together at night among the pleasant vine-yards that belonged to Abelard's patrons, the Garlandes, on the left bank of the Seine. The eerie, disorienting landscape that is created by moonlight seems at first sight to have much more to do with fear and death than love, yet it frequently provides the scenery against which couples appreciate briefly together the universal potential of love. If Abelard and Heloise had been accustomed to looking at the stars together, appreciating love in all its forms, it might explain their ref-erences to the celestial universe. An interest in astronomy is the best explanation anybody has for the fact that the couple were soon to take the bizarre step of naming their son after a medieval scientific instru-ment that is itself a model of the heavens.

SIX

Love and marriage

1116

*Those who are in the grip of sexual desire's numerous incitements
perceive little or nothing.*
Fulk of Deuil, Letter to Abelard

ARLY ON in the correspondence Abelard had expressed the wish, "may I gaze endlessly at you alone, ignoring the light of day."[1] This feeling is familiar enough to those who are deeply in love; but it is not advisable to ignore the light of day for too long. His all-consuming passion began to consume too much of his energy as a scholar and teacher. The ideas he discussed between kisses with his most intelligent and beautiful pupil had become the only philosophy that interested him:

> *It was utterly boring for me to have to go to the school and equal-
> ly wearisome to remain there and to spend my days on study
> when my nights were sleepless with lovemaking. As my interest
> and concentration flagged my lectures lacked all inspiration and
> were merely repetitive of what had been said before.* (Abelard,
> Autobiography)

It is indicative of Abelard's high standards as a teacher and perhaps even of the general quality of debate in a medieval school that he is concerned that his lectures might be mere repetition. Some would say that this was the definition of a lecture.

A note in the early letters reflects this breakdown of Abelard's habitual philosophical activity: "This laziness must be shaken off, and along with the fervor of the season a new fervor for composition must be taken up."[2] He tells us in the autobiography that his creative energies, such as they were, found an outlet more often in his other talent, the gift for songwriting for which Heloise says she first loved him. He cannot resist pointing out to his monk friend that his musical offerings have, fifteen years later, stood the test of time and did indeed reach their target audience: "A lot of these songs as you know are still popular and sung in many places, particularly by those who enjoy the kind of life I led."[3]

Heloise does tell us that it was the beauty of the tunes that made these songs well known even among the unlettered, thereby indicating that they were written in Latin. To those who knew Latin, however, the songs must have been laden with clues as to the identity of the lady who was being celebrated. For those who could not understand the words they would be accompanied by anecdotes and mistranslations. Stories about Canon Fulbert's lodger who melodramatically threw himself on the bed when dispatching a letter to his student would have combined with the songs to make a first-class piece of gossip. Heloise when recalling this time seems to have been well aware that the affair was far from secret. She remarks that Abelard was so popular that "even queens and great ladies envied me my joys and my bed."[4]

As his pride in the success of his songs shows, Abelard was not displeased with the idea of being a celebrity lover. On the other hand he had much to lose from exposure. Stories of impropriety would jeopardize his position as master of the school, which was after all a religious appointment. The reforming movement, which was already against him because of his association with his antireformer patron, Stephen de Garlande, was concerned with the imposition of a stricter sexual morality on all levels of society. A scandal might give his detractors the excuse they needed to get rid of him.

It is not certain how long the affair continued before anxieties began to intrude on their private world. From the dates we know, the duration of the affair, from first meeting to final catastrophe, cannot be more than two years. Quite soon in the early correspondence that covers this period he is warning Heloise, "you should not be sur-prised if twisted jealousy should turn its eyes towards such a conspic-uous and fitting friendship as ours."[5] He urges caution, spoiling the joyous affirmation of philosophical closeness – "Now that our love has grown so strong that it shines forth by itself there is little need of words" – by using it to soften the blow of a suggestion to take things easy:

> ... nevertheless it is not unreasonable if sometimes, or now for example, we alternate between visiting each other and having a letter take the place of physical presence. (Abelard, Early Let-ters, 54)

Heloise's reply to this suggestion is finely judged and firm. As far as she is concerned the relationship is not capable of being toned down:

> I think you are not unaware, my sweet light, that ashes placed on a sleeping fire never put it out ... and so not for any reason will external events be able to wipe out the thought of you that is bound to my heart with a chain of gold. (Heloise, Early Letters, 55)

Nevertheless they seem to have reduced the frequency of their meetings. Heloise in her next letter describes herself as "unjustly deprived of the privilege of love." Abelard then replies that "an unavoidable matter has put its foot against my desire." Is this the gen-eral threat of scandal or some other problem? It doesn't make much difference to the course of the dialogue because he makes the mistake of signing off with "I am guilty, I who compelled you to sin."[6]

This remark triggers a lengthy complaint from Heloise. To claim that he was the only sinner is to deny that Heloise has made choices for herself. This would be hurtful enough to anybody, but especially so for someone who is trying to build a philosophical partnership and who, more than once, greets the greatest philosopher of the age as "an equal." It is in effect saying that her intention – the part of her that, in their philosophy, God judges – has been valueless or at least inactive. Abelard was to make a similar denial of Heloise's inner responsibility when, fifteen years later, he asserted in the autobiography that – now that the affair was over – Heloise was holy and free from sin. She reacted in the same way on both occasions.

She tells him in the next letter that she is disappointed in him: "I had placed all my hope in you, as though you were an invincible tower . . . take your complaints away from me, I will not hear your words anymore." She must, one imagines, still be referring to Abelard's ill-considered "this is all my fault," or maybe he had made other remarks on what she felt were slightly self-pitying lines. Heloise's fury is in any case unambiguous; she nearly ends the affair with a final, "from now on may all our writing cease."[7]

It does not cease. Abelard replies with (feigned?) puzzlement: "I do not know what so great sin of mine preceded that in such a short time you could wish to throw away completely all feelings of compassion and intimacy for me."[8] A series of loving letters from Abelard follows until Heloise puts an end to the fighting with a final reference to her philosophical self: "My intention has decided this: that further conflict between us should cease. Dreadful anger has already swelled enough with words thrown at each other."[9]

From this point the letters continue to show the tensions inherent in the relationship. It is quite difficult to know exactly what is happening: successive letters do not always answer each other and often seem to refer to events of which we have no record. What is clear is that there is a constant rise and fall of emotion as the lovers alternate between reassuring each other of their love and chiding each other for failing to respond in the right way. Heloise complains, "you have changed your ways and so trust is not secure anymore."[10] She even says at one point that she regrets having fastened her heart so firmly to him alone. Abelard takes up the role of reassurer, signing himself "the same friend that he has always been" sending "the same constancy of love,"[11] and later simply "I am the person I was." The need for reassurance is probably never far from the need for love in any affair, but one cannot help feeling that the relationship is showing the strain of having to be kept secret and the growing realization, certainly on Abelard's part, of the potential consequences of letting this private matter become public.

Despite the (probably only intermittent) attempts at increased security, or even apparent attempts to end the liaison, their affair became more and more public:

> Few could have failed to notice something so obvious. In fact no one, I fancy, except the man whose honor was most involved — Heloise's uncle. Several people tried on more than one occasion to draw his attention to it, but he would not believe them.
> (Abelard, Autobiography)

Abelard attributes Fulbert's failure to realize what was going on, even when well-wishers attempted to bring the matter to his attention, to his own reputation for chastity. We might also be inclined to wonder whether, for Fulbert, the idea of Abelard making love to his beautiful niece might have been so abhorrent that it would be impossible for him to accept it. It does seem plausible that he had for some time been blocking the very possibility from his mind. There must have been clues in his own house. Lovers who are completely wrapped up in themselves seldom fail to display some outward signs of inner reality — the laughter that stops as a third person enters the room or covert glances, exchanged in conspiracy or perhaps mockery. When Fulbert finally did find out he might well have spent some time running incidents over in his mind and feeling the extra pain of a long-term deception:

What is last to be learned is somehow learned eventually, and common knowledge cannot easily be hidden from one individual. Several months passed and then this happened in our case.
(Abelard, Autobiography)

It was only by stages that Fulbert found himself forced to con‚ front the truth. When he first began to realize what was going on he obliged the couple to separate. The affair continued, however, both through letter writing and through meetings. According to Abelard frustration inflamed their passion and lessened their inhibitions:

Separation drew our hearts still closer while frustration inflamed our passion even more; then we became more abandoned as we lost all sense of shame and, indeed, shame diminished as we found more opportunities for lovemaking. (Abelard, Autobiography)

He also reminds Heloise in a later letter that he had made love to her during Easter and other significant religious festivals. Although to us it seems that if making love is a sin, then the day on which one does it is neither here nor there, this was not the view of many at the time. Ivo of Chartres, the reforming bishop and enemy of Abelard's patron, Stephen, was of the opinion that not only sex but also sexual fantasies were inherently evil. His law book codified specific rules about how and where people were permitted to indulge their regret‚ table appetites. These rules were not his own invention; they were the cumulative prohibitions of centuries. Celibate clerical lawgivers had amassed so many rules that they had succeeded in making marriage more frustrating than celibacy.*

---

* Historian James Brundage imagines a series of questions to which an aspirant lover must give the right answer if he was to achieve sexual fulfillment with the approval of the church authorities: Feeling randy? – Are you married? No? Stop, sin! – Is this your wife? No? Stop, sin! – Married for more than three days? No? Stop, sin! – Is your wife menstru‚ ating? Yes? Stop, sin! – Is your wife pregnant? Yes? Stop, sin! – Is it Lent? Yes? Stop, sin! – Is it Advent? Yes? Stop, sin! – Is it Whitsun week? Yes? Stop, sin! – Is it Easter week? Yes?

It is not easy to tell how much notice ordinary people took of these rules in their daily lives. Other people's sexual behavior is notoriously hard to determine even in the case of contemporaries, and in the case of the Middle Ages there is almost no record of any aspect of the behavior of the majority of ordinary people. Below a certain level in the social hierarchy a person's life does not show up in the historical record in any form. The common folk were just not of interest to the people who wrote down things. Abelard himself mentions the feastday transgression only when he is compiling a list of the enormity of their sins in order to illustrate to Heloise how much better off they are now that they are sinning no more.

It is clear, however, that, outside the uninhibited private world of the lovers, there were reserves of moralistic disapprobation that could easily be directed at them. It might be observed that not all of it was misplaced: there is an argument, not fashionable at the moment but comprehensible none the less, that the sexual urge does indeed distract men and women from more worthwhile pursuits. Few people, if they look into their souls, can deny that at some time in their lives they would have achieved more had they not spent so much time in the pursuit of carnal gratification.

But medieval moralists took the argument a stage further and considered sex not only a distraction but also a base motivation capable of taking over the human mind. Sexual desire is a constant invitation to sin and therefore to be continually repudiated. Religious disapproval of sex does often seem to be driven less by theology and more by a visceral reflex of disgust at the physicality of sex. Anselm of

---

Stop, sin! – Is it a feast day? Yes? Stop, sin! – Is it Sunday? Yes? Stop, sin! – Is it Wednesday? Yes? Stop, sin! – Is it Friday? Yes? Stop, sin! – Is it Saturday? Yes? Stop, sin! – Is it daylight? Yes? Stop, sin! – Are you naked? Yes? Stop, sin! – Are you in church? Yes? Stop, sin! – Do you want a child? No? Stop, sin! If you answered all the above correctly you can go ahead but no fondling, no lewd kisses, no oral sex, and no strange positions. Do it only once. Try not to enjoy it and wash afterward (*Law, Sex, and Christian Society in Medieval Europe* [Chicago: Univ. of Chicago Press, 1987]).

Canterbury (later St. Anselm), for example, in a letter written in Abelard's lifetime tries to persuade an aristocratic lady to return to her convent by describing what had become of her former lover:[12]

> *Go now sister, lie down with him on the bed in which he now lies; gather his worms to your bosom; embrace his corpse; press your lips to his naked teeth, for his lips have already been consumed by putrefaction.* (Anselm of Canterbury, *Letters*, p. 70)

A century earlier the reforming cleric Peter Damian had written to a certain Countess Blanche dissuading her from the pleasures of the flesh:[13]

> *Call to mind that the flesh that now is nourished by dainty food will in a little while be swarming with worms: that it will become the food of rodents . . . that it will admit an overwhelmingly fetid and putrefying odor proportionate to the gentle sweetness on which it was reared.* (Peter Damian, *Letters*, 169)

In both these examples disgust is mixed with an almost sadistic desire to make the object of the homily wallow in decaying flesh. It is hard not to wonder whether the writer's own struggle to wrench himself free of his desires has generated this revulsion, or even a need for vengeance against someone who has tasted the joy that he has succeeded only in transforming into horror.

That Fulbert merely obliged the lovers to separate without taking any further action seems to indicate that he was not at first driven by such a vehement level of disapproval. It is possible that up until that time, if not actually telling himself that it wasn't happening, Fulbert was still able to prevent himself from confronting the tormenting image of his niece with Abelard. But the lack of inhibition that the couple were showing during their "separation" led to the worst possible outcome: they were caught in the act by Fulbert. Perhaps they had taken the opportunity to sneak back to the house when they thought Fulbert was out. When he walked in on them he faced a picture that could no longer be excluded from his imagination.

Whatever revulsion he felt must have been mixed also with regret. The intelligent young niece who had quite suddenly entered his life had by then become something very close to a daughter — a means of fulfillment that his clerical calling denied him. No doubt she had been always respectful and polite; someone for him to educate himself, thoughtful and devout; a pupil who understood what he understood; a conduit through which the things that he perceived as most noble and beautiful could be transmitted into the future. Without the inhibitions created in a family home the distinction between paternal affection and erotic interest can become blurred. We do not even have to imagine any grosser intimacy to imagine how Fulbert must have soon come to take pleasure in the physical presence of his niece. It would have been easy for him, a man with little experience of women, to overestimate the intensity of their emotional bond; politeness and good nature would be easy to mistake for deeper feelings.

Now, having discovered them together, he was forced to confront a single, undeniable picture that destroyed forever any hope of fulfillment through Heloise. Abelard attests later in the autobiography to the fact that Fulbert was prone to rages; it is not hard to imagine the powerful emotion that the discovery might generate. Abelard's carnal union with her would seem to block him from any kind of intimacy, physical or spiritual, with her. He now felt maliciously excluded from the world that the two of them had built, in which they had enclosed for themselves everything beautiful that he had thought to attain through Heloise. She had deceived him not just in a single act but continually for a long period; now his whole world was undermined. She had mocked him and the hoped-for beauty that he saw in her was made worthless by this selfish and disgusting act.

Even if the pain that followed his discovery was insufficient to push Fulbert to the act for which he has entered history, there was more to come. The next event has an inevitability about it. "Soon afterward," says Abelard with his usual vagueness but that we can interpret as "soon enough to preclude any action from Fulbert," Heloise discovered that she was pregnant. She wrote to Abelard (by now it was presumably impossible for them to meet) "a letter full of joy" asking what he thought they should do. It is not hard to understand her joy: she now had the very conduit to the future that Fulbert had longed for, a physical manifestation of her love, a spiritual friendship in human form. Nor is it hard to imagine that Abelard's immediate response might have been more complex. Added to the uncertainty that all men feel at the prospect of fatherhood was his knowledge of the medieval disapproval of all sexual liaisons, and quite possibly his appreciation of the strength of Fulbert's feelings.

There may be a clue as to what passed between them in the brief and poignant note that is Heloise's final contribution to the early letters. There has plainly been a great deal of argument; we are not told what about but it is clear that she is exhausted:

> *Where there is passion and love there is always struggle and turmoil. Now I am tired. I cannot reply to you because you are taking sweet things as burdensome and in doing so you sadden my spirit. Farewell.* (Heloise, *Early Letters*, 112a)

Whether one of the "sweet things" that Abelard is "taking as burdensome" really is her pregnancy will never be known. Although the overall picture that the letters provide is clear – love, adversity, secrecy, separation – the exact correlation between the story of the lovers and the twists and turns of the letters is very hard to ascertain. But whatever the exact event to which it refers, this paragraph sets very well the closing scene of the golden age of the love of Abelard and Heloise. From this moment on, outside events would drive the lovers. They were never again to inhabit the universe of two.

Heloise had asked Abelard what he thought they should do. His answer was that she should go to his sister-in-law in Brittany. He waited until Fulbert was away and took Heloise out of Paris, presumably by the road south, across the river and through the vineyards and on toward Orléans, from where she would travel by boat. He notes later that he disguised her as a nun. The disguise would have been needed only in the cathedral precincts and in the immediate vicinity of the Ile de la Cité where she might have been recognized. A nun's habit is possibly the ideal disguise: face and hair would be covered; with a hood drawn forward it would be very hard for any⁄body to recognize her, nor would her presence on the street provoke any comment. To use this disguise, of course, broke the sacred sym⁄bolism of the garments. The veil symbolized the vows, the marriage to Christ. To use it for frivolous or immoral purposes could be con⁄strued as blasphemy.

Abelard documents Fulbert's rage with something like the detachment of a philosopher; his anger had to be seen to be believed:

> *Her uncle went almost out of his mind — one could appreciate only by experience his transports of grief and mortification. What action could he take against me?* (Abelard, Autobiography)

Fulbert did not know what had happened to his beloved niece; he probably did not know that she was pregnant. His already intense agony was now compounded with fear and uncertainty. He knew, of course, that it was Abelard who had removed her and, judging by later events, his instinct would have been to take measures against him. However, in the autobiography Abelard explains that he has made a clever move. With Heloise in Brittany, Fulbert could take no action against him for fear of what Abelard's own people might do to Heloise:

> *What traps could he set? He did not know. If he killed me or did me personal injury, there was a danger that his beloved niece might suffer for it in my country. It was useless to try to seize me or confine me anywhere against my will, especially as I was very much on guard against this very thing.* (Abelard, Autobiography)

In these remarks we see an aspect of the world of Fulbert and Abelard that the autobiography generally underplays: the role of legitimized vengeance. This is a society where the rule of law is still emerging. Justice can be administered not only by the state but also by the individual or their family. Medieval law books include, along with lists of penalties, lists of acceptable acts of revenge for specific acts. A wronged family could, within certain defined limits, legally exact their own punishment for a perceived wrong. The recipient of the revenge then had redress in law if he or she felt it to have been excessive or inappropriate. This is the world of the blood feud, more familiar to us from *Romeo and Juliet* than from *Abelard and Héloïse*. On the Ile de la Cité Abelard might have been just a brilliant but difficult academic, but back in Brittany he was a member of a prominent family and an attack on him would have been seen as a matter for revenge. The removal of Heloise to Brittany served not only to protect her from scandal, it protected them both from the still-growing rage of Fulbert.

Heloise was to stay in Brittany for several months – from shortly after she was certain she was pregnant until after the birth of their son – probably with the family of Abelard's brother Dagobert, who had inherited the family estate, and, we know, had a wife and children of his own. In a large household it was probably not too much trouble to look after the clever girl from Paris.

Abelard says that it was Heloise who chose the name Astralabe. But, given the proprietary feeling a man normally has for his first-born, it is likely that had he objected he would have mentioned it. It is the name of a medieval scientific instrument and a bizarre choice for a baby's name in any language. In the Middle Ages Christians were expected to have a saint's name. Even though this rule was not very strictly enforced at this time, the couple's eccentric choice was guaranteed to shock. The nun transcribing the son's name into the records of the Paraclete writes it as Peter Astralabe, but there is no other evidence that he was ever called Peter. It seems quite possible that she was just trying to take the edge off the apparent irreligiousness of the name.

To call one's child after a scientific instrument must have been a sort of joint declaration of uniqueness by the couple. Such an un-christian name must have caused comment in the isolated village of le Pallet. There is a fragment of a sixteenth-century Breton song that describes Heloise as Abelard's witch. That is an accusation that only the superstitious Bretons ever made and it seems quite possible that the rumor started at this time with gossip about Master Peter's weird Parisian girlfriend.

But the name is not one that a witch would choose; on the contrary, it is most likely to appeal to a Parisian intellectual. Nor, although it is the name of a piece of sophisticated technology, is it quite the equivalent of naming one's child today something like "Microprocessor." The astrolabe (as the name of the instrument is usually spelled) is more than a piece of technology: it is a handheld model of the universe. A fretwork disc rotates over a solid backplate; as it does so it demonstrates the daily motion of the heavens, the rising and setting of the sun, and the stars. An astrolabe can theoretically be used to tell the time and this is often stated as its purpose, but in fact the instruments from the early Middle Ages are so small — the whole of the sky is shrunk to a 12cm disc — that they are hopelessly inaccurate.

The astrolabe is not a practical instrument at all; it is a sort of aid to meditation, a way of contemplating the complex motions of the heavens. By tracing out the yearly motion of the sun we can under-stand why there is summer and winter; we can see why the sun climbs higher in southern lands; we know that there must be a place on the earth that spends six months in darkness and six in light. It is astro-nomical knowledge crystallized into solid form. Beautifully crafted examples, mostly based on models from the Islamic world, were among the possessions of every medieval scholar who professed to understand the nature of the universe.

The couple who had watched the stars while lying together among the vines on the left bank of the Seine and called each other sun and moon in their love letters must have understood the significance of the name. They prided themselves on their rational understanding of the world. Just as the astrolabe was a physical sign of the possibility of understanding through reason, the child was a physical expression of their love.

Little Astralabe was to be left in Brittany, in the care of Abelard's family. To modern eyes this might be seen as bad parenting but it was not uncommon at the time for children to be "farmed out" to relatives. There is also some telling evidence that they both loved and cared about their child. In the autobiography Abelard calls him "our little fellow" (*parvulus noster*), hardly the words of somebody who didn't care. He seems to be aware of both the vulnerability of the young Astralabe and the fact that he was the responsibility of them both. He was also to write a lengthy poem, known as *Carmen ad Astralabium* (Song for Astralabe), which opens with the words "Astralabe, my son, the delight of your father's life, I have a few words for your instruction." The version of the poem that survives is plainly only a draft; it is repetitive and contains fewer insights than one might expect. He does at one point, however, refer rather charmingly to Astralabe's mother as "our Heloise" while quoting her remark that her past sins were so pleasurable that she could not regret them. This again is not the language of somebody who had abandoned his son. On the contrary, it gives the impression that the three of them did indeed think of themselves as a family. We also find Heloise much later using her influence and writing to the abbot of Cluny asking him to get Astralabe a job. Significantly she specifically requests a monastery near to her. Evidence about Astralabe's later life is sparse, but it is possible to fit him into his parents' story with some certainty.

In Paris Fulbert's rage continued unabated. Abelard eventually went to see him. He says that he did this out of pity, but he might also have realized that the situation could not be allowed to continue if he was to remain master of the school. Abelard apologized to Fulbert, offered to make amends, and threw himself on his mercy. He entered a plea of mitigation, claiming that he had "done nothing that a person familiar with the power of love would find unusual." There is an element of truth in this remark. It is made less attractive, however, when it emerges that Abelard was plainly not distinguishing between the power of love and the wickedness of women. He went on to say that he was just another victim: "I reminded him how since the beginning of the human race women had brought the noblest of men to ruin."

However craven this shifting of blame onto an absent Heloise, it seems to have struck the right note with Fulbert. He was still in torment, playing over and over in his mind the circumstances of Heloise's systematic deception. In his despair he was probably ready to hear a version of events that painted her as evil. He accepted Abelard's offer that, by way of righting the wrong that he had done to him, Abelard would marry Heloise. Abelard stipulated one condition: that the marriage should remain secret. A public marriage would wreck his career; the rising tide of monastic reform meant that rules were being tightened up — it was now impossible for a cleric in such a prominent position to have a wife. Fulbert agreed:

> He agreed, pledged his word and that of his supporters and sealed the reconciliation I desired with a kiss. (Abelard, Autobiography)

It was a negotiated settlement, an uneasy accommodation worked out to avoid what could have been a very ugly situation. And it might well have achieved its aim had it not been for Heloise.

Back in Brittany she knew nothing of their meeting. Abelard therefore made the journey himself to fetch his mistress and to tell her what the men had decided. In almost all stories of unexpected or unwanted pregnancy marriage is offered as the morally optimal solution to which the woman in question is drawn by her instinct for homemaking. But Heloise said no. She had a number of reasons for opposing the marriage and Abelard records them in the autobiography; it constitutes a large section of the book. In her first letter, which is her reply to the autobiography, she goes over some of them again because she doesn't feel he has represented them quite correctly. As they cut their deal, Abelard and Fulbert — two men who loved her — should surely have expected that Heloise, who spent her time examining the nature of love and of her own feelings, would have something to say. In fact her thoughts on this subject provide some of her most startling writing.

Her first objection was that marriage would damage Abelard's career. To stand in the way of the natural development of his genius would be one of the worst things she could imagine. Abelard related her argument to his monk friend:

> *What honor could she win, she protested, from a marriage that would dishonor me and humiliate us both? The world would justly exact punishment from her if she removed such a light from its midst . . . Nature had created me for all mankind . . .*
> (Abelard, Autobiography)

This argument doubtless sounded eminently reasonable to Abelard, who retells Heloise's remarks about his luminous uniqueness as if they were quite unremarkably factual. She, he says, went on to detail exactly how marriage might damage the life of a philosopher:

> *"Who can concentrate on scripture and philosophy and be able to endure babies crying, nurses soothing them with lullabies, and all the noisy coming and going of men and women about the house?"*
> (Heloise, quoted in Abelard's Autobiography)

She continues, like a true medieval writer, with a list of authorities and historical examples to back up her case. From the Christian world she quotes St. Paul who says that those who marry shall have "pain and grief in this bodily life."[14] Moving on to the Greeks she mentions the philosopher Theophrastus, who details the pain and annoyance of a marriage. Among the Romans, she says, Seneca said that philosophy is not a subject to be pursued in leisure time and that for that reason all the pagan philosophers had led blameless and chaste lives. Cicero, the master of Latin letter writing and therefore a particular hero of hers, she points out, refused to marry a second time on the grounds that it would interfere with his life as a philosopher.

It is possible to quibble with these arguments, or at least Abelard's representation of them. Their child would be cared for elsewhere, for example, so that particular problem would not apply to them. As for "blameless and chaste lives," she is arguing against marriage, not against the affair, so the remark is hardly to the point. None of this matters, however, because Heloise is absolutely right: a public marriage would have destroyed him as a philosopher. He would have had to resign from the cathedral school. Although he could have set up his own school or perhaps even obtained some other living he would have stepped down from the pinnacle of achievement that it had taken him sixteen years to attain. That would be like admitting that he was no longer "the only philosopher in the world." It was fundamental to the relationship that they both believed that, in her words, "nature had created him for all mankind." If they turned their back on that destiny they would no longer have been Abelard and Heloise.

A secret marriage might have answered these objections and allowed him to continue as master of the school – this was Abelard's plan. Heloise's answer was that a secret marriage would not satisfy Fulbert. She had, after all, lived with him; she had no doubt sensed his passion for her and been a witness to his rage. She knew that a negotiated compromise would not hold back his emotions for long.

Heloise's final argument, which she expands in her first letter to Abelard, is drawn from her ideas about love. The spiritual and philosophical love that Heloise is trying to construct is not compatible with the socially defined formal ties of marriage. She has observed, as many women have since, that marriage is often an essentially economic union:

> *A woman should realize that if she marries a rich man more readily than a poor one and desires her husband more for his pos-*

sessions than for himself, she is offering herself for sale. Cer-
tainly any woman who comes to marry through desires of this
kind deserves wages not gratitude . . . (Heloise, First Letter)

Her love for Abelard binds them by its own nature; it doesn't need
any public sanction, much less a commercial transaction. Marriage,
in the opinion of Heloise, is for other people. She makes her point
with a combination of philosophical thought, submissiveness, and
eroticism, which one feels can only have come out of those now
longed-for sessions behind closed doors in Fulbert's house:

> *The name of wife may seem more sacred or more binding, but*
> *sweeter for me will always be the word mistress, or, if you will*
> *permit me, that of concubine or whore.* (Heloise, First Letter)

The extravagant sensuousness of offering herself to her lover as
his whore disguises what might actually have been a practical option
for the couple. Heloise could simply have remained Abelard's mistress and friend (the word *amica* in medieval Latin can mean both).
Abelard could then have continued as master of the school,
Astralabe would have remained in Brittany and the affair could have
continued discreetly. Clerics of minor orders (those who were not
fully fledged monks or priests, including cathedral canons) had traditionally had concubines. There were attempts to end this state of
affairs but the reformers were by no means yet victorious. Heloise as
concubine would have been less of an impediment to Abelard's
career than Heloise as wife. Marriage was seen as, in historian
Michael Clanchy's phrase, "a formal commitment to repeated acts of
sexual gratification,"[15] and therefore actually one step worse than
occasional lapses into casual fornication.

Viewed today this might seem a very sensible solution. So why
was Abelard so insistent on getting married? He gives one answer in
a later letter saying, "I desired to keep you whom I loved beyond
measure for myself alone,"[16] but that hardly seems a strong enough

reason. Heloise never tires of telling him that she is his alone; he can have had no doubts about her devotion and he never displays any in his writing. One can only speculate that Abelard may have been driven by fear of Fulbert. Heloise may have had no desire whatsoever to be made an honest woman of, but it does seem very likely that it was a sine qua non for Fulbert. The threat either of violent retribution or of damage to Abelard's standing as master of the school must have been voiced at the meeting in a way strong enough to make Abelard insist on marriage. Heloise eventually gave in, not because she was persuaded by Abelard's arguments but by her desire to obey – the first of her two fatal acts of submission. She cannot resist one chilling last word:

> But at last she saw that her attempts to persuade or dissuade me were making no impression on my foolish obstinacy, and she could not bear to offend me; amidst deep sighs and tears she ended in these words: "We shall both be destroyed. All that is left to us is suffering as great as our love has been." (Abelard, Autobiography)

Abelard comments wryly, "in this the whole world knows that she was a true prophet."

They left Astralabe in Brittany and returned to Paris. Abelard describes the wedding in a single, short sentence: "After a night's private vigil and prayer in a certain church at dawn we were joined in matrimony in the presence of Fulbert and some of his, and some of our, friends." Abelard refers almost coyly to "a certain church" as if there is something special about it that he is not at liberty to divulge. This has led some people to suggest that it was in fact the chapel of the sumptuous house that his patron, Stephen de Garlande, had recently built on the northern perimeter of the cathedral precinct. Stephen had reputedly imported craftsmen from the great monastery of Cluny to build the little chapel of St.-Aignan, which still exists and is one of only two buildings in Paris from Abelard's time that are still standing.

The all-night private vigil would have been the culmination for Abelard and Heloise of long sessions of serious talk as they made their way back to Paris. It was a chance to think together, perhaps for the last time, of the relationship between their love and the great truth that religion sought to express. The marriage itself was more for the benefit of the witnesses than for God. By canon law the ceremony was required to take place in daylight. Abelard does not mention a priest and there might not even have been one: the exact rules for a marriage were still being worked out and it was not universally agreed that a priest was necessary. Even less certain is the legality of a secret marriage. Ivo of Chartres, the reforming jurist, specifically states that such a marriage would not be valid. The point of a wedding is public affirmation of commitment. If it was not known to all, went the argument, it would be too easy to renege on the promises later. But nobody raised this point at Abelard's wedding. Fulbert was the person who needed to be convinced. If he had no objections, the negotiated settlement was working.

After the wedding the couple lived apart; she in Fulbert's household and he in nearby lodgings. This was marriage as divorce. It must have quickly dawned on all parties that the agreement was in fact very unsatisfactory. For Abelard and Heloise, since no public acknowledgement of the marriage was possible it was difficult for them to continue to enjoy a full relationship. Fulbert's situation was even worse: the required secrecy made it impossible for him to console himself with the thought that at least the damaged honor of his family had been repaired for all to see.

His solution to this problem was, as we would say now, to leak the story. Abelard says that he engaged his servants in the task of making sure people knew about the marriage. As the rumor spread people naturally enough asked Heloise whether it was true. When Heloise was confronted she saw no way of defending Abelard but to deny it. Doubtless embarrassed at being forced to lie, she turned on her inquisitors and a public row ensued. Her proven ability with words makes one think that a stream of invective from Heloise would be worth hearing, but sadly Abelard does not give us a verbatim account of what she said. He merely tells us that she became angry, swore, and cursed (literally "anathematized") them.

When Fulbert heard about this vehement denial of what to him was the linchpin of the whole arrangement, he felt that his niece had betrayed him. She was after all one of his family. He had taken her in and offered her access to the life of scholarship that she loved so much; if she had no regard for the honor of her own family she should at least think about that – she owed him that much. These arguments had little effect on Heloise. To her anything anyone could say would always be secondary to her love of Abelard. Relations evidently broke down completely. Fulbert heaped abuse on her repeatedly and made her life intolerable. Abelard decided to act. He removed Heloise from the household, once more disguised as a nun (he tells us this time that he specifically did not include the veil in the outfit), and sent her the few miles downriver to the convent of Argenteuil, where she had been educated.

Abelard does not tell us what his plan was at the time. Perhaps he was merely seeking a breathing space while he tried to find a more workable arrangement with Fulbert. Given Heloise's later objections to taking holy orders it seems unlikely that they were planning for her to become a nun, which is what Fulbert was later to claim that he had believed. Monasteries and convents were populated not just by fully fledged monks and nuns but by many others of varying degrees of devotion and commitment. Those awaiting ordination (who did not wear the veil) followed the rules without having taken vows. In addition, many houses permitted laypersons who wished to follow the rule but who did not intend to become fully ordained, on the principle that a committed layperson was better than a bad monk. There were thus a number of ways in which Heloise might remain at Argenteuil not as a nun. She was an "old girl" of the convent and so would have friends there. It was in many ways the perfect refuge.

While she was at Argenteuil the couple were able to meet. It may even have been easier for Abelard to get into a boat and go down to

Argenteuil than to make a conjugal visit in Fulbert's house. On these visits they were not allowed privacy, but Abelard tells us that on at least one occasion they managed to make love in a corner of the refectory. The refectory of a convent is a large open hall in which the whole community dines together. One is tempted to wonder whether Abelard has invented this detail in order again to demonstrate how mired they were in the pit of degradation. But the remark comes not from the autobiography but in a later letter to Heloise, the one person who would know for certain whether or not it was true.* This is not just an exaggeration for effect; it really happened.

Abelard and Heloise were now separated from each other and from their baby but they at least were in contact and had some hope of finding a way out of their predicament – love might quite possibly have found a way. Fulbert by contrast was in a literally hopeless position. The honor of his family had not been saved. His relationship with Heloise had been destroyed. Now she belonged formally to Abelard and the existence of a baby served as a constant and indelible reminder that she had given herself to another man's future. Once again she had been removed from her uncle's household. This time, however, he was irked by the realization that, as her husband, Abelard probably had the right to do what he had done.

As he brooded it must have become more and more obvious that he had lost everything. He contemplated over and over the drastic action that might restore the balance, at least give him some sort of restitution for the pain he was enduring, the action that he could have taken – should have taken – earlier.

---

* He also remarks that he on occasion forced himself on Heloise against her will. She may have had a slightly more developed sense of propriety than he did.

SEVEN

"The story of my misfortunes"

1117

At this her uncle and his friends imagined that I had tricked them,
and had found an easy way of ridding myself of Heloise by making her a nun.
Wild with indignation they plotted against me . . .

Abelard, Autobiography

 ULBERT DID NOT GO TO ABELARD to ask him why he had sent Heloise to her old convent at Argenteuil. To have discussed it with him would have been an admission that there was something to negotiate. Fulbert's experience of negotiation was that it had robbed his family of its honor and himself of the niece who had brought the promise of happiness into his life. He preferred to interpret Abelard's action as preparation for divorce. The resulting dishonor to Fulbert's family that that would have entailed could be used as a justification for an attack on him.

Fulbert was, we know, a man prone to rages; Abelard confirms he was "wild with indignation." Perhaps he was just so enraged that he was incapable of holding a conversation with Abelard. He was now planning action; the last thing he was looking for was an expla-nation that might have diluted his feeling of righteous anger.

When describing the attack Abelard always refers to plotters in the plural: "they," "her uncle and his friends." Fulbert was to call on his clan, the extended group of relatives and associates – the family – to help him take vengeance. He needed the help of his kin, not just to make the operation more legitimate (a family wrong should be avenged by a family) but also because what he intended required planning and even specialist expertise. Abelard's circumstances had to be secretly ascertained; one of his servants had to be approached and their services bought; the right people had to be assembled and a time for the operation had to be selected:

> *. . . and one night as I slept peacefully in an inner room in my lodgings, they bribed one of my servants to admit them and there took cruel vengeance on me of such an appalling barbarity as to shock the whole world; they cut off the parts of my body where-by I had committed the wrong of which they complained.*
>
> (Abelard, Autobiography)

Nowadays the surgical procedure of castration can be performed under a local anaesthetic, even on an outpatient basis.* Two incisions are made in the scrotum through which each of the testicles is removed in turn. The spermatic cords are cut, sewn up and the incisions are closed. In surgical terms it is a relatively simple operation and recovery from the wounds is usually rapid and complete.

The castration of farm animals has been practiced throughout the history of agriculture† without anaesthetic and is still widespread, although animal welfare groups discourage it because it always involves some suffering. The method used by farmers in the Middle Ages would presumably have been similar to the one that is used now: a cord is wound tightly round the scrotum, which is then cut open and the testicles removed swiftly. The cord is then left in place to prevent bleeding. The people who castrated Abelard might well have

---

* In modern medicine surgical castration is performed as part of gender transformation as well as a treatment for testicular cancer and (more controversially) advanced prostate cancer.

† Castration increases the weight of the animal, reduces aggression, and, in some cases, removes an unpleasant flavor in the meat. It can also be used simply to prevent the wrong animal from breeding.

been experienced in this technique. An illustration from a thirteenth-century law book shows the castration of a knight. The victim's tunic is pulled up over his head both to allow access for his attackers and to render him helpless. The method involving a cord is apparently about to be used.

Abelard says in the autobiography that the wounding itself did not hurt as much as the breaking of his collarbone on a later occasion. If the operation was performed swiftly and skillfully that might just be credible, although he might also be exaggerating to emphasize the injury to his pride, which he says was overwhelming. He does also make a curious remark about being drowsy at the time, which may suggest that part of the treacherous servant's job might have been to drug his food. Historians are agreed that in Abelard's case it is most likely that only the testicles were removed. Removal of both penis and testes was not the common practice in the documented cases of revenge castration. It inevitably involves much more blood loss and risk to life (although as modern examples show, it is still survivable), which was undesirable. If Abelard had died Fulbert would have been liable to much more severe penalties.

When the intruders had accomplished their task they made their getaway, leaving Abelard, presumably, in a state of extreme shock. They did not get clean away, however:

> *Then they fled but the two who could be caught were blinded and mutilated as I had been, one of them being the servant who had been led by greed while in my service to betray his master.*
> (Abelard, Autobiography)

It is surprising that revenge was taken so swiftly on the perpetrators. After the attack they had only to leave the house and run to safety. Abelard was not in a state to follow them so who waylaid them? No one they met in the street would have yet known of the crime and, even if they did, a group of men capable of a violent assault would surely have had little to fear from the odd citizen they might chance to run into late at night. The reprisal could only have been taken by people in or close to the house who knew what had been done. Abelard describes his accommodation at the time as a *hospicium*: a guest room or lodgings. Could he perhaps have been staying in a household whose servants had strength and numbers enough to over﹣ power some of the gang and whose master had the authority and the nerve instantly to approve violent retribution? One can only speculate, but the person with that kind of power most likely to side with Abelard without question is Stephen de Garlande, Abelard's patron and also, among his other posts, dean of the cathedral. His new house was on the Ile de la Cité, on the very perimeter of the cathedral enclo﹣ sure. If Abelard was lodging with him, men of his household might very well have caught two of the perpetrators and, acting on Stephen's authority, inflicted a brutal revenge. If this is the case it is not surpris﹣ ing that Abelard does not mention it: Stephen is hardly likely to have welcomed written testimony about his activities. In any case, at the time it is likely that he was going through one of his periods of royal disfavor, so it might have been inadvisable to mention him at all.

The Garlandes would have seen an attack on their protégé, for whatever reason, as meriting exemplary punishment. In the manner of many organizations that derive their authority from their own capacity for violence it was probably prudent for the family, every now and again, to demonstrate in a graphic way what happened to those who displeased them. In this case, by blinding the attackers as well as castrating them, they inflicted on them a fate worse even than Abelard's. What could have been a more eloquent statement of the implacable power of the Garlandes than to release the two men to grope their way bleeding through the streets at dawn?

By his action Fulbert had invoked the violent world of family vengeance and blood feud inside the cathedral precinct to a degree far beyond the normal experience even of medieval life. This was a rare and shocking event and it is not surprising that news of the night's carnage spread quickly, horrifying and fascinating the whole of Paris:

*Next morning the whole city gathered before my house, and
the scene of horror and amazement, mingled with lamentations,
cries, and groans that exasperated and disturbed me, is difficult,
no impossible, to describe. All sorts of thoughts filled my mind —
how brightly my reputation had shone, and how easily in an evil
moment it had been dimmed or rather completely blotted out.*

(Abelard, Autobiography)

The fuss in the street was evidently distressing. Inside his lodgings
Abelard wanted to be quiet and to think. He was a man who lived by
ideas and he would have begun immediately to contemplate the nature
of the irrevocable mutilation that he had undergone. Human consciousness is embedded in the physical body, even in the most cerebral
of people. Suddenly to be deprived of an organ of sensitivity is to lose
an integral component of the model of one's physical self to which the
thinking mind makes constant reference. Abelard was now altered in
a fundamental sense. Whether overtly sexual or not, every encounter
with another person, almost every conceivable action, would be performed, as it were, by a different Abelard. He was now obliged to
reassess himself and adjust his self-image in order to take account of
his new state. Even in the best of times he often let the inner workings
of his own mind distract him from the thoughts and feelings of others.
On this occasion it is understandable that his absorption in that press-
ing and vital process of inner readjustment gave rise to an apparently
graceless reaction to the sincerely expressed sympathy of his students:

*In particular the clerks and, most of all, my pupils tormented me
with their unbearable weeping and wailing until I suffered more
from their sympathy than from the pain of my wound, and felt
the misery of my mutilation less than my shame and humiliation.*

(Abelard, Autobiography)

Abelard refers repeatedly to his shame after the castration. He
tells his monk friend that the shame was much harder to bear than the

pain. At first sight it is not obvious why he was ashamed – surely anger would have been a more appropriate reaction. We know from other accounts of Abelard's behavior that he did feel anger, but this is not the emotion he chooses to emphasize in his autobiography. There may have been several contributory reasons for this evidently overwhelming feeling. He was humiliated that he was no longer fully a man, ashamed because the most intimate aspects of his body were now the subject of conversation in Paris:

> *I thought how my rivals would exult over my punishment, how this bitter blow would bring lasting grief and misery to my friends and parents, and how fast the news of this unheard of disgrace would spread over the whole world. What road could I take now? How could I show my face in public, to be pointed at by every finger, derided by every tongue, a monstrous spectacle to all I met?* (Abelard, Autobiography)

His private life was now open. He had shared with Heloise a sensuous and necessarily clandestine world where philosophy, love, and sex met and provided not just a shelter from the pain of the world but a key to its understanding. Now what had been a universe of two was the subject of conversation in the streets.

Few people would be able to watch with equanimity as their most intimate world was subjected to public scrutiny. For Abelard the situation was even worse: at the same moment that everybody else saw into his secret world he himself was removed from it. He was separated from the sexual element that had kept their universe together. Without an acceptance of carnal desire the whole of his life with Heloise was incomprehensible – a diversion based on a mistaken appetite, a shameful waste of time. The more he pieced together a new picture of himself as a person without sexuality, the more his previous involvement in it seemed ludicrous. In order to cope with what had happened he was to separate what could be salvaged of his idea of himself, the philosopher, from what had to be abandoned, the lover and friend. It was in a way the very opposite of what Heloise had worked for in their affair. She had tried to build a philosophical friendship, uniting intellectual and emotional intimacy. Now what she had tried to unite, Abelard felt obliged to pull apart.

As well as those in the crowd who were expressing their distress so volubly others must merely have turned up just to see the home of the philosopher who had been castrated because of a love affair, hoping perhaps to derive some kind of unrefined enlightenment from the scene, as people do to this day at a road accident. There would no doubt have been things to see: servants coming and going; doctors visiting; representatives of the bishop; also perhaps a servant from a frantic Heloise, sent in secret to find out what he could. Anyone in the crowd who had not heard the rumors about Abelard and Heloise would have learned about them there. The general opinion – both informed and uninformed – was that Abelard was the tragic victim of an unjust act of extreme spite. This is attested to not just by Abelard but also by Fulk, prior of the monastery of Deuil, just out-side Paris. A letter from him to Abelard has survived among cathe-dral records. Writing within a year of the event, Fulk (who does not give Abelard unqualified sympathy) confirms that in his opinion as well as in that of the city Abelard was an innocent man:

> *You were resting your limbs, not preparing to do evil to anyone when, behold, the hand of impiety and the deadly blade did not hesitate gratuitously to shed your innocent blood . . . The multi-tude of canons and noble clerics laments. The citizens lament, because they consider this a dishonor to the city and are troubled by the fact that their city has been violated by the shedding of your blood . . . Almost the entire city has wasted away in griev-ing for you.* (Fulk of Deuil, letter to Abelard)

If Abelard was self-evidently innocent then Fulbert was surely equally self-evidently guilty. Nobody who comments on the event has ever been in any doubt that it was Fulbert who caused the castration. There seems little doubt either that Fulbert's true motivation can be found in his passion for Heloise – what more clear manifestation of sexual jealousy can there be than to castrate one's rival? Symbolically, Fulbert's actions make sense: he was trying to remove the physical symbol of another man's relationship with Heloise and with the same stroke remove the cause of the child that was a sign of his failure and his rival's success. But what was a perfect outcome in the world of symbols was, of course, a disaster for Fulbert in the real one. His action merely ensured his complete separation from Heloise.

Psychiatrists who study violence distinguish between two types of act: self-preservative and sadistic. The first kind of violence is the result of desperation: the perpetrator's situation has become so agonizing that their psychic survival depends upon the immediate removal of the element of their life that is causing the pain. Self-preservative violence is an almost blind response – there is no pleasure in the act, no particular feelings even directed toward the other person. The target of a self-preservative attack is like an object; they are attacked in order to remove the pain. Although both Fulbert's desperation and his agony are attested to by Abelard, the premeditation and planning indicate that what might once have been a desperate act of psychic self-preservation had been transformed, by the time it was actually perpetrated, into sadistic violence. Hurting Abelard, knowing that he had been hurt, and that he was continuing to suffer, was now a source of pleasure to Fulbert, a balm that soothed the pain of his soul.

Abelard himself would have understood this distinction. His ethical theory of intentionalism brought his moral philosophy close to the, as yet undiscovered, science of psychology. Following his philosophical position, we might reason that if Fulbert's crime had been self-preservative, a visceral reaction to psychic pain, then his action could not be counted as a sin since he would not have given rational consent to an evil act. If, on the other hand, it was a considered act whereby Fulbert consciously wanted to hurt Abelard, then plainly he gave consent and his actions were sinful. Abelard does not discuss his own case in his ethical writings but he does consider a related case in his book on ethics, *Know Thyself,* which was written twenty years later. He uses the example of a servant whose life has been threatened by his master. The servant runs away but, as an act of self- preservation, returns to kill him. He could not have written about this example without thinking of his own betrayal by a servant. After following the arguments back and forth Abelard comes to the conclusion that, whether or not he was acting for self-preservation, the servant had sinned.

Apart from the issue of the guilt and innocence of the main pro- tagonists, which is a timeless question, there are possible justifications for the attack in the context of medieval law that made allowance for, and even legitimized, individual revenge. Abelard himself appears to give more than one reason for the assault. He says first that it was the removal of Heloise to the convent that moved Fulbert to act. When he describes the actual castration he implicitly gives a different one: "they cut off the parts of my body whereby I had committed the wrong of which they complained." This must refer to his original seduction of Heloise. In writing of the thoughts that went through his mind after the attack he even talks about the "just reprisal that had been taken by the very man I had myself betrayed." Later on, how- ever, it is quite clear that he does not consider it a just reprisal at all. But did Fulbert and his family consider that his original seduction justified their actions? Such an argument might have given them a chance, albeit slim, of mounting a defense within the culture of legit- imized revenge.

A twelfth-century book that summarizes English law at the time of Abelard states that a man is entitled to use force against anyone he finds "under the same cover" with either his wife, sister, mother, or daughter. The French legal statutes have not survived but there is no reason to believe that they were not similar. If this was the case then Fulbert would certainly have had the right to attack Abelard when he had found him together with Heloise several months earlier. On the other hand Abelard could point out that by the time the attack took place he had done his best to make amends by marrying Heloise. This would be an effective defense – marriage is almost always seen as countering whatever dishonor seduction might bring upon a family. Fulbert's clan, however, might have counterargued that in this case they had evidence that the marriage had not been sincerely entered into by Abelard. Had he not, only weeks afterward, sent his bride away to a convent? The alleged removal of Heloise to Argenteuil might well be seen as negating any mitigation of the offense that the marriage might have offered, and therefore justifying the attack.

It is less clear whether there could be any justification for castration specifically. The English law book permits the castration of adulterers but limits it to those who have been caught three times in the act, and only then when genital contact between the couple has actually been witnessed – it seems to have been intended only as a last resort for persistent and careless offenders.* Castration as part of war – beyond the scope of statutes and legal argument – was also not unknown. The biographer of Louis VI gives an account of how the monarch blinded and castrated an erstwhile favorite who had betrayed him. The writer adds that this was a lenient punishment as the man plainly deserved to be hanged. Abelard himself must have been familiar with the concept of revenge castration. When he was a boy, the brother of the Duke of Brittany, one Mathias, seems to have got himself into some trouble over an affair and eventually died after being castrated by an aggrieved husband.

It would have been difficult, however, for the family of Fulbert to justify the castration of Abelard on legal grounds. He had never been guilty of adultery, only of the lesser sin of fornication. Adultery tended in medieval law to be given a special legal status and attract more severe

---

* In the Italian town of Belluno, slightly later than Abelard's time, castration was also specified as the punishment for bigamy, but again only as a last resort: in this case if the offender was unable to pay the fine.

punishment because it constituted not only an attack on another man's property but also a potentially serious disruption of the pattern of inheritance, which is all-important for a stable, property-owning society. Heloise in a later letter echoes this impression of the legal situation: "The punishment that you suffered would have been proper vengeance for men caught in open adultery. But what others deserve for adultery came upon you through a marriage that you believed had made amends for all previous wrong doing." The paradoxical injustice of what had happened to them was evident to her. They were being punished for doing the right thing: "while we enjoyed the pleasures of an uneasy love and gave ourselves over to fornication we were spared God's severity. But when we amended our unlawful conduct by what was lawful, and atoned for the shame of fornication by an honorable marriage, then the Lord in his anger laid his heavy hand upon us."[1]

But Abelard's case did not go to a court of law. Gilbert, bishop of Paris, investigated it himself, as Abelard's correspondent Fulk tells us. Since the crime had happened on church land and was therefore subject to church law he was the most appropriate person. Fulk, who was trying to persuade Abelard to accept the decision of the authorities and not make a fuss, could hardly be more obsequious about Gilbert, who, he assured him, had everybody's best interest at heart:

> *The venerable bishop in his kindness laments this wound and injury of yours, and he has taken pains to spend as much time seeking justice as has been allowed to him.* (Fulk of Deuil, letter to Abelard)

The case was a difficult one and the bishop, who was a professional politician as well as a cleric, would need all his skill. It was full of pitfalls: two high-ranking members of the chapter involved in a violent quarrel with a background of scandal, all coming just at a time when the church was meant to be undertaking reform by rooting out all sign of sexual impropriety. Gilbert himself was a onetime student of

Ivo of Chartres, the chief architect of the reform movement, and so he probably found the whole affair interesting if distasteful. Any measures that he took would also have to take into account the fact that each of the parties had powerful supporting factions behind them. Abelard might be a troublemaker but with the Garlande family taking an interest he could not just be sent away into obscurity. The case would require delicate handling.

It was clear, however, that action had to be taken. Abelard could not remain master of the school: there was no telling what further trouble his presence might cause and anyway he was, it now turned out, married and therefore ineligible for the post. For Abelard's case Gilbert did manage to find a solution that eventually met with his approval: he was to become a monk. Although to us this sounds like a kind of imprisonment we should remember that as many as a quarter of young men of Abelard's class chose a monastic career. It was a respected option and although it did involve surrendering one's will to the head of a monastery it was not quite the isolated withdrawal from the world that it might at first seem. Abelard could and did continue writing and teaching, although he could no longer receive fees for his work. The monastery chosen was St.-Denis, the most prestigious in France. It was not far from Paris, so he could have access to students and even to rival thinkers. St.-Denis today is the burial place of no fewer than thirty-three French monarchs, many of whose remains were moved there in the seventeenth century. In Abelard's lifetime its association with royalty was already well established, partly because of its strategic significance as protection for the northern approach to Paris. Abelard tells us that he complied with the bishop's suggestion, but without commitment:

> *I admit that it was shame and confusion in my remorse and misery rather than any devout wish for conversion that brought me to seek shelter in a monastery cloister.* (Abelard, Autobiography)

He was temperamentally incapable of becoming a quiet and unobtrusive member of an enclosed community but eventually, although he would never cease to provoke and enrage his brothers in the cloisters, he was to become a champion of monasticism, at least in theory.

In the case of Fulbert, Bishop Gilbert also had no option but to act. It would plainly not be acceptable to the Garlandes, never mind to Abelard, if he were to remain unpunished. Abelard remains silent about this part of the story but Fulk tells us what happened:

> *The man who denies that it happened on his account has already been utterly destroyed by the seizure of all his possessions.* (Fulk of Deuil, letter to Abelard)

Evidently, rather than trying to mount a weak legal defense, Fulbert had chosen to deny his involvement entirely. Apparently he was not believed by Gilbert because his possessions were forfeited. We do not know whether this really meant that he was left destitute, reduced to living on the charity of his (evidently supportive) family, or if, as one might imagine from modern analogies, he was in fact able to protect a significant proportion of his possessions by such familiar strategies as claiming that they were in somebody else's name or by failing to declare them at all. There is corroborative evidence from the cathedral records that he was dismissed from the cathedral chapter. In the year 1117 his name suddenly disappears from the usual list of signatories that was appended to charters and other legal documents.

Abelard plainly felt that the punishment was too lenient. The purpose of Fulk's letter was to persuade him to accept the judgement of Gilbert and stop making what were evidently quite intemperate protests. The authorities were no doubt anxious that the notoriously combative Abelard didn't wreck a finely wrought solution to a difficult situation:

> *Do not call the canons or bishop "the shedders of blood" or "destroyers of your blood," for they set their minds on justice for*

your sake and for their own, to the extent they were able. Listen instead to the good advice and consolation of a true friend . . . "Pursue peace and holiness with all," says the Apostle, "without which no one shall see God."[2] . . . "Vengeance is mine, sayeth the Lord, and therefore I shall repay."[3] . . . Stop pouring forth threats and bombastic words for nothing. (Fulk, letter to Abelard)

Abelard might reasonably have replied that on this occasion vengeance seemed to have been Fulbert's rather than the Lord's. Fulk, however, continues with his platitudes, trying to reassure Abelard that Fulbert's crime is really its own punishment: "an injury unjustly inflicted is infamy not for the one upon whom it is inflicted but for the man who inflicts it." He even counsels Abelard to forget the present and set his gaze on the hereafter, when "Christ shall reform everything you have lost marvelously and many times over . . . then finally the rule of the dialecticians shall appear false who habitually say that a privation can never be restored." It was quite normal then to look forward to rewards in heaven – Abelard himself writes in these terms – but there is something a little too glib in Fulk's very specific interpretation of it, cunningly tailored as he sees it to Abelard's specific needs.

It appears that Abelard was so aggrieved by what he perceived as Fulbert's lenient treatment that he was threatening to take his case to the papal court in Rome. This was a proposal that would not have pleased the reformers, whose agenda included increased autonomy for religious institutions and the weakening of ties with Rome. Fulk tries to talk him out of it. The Romans, he says, are corrupt and unreliable:

O what a truly wretched plan, devoid of all profit!! Have you never heard about the avarice and the impurity of the Romans? Who has ever been rich enough to satisfy the greedy maw of those harlots? Who has been able to fill the bags of their cupidity with their purses? Therefore, as far as I can reasonably gather, even to contemplate this is not known to be wise counsel for either you or your Church. (Fulk of Deuil, letter to Abelard)

He points out that Abelard's resources are running low and will not cover the expense of a journey that would entail his supporting himself as well as paying for transport over a period of months:

The substance of your property, since it is either modest or nonexistent, will not be enough for a visit to the Roman Pontiff. Since all of your relatives and friends hate you because of your behavior, the support of family property or that of others shall in no way serve you. (Fulk of Deuil, letter to Abelard)

He paints a sad picture of Abelard, alienated from his family and friends because of his scandalous behavior. It is impossible to judge how true this is. Is he referring to lack of support from the Garlandes, or from other friends? How does he know about Abelard's family? It is true that we hear no more of Abelard's family in the autobiography but several of his relations find themselves commemorated in the records of Heloise's convent and some of them seem to have joined the community. This hardly seems consistent with the entire family having turned its back on Abelard. But these records date from at least twelve years later – it is quite possible that there was a rift for a time, which eventually healed.

Although Fulk tries to represent Abelard as bereft of support he is at the same time evidently alarmed that he might still have influence enough to obtain funds for the proposed trip from the monastery of St.-Denis, where he was by then a monk. Fulk warns that this course of action would have dire political consequences. It would, he says, "turn the bishop and canons of the Church of Paris into the most bitter and troublesome enemies of your monastery and your brethren." It is quite likely that this is the real purpose of Fulk's letter: to prevent Abelard's continued complaint from becoming the focus of conflict between political factions – the reforming bishop and chapter on the one hand, and the monastery of St. Denis, backed by the pope, on the other.

Abelard did not go to Rome over the issue; he never mentions the question of Fulbert's punishment again. There is, however, some indication that his disquiet about leniency was not groundless. On 1 April 1119 the signature of Canon Fulbert appears once again at the bottom of a cathedral document. It had apparently taken him as little as two years to get his old job back – somebody in high places liked him. With the exception of a couple more signatures, Fulbert then disappears from history, destined to be remembered only for what is surely – irrespective of any debate then or now – an irreducibly evil act.

Despite affecting superficial sympathy, Fulk does nothing to comfort Abelard in his letter. He manages, in almost every paragraph, to include jibes about what he refers to as "the small part of your body that you have lost." His attempt at consolation for what he insists on claiming is the complete collapse of Abelard's reputation (despite his acknowledgment of the general sympathy of the crowd) consists in saying that although everybody does indeed think that he is worthless he should not worry because they are merely reflecting the emptiness of this world. He has clearly thought a great deal about Abelard's reputation as a lover and finds it hard to leave the subject alone. He slyly tells Abelard how much "single women" – a term he seems to use synonymously with "prostitute" – lamented Abelard's tragic loss. On the bright side, though, at least he can encounter a crowd of virgins, "shining in the flower of youth, who can usually kindle even old men to the heat of lust with their motions," and still be able to walk among them "safe and sinless." Just think of the advantage, he says: Abelard will be received with complete confidence by every host. Never again will a husband fear that he may violate his wife and wreck his marriage bed. With friends like Fulk who needs enemies?

The other surviving letter that touches on these events is definitely from an enemy. Roscelin was a philosopher of the previous generation who had taught Abelard as a very young man, before he came to Paris. A letter exists, written after they had already had a vicious philosophical row about the nature of the Holy Trinity. So vicious was it that when he came to write his autobiography Abelard failed to mention that Roscelin was ever his teacher. Roscelin manages, in his letter to Abelard, to get in some nasty personal remarks. He starts by refusing to call him Peter, because it is a masculine name no longer appropriate as Abelard is no longer of that gender. He makes some dubious illusions to grammatical "parts" before going on to warn Abelard that if he doesn't change his attitude other appendages could be removed: "your tail of impurity with which you used to sin at every opportunity could be followed by your tongue with which you are stinging at the moment." It is known that Roscelin was in his own right an eminent and adventurous philosopher. He was once accused of heresy, but he recanted his questionable beliefs and remained highly influential on the thought of his generation. This piece of hate mail to Abelard, however, is the only surviving writing that can be ascribed to him with certainty.

Otto of Freising, a German bishop who wrote a biography of the emperor Frederick Barbarossa, also makes a lengthy digression about Abelard's life. Otto gives a glowing account of Abelard's talents. He may even have studied under him; he was in Paris at the right time. Otto takes what is a relatively compassionate view of the castration. Afterward, he says, Abelard was freed from all distractions. He "devoted himself day and night to reading and thinking; from being clever, he became even cleverer and from being learned he became doubly learned."[4] The castration, in other words, was a good thing.

This is close to the view that Abelard himself would eventually take in his later exchange of letters with Heloise. He uses the same argument that supports the notion that marriage is a morally inferior option to celibacy. Sex is first a distraction and second a source of powerful desires that, if yielded to, give rise to evil. How much better, then, to be freed by castration of the desire and even the means to commit sin? In fact removal of the testicles does not necessarily remove sexual desire in an adult, nor does it necessarily remove the ability.* We know that some people in the Middle Ages were aware of this because Pierre de la Palude, writing in the fourteenth century, was to assert that if a man who was castrated was able to achieve an erection and to penetrate then he was legally entitled to marry. But neither Abelard nor any of his correspondents seems to have been in any doubt that castration precluded any sexual activity and was a total cure for sexual desire. Perhaps in his case the shock and the shame he alludes to contributed to his impotence.

Religious tradition discourages the act of deliberate self-castration as a preventive measure against sin or even an act of devotion. It is not, the argument runs, for man to remove what has been provided by God. Perhaps there is even a suggestion that removing the physical cause of temptation is a kind of cheating. This was enough of an issue in the early stages of Christianity for it to be considered by the first council of Nicea, which in the year 325 codified and fixed many of the basic tenets of the faith. The council specifically excluded men who had been castrated from joining the clergy. Abelard's consciousness of these arguments contributed to his feeling of shame:

> *I was also appalled to remember that according to the cruel letter of the law, a eunuch is such an abomination to the Lord that men made eunuchs by the amputation or mutilation of their members are forbidden to enter a church as if they were stinking and unclean.* (Abelard, Autobiography)

Christianity does, despite the Old Testament warnings, also have a marginal and mostly uncelebrated countertradition, derived probably from the pagan religions that preceded it, of voluntary castration for religious purposes. Abelard draws on this in his later letters to

---

* A survey in America in the 1980s showed that 10 percent of men whose testicles had been removed were still having sexual intercourse up to twenty years after the castration.

Heloise when he argues that his castration has purified him and made him pleasing to God: "divine grace has cleansed me rather than deprived me." The main authority for this was St. Matthew who, quoting Christ in his gospel, plainly approves of "eunuchs which have made themselves eunuchs for the kingdom of heaven's sake."[5] There are also examples in the later history of Christianity where emasculation is plainly seen as a route to sanctity. Origen, a theologian of the second century AD, was believed to have castrated himself in order to concentrate better on his studies. St. Hugh had reputedly been so beset by lust that in answer to his prayers angels removed his private parts and liberated him thereby, in the words of his biographer, from the "law of sin and death that is in our members." Nor is the practice restricted entirely to the Middle Ages. There was an ecstatic Russian religious sect, which began in the eighteenth century, known as the Skoptsy (Castrati). Not only did the men practice voluntary castration but the women had their clitorises and even their nipples excised in order to intensify their religious experience. There is no evidence that the adherents who underwent these operations were anything but happy with their transformation. The sect survived into the twentieth century, even resisting for some time the disapproval of the Soviet state.

Abelard must have contemplated all the theological and philosophical aspects of his fate. His most cherished view of himself had not changed: he was, as he always would be, Abelard the philosopher. He was very soon afterward to pick up his intellectual work with undiminished vigor, taking advantage of the extensive library of his new monastery of St.-Denis eventually to produce a book that would yet again make him the target of official disapproval. It may seem strange to modern sensibilities that he genuinely came to think that the castration was a gift from God. His attitude can be seen as a naive, possibly even sinister, act of self-deception or, as the result of courage and resolution, a determination to fulfill his destiny come what may. Both interpretations may be in part correct: he had struggled, as we all must, to complete a process of self-analysis, to turn his life into

a story that he could tell himself that was both bearable and consistent with the facts. Within that process there is plenty of room for
both self-deception and courage.

Having described the events, his reactions, and what his future
was to be, Abelard reintroduces Heloise into the narrative of his
autobiography. She had, he said, "already agreed to take the veil in
obedience to my wishes and entered a convent." This is a little puzzling. Does he mean that she had agreed to become a nun before the
castration and that by sending her away Abelard had indeed been
effectively divorcing her, as Fulbert and his family suspected?
Abelard says in his account of the prelude to the castration only that
they imagined that he was putting her away. Had what they imagined
been the truth? Or did Abelard only insist on this course in the aftermath of the castration, as a reaction to the couple's own emotional
turmoil?

It is hard to decide, just as it is hard to evaluate at this distance in
time quite what Heloise's options were. It seems very unlikely that she
could have continued living with Fulbert, even if he had not forfeited his possessions. Could she have made a life, or even what we
would now call a career, by herself? There are examples of intelligent
and gifted women doing so throughout the Middle Ages: Heloise's
contemporary Hildegard of Bingen springs to mind. None of them,
however, lived their lives without the support of either family, in the
case of those of high birth, or of a religious community, in the case of
the others. There is no evidence of any other members of her family
who might have supported Heloise. She might perhaps have been
able to maintain what she would have considered a fulfilling life
within a religious organization without being committed to actually
taking the vows of a nun. She was an exceptional and already famous
woman and many houses might well have been willing to accept her
on her own terms. Emotionally she might have wished to live with
Abelard but that would be precluded for the reasons she had already
given against marriage. It would have damaged Abelard's career and
would therefore be acceptable to neither of them.

Whatever the range of other possibilities that existed for her, she makes one thing clear in all her writings: she took the veil only because Abelard wanted her to. "It was your command rather than God's that made me take the veil." This is in fact against the spirit of monasticism. The rule of St. Benedict is clear that a monk or nun must decide to take the vows of their own free will. In the aftermath of the Abelard affair nobody in authority would have been concerned with such a technical nicety, but Heloise was to be aware of it for the rest of her life.

Abelard gives no reason for his insistence on Heloise becoming a nun. He may have been genuinely solicitous about her spiritual welfare. He was coming quickly to the conclusion that life in the cloisters was not just his best available option but a manifestation of divine will. It would be illogical not at least to consider applying the same thinking to Heloise. Abelard was indeed to remark later that God "in his mercy had intended to provide for two people in one." This line of reasoning is, however, very close to a less noble one: sending her to a convent was the perfect way of keeping Heloise from other men.

The feelings of shame, inadequacy, and powerlessness that overwhelmed Abelard cannot have failed to lead to a fear of being rejected and usurped. This is a common enough concern even in men who have not been mutilated. The fact that Heloise had directed such fierce erotic energy toward him would only increase the anxiety – it would be all too easy to imagine that energy being channeled toward someone else. The convent provided a strategy whereby Heloise could be prevented even from meeting other men as well as being set on the path to spiritual improvement. With the anachronistic notion of the unconscious mind we can allow Abelard to pursue both arguments. Inside he is protecting his male self-respect while at the same time sincerely believing that by entering a convent Heloise had done the right thing. As he says in a later letter, she had turned the curse of Eve into the blessing of Mary.

Abelard describes the scene of her vow-taking. Bishop Gilbert himself officiated in the church, thereby giving his approval to this final, and presumably to him least important, part of the solution to a tricky problem. There were those present who did not share his feel/ings, however. Some of them were moved apparently to make a last/minute appeal to Heloise:

> *There were many people I remember who in pity for her youth tried to dissuade her from submitting to the yoke of monastic rule as a burden too hard to bear.* (Abelard, Autobiography)

But Heloise was, as one would expect, resolute. She had made up her mind long before entering the church. This moment symbolized her total commitment not, as the ritual implied, to God but to Abelard. In the middle of the ceremony, which was meant to denote the sup/pression of her will and her acceptance of the authority of a convent, she made one final personal act of will. She quoted aloud a passage from a classical poet. Lucan's *Pharsalia* is a story of the Roman civil war. It contains a scene in which Pompey's wife, Cornelia, blames herself for her husband's defeat in battle. When he comes home bloodied from combat she greets him with these words:

> *O noble husband, too great for me to wed, was it my fate to bend*
> *   that lofty head?*
> *Why did I marry you and bring about your fall?*
> *Now accept the penalty and see me gladly pay.*[6]

Heloise spoke the words aloud "as best she could through her tears and sobs." It was an extraordinary thing to do, then or now – a moment of premeditated theatricality through which Heloise was able to achieve the paradoxical effect of asserting her submission. The poem was well known and most of the hearers would have understood the context. In the charged atmosphere of the church, those who sympathized with her must have felt that she deserved to have her moment. As they listened they must have realized that she had chosen her text with precision. In the *Pharsalia* Cornelia offers her life as a sacrifice to appease the gods and bring her husband victory. This ceremony was Heloise's sacrifice. Even before the horrific events she had seen love as a debt. She had promised "to always repay you and in all ways obey you." Now feelings of responsibility and desire made her pay gladly. The price she paid was to spend more than half her life as a nun:

> *So saying she hurried to the altar, quickly took up the veil blessed*
> *by the bishop and publicly bound herself to the religious life.*
> (Abelard, Autobiography)

Writing to Abelard after a gap of twelve years she chose to recall not the scene itself, but her feelings. She had become accustomed to study them as part of philosophy and part of love and she is unflinching in her analysis of her mental processes:

> *I carried out all your orders so implicitly that when I was pow-*
> *erless to oppose you in anything, I found strength at your com-*
> *mand to destroy myself. I did more — strange to say — my love*
> *rose to such heights of madness that it robbed itself of what it*
> *most desired beyond hope of recovery, when immediately at your*
> *bidding I changed my clothing along with my mind, in order to*
> *prove you the sole possessor of my body and will alike.* (Heloise,
> First Letter)

This is the Heloise who would rather be called a whore than an empress. Even though they were now to part, each one into a separate closed world, to her Abelard was still the sole possessor of her body and her will. Historian Michael Clanchy even suggests that the proceedings should have been stopped because she was plainly in no state of mind to take her final vows.[7] She was certainly in a highly charged condition as she stood at the altar, already in the simple white habit of a novice nun, and accepted the veil from the bishop. Did she feel for the last time the frisson she had felt when she had given herself completely to Abelard during their lovemaking? Perhaps as she took the veil she had, for a blissful instant, that feeling of reckless freedom that comes from the total surrender of the will — the emotional equivalent of stepping blindfolded off the edge of a cliff.

EIGHT

St./Denis

1117–1123

I had still scarcely recovered from my wound when the clerks came thronging
round to pester the abbot and myself with repeated demands that I should
now for the love of God continue the studies that hitherto I had pursued only in
desire for wealth and fame.

Abelard, Autobiography

F THE BISHOP OF PARIS, or anyone else,
had expected that the contemplative life of a monk
would from now on keep Abelard clear of controversy they had failed to appreciate his innate ability
to generate conflict. He had come to St./Denis with
the intention of continuing his philosophical work. This was probably his best strategy for coping with the trauma of castration and its
aftermath – it is hard to imagine that it would not have been his over-
riding ambition whatever the circumstances. But it was precisely the
pursuit of pure philosophical truth that generally led him to clash
with the authorities.

The abbey of St./Denis was in some ways even better suited to his
studies than the school of Notre-Dame. It was famous for its library
and its scriptorium, the almost factory-like writing room where teams
of monks worked for long hours to copy manuscripts by hand. If the
librarian felt that St./Denis needed a certain book it would be obtained
and a copy made in the scriptorium. In this way one of the most comprehensive collections of books in Europe had been amassed.

Abelard now had a chance to study and make comparisons between the writings of the various thinkers whose ideas had shaped the religious thought of the time. The major authorities were writers such as St. Augustine, who was the first thinker to try to reconcile classical philosophy with Christianity, or St. Jerome, who was responsible for the Latin translations of the Bible, but there were also a host of less well known authors, each of whom had made some contribution. These authorities had interpreted and extended scriptural ideas; they formed a sort of second rank of authority deferring in matters of doctrine only to the Bible itself. Inevitably not all of these authorities said the same thing. Abelard applied his logical mind to documenting the apparent contradictions and inconsistencies among them. This study was to be the basis of one of Abelard's most famous books, called in Latin *Sic et Non,* which can be translated as "Yes and No," or "On the One Hand . . . On the Other Hand."

The comprehensive range of texts in the library at St.-Denis meant that he was able to include upwards of 2,000 quotations, making *Sic et Non* a monumental work of comparative scholarship. The book seems to have been intended, like most of Abelard's philosophical works, for the use of students. It was in effect a set of exercises, pointing out useful topics for practice at interpretation and analysis. It does not include information on how these conflicts may be resolved; it merely states, with copious references, the case for and against. The book includes moral questions such as whether it is lawful for Christians to kill people or (significantly?) whether one is allowed to take in marriage the woman with whom one has fornicated. It also has questions of pure theology and biblical interpretation, dealing even with contradictions among the Gospels themselves, such as a disagreement in the accounts of the crucifixion as to the exact time of Christ's death. Abelard tactfully attributes these particular inconsistencies to copying errors by the scribes. With the exception of the scriptures themselves, however, he is adamant that to expose and discuss these contradictions is an essential project:

All writings belonging to this class are to be read with full free-
dom to criticize, and with no obligation to accept unquestioning-
ly; otherwise the way would be blocked to all discussion, and
posterity be deprived of the excellent intellectual exercise of
debating difficult questions of language and presentation.
(Abelard, Instruction to *Sic et Non*)[1]

Historians tend to agree with Abelard that the effect of *Sic et Non* was beneficial in the long run; as one historian puts it, he taught scholars what they did not know.[2] Although the book was the result of rather daring questioning –"By doubting we come to inquiry, by inquiry we come to truth" is the keynote phrase with which he choos-es to end the introduction – Abelard managed to avoid censure for this particular work, probably because he was not expressing opin-ions of his own. He did not exercise the same restraint when it came to assessing his new home.

Abelard's first conflict with authority at St.-Denis was occa-sioned by his enthusiasm for his new calling. He wanted to be a good monk. Not only was it, no doubt, desirable psychologically for him fully to embrace his new role, it was also professionally expedient. Nobody would accept teaching from a monk who was considered to be lax in his observance of the rule of St. Benedict or in some other way imperfect. In view of his previous history he might well have felt that he had a little catching up to do if he was to gain a reputation for rectitude. Whatever the reason, he seems to have taken on the mantle of the reformists in pointing out the numer-ous infringements of the rule that he observed around him. He took it upon himself to share his opinion with his fellow monks and he is certainly happy to expand on his judgement in the auto-biography:

The abbey to which I had withdrawn was completely worldly
and depraved, with an abbot whose preeminent position was
matched by his evil living and notorious reputation. On several

occasions I spoke out boldly in criticism of their intolerably foul
practices, both in private and in public. (Abelard, Autobiography)

Although Abelard was possibly exaggerating for effect, there is
corroboration in other documents for the general tenor of his remarks. Bernard of Clairvaux, who was fast becoming the spokesman
of the reformers, actually sounds very much like Abelard when he
says of St.-Denis at the same time that it was "crowded with knights,
with deals being negotiated, with disputes being conducted, and
sometimes open to women."[3]

After Abelard's outspoken criticism he tells us that Adam, abbot
of St.-Denis, had him removed to a smaller daughter-house away
from the main abbey.* This was a pattern that would be followed
throughout his life: almost every large institution in which he found
himself would, after a brief interval, transfer him to a smaller outlying unit where there were fewer people for him to upset. Even in
partial exile, however, he was allowed to continue teaching and he
proudly relates that students "gathered in crowds until there were too
many for the place to hold or the land to support."

Perhaps because he no longer had access to the main library,
Abelard turned his attention to new areas of study. He started once
again to apply his logic to questions of belief, as he had done as a student in Laon until the aged Master Anselm made him stop. He chose
to examine the theoretical nature of the Holy Trinity, probably the
most problematic, complex, and controversial topic in the whole of
Christian theology. Abelard was encouraged in this direction of
inquiry by his students:

I first applied myself to lecturing on the basis of our faith by
analogy with human reason, and composed a theological trea-
tise "On the Unity and Trinity of God" for the use of my

---

* Traditionally believed to have been at Maisoncelle-en-Brie, quite distant from Paris, in
the county of Champagne.

students who were asking for human and logical reason on this
subject, and demanded something other than mere words.
(Abelard, Autobiography)

A desire for "something intelligible rather than mere words" was central to the spirit of Abelard's philosophical teaching. He believed that words were useless if intelligence could not follow them. The optimistic belief that there were new things to be discovered in the field of ideas was part of the twelfth-century renaissance. It was quite understandable, therefore, that Abelard saw his destiny as a scholar in this field of inquiry.

To publish views about the Trinity was to run the risk of attack. Almost since the beginning of Christianity the idea of the Trinity had been the focus of bitter doctrinal conflict. This is partly because it is such a central one. All religions try in some way to offer to their adherents a link between the divine world of heaven and the mundane world of everyday experience. Christianity's unique feature is to construct this link around an event – the incarnation – in which God becomes a human being, Jesus Christ. Potentially this makes for a compassionate religion in which the creator understands the trials of humanity because he has experienced them and whose adherents feel they have formed a human relationship with God rather than having to grapple with the concept of a numinous universal spirit. Problems arise, however, when attempts are made to be precise about how this arrangement works. There is plainly more than one entity involved: while Christ was a man, for example, he prayed to God, whom he called Father. There are also references in the Bible to a more mysterious entity known as the Holy Spirit. It seems that we are faced with a situation where three persons (as theologians call them) – Father, Son, and Holy Spirit – are all struggling to become one deity.

It is probably easier to understand the conceptual nature of the Trinity – as it was understood then and still is by contemporary Christians – by listing some of the things that are not true about it. It is not, for example, the case that there are three separate Gods. Christianity, like Judaism and Islam, has a deep-seated horror of having more than one God — that is seen as a pagan and degenerate notion. People who talked themselves into a position where they seemed to believe in more than one God were inevitably condemned. This is exactly what had happened to Abelard's first teacher, Roscelin, who apparently gave the impression that he believed that the persons of the Trinity were separate deities. He had been forced publicly to retract his teachings — Abelard is always at pains to make sure that nothing in his own writings might be read as containing a similar heresy.

Neither is it true that Christ, when he was on earth, was in some way God disguised as a human being. He was a man in all respects — it is fundamental to the religion that he lived and suffered as a man. The nature of the Son is, therefore, necessarily complex for, although he is human, he is also divine, existing in heaven alongside the other persons of the Trinity both before and after his spell on earth. Also, although the persons of the Trinity have different qualities, they are all equal aspects of the one God. It is not true, for example, that one of the persons has powers that the others do not.

It is a subject of great subtlety and Abelard made a novel and, to the eyes of many contemporary churchmen, eccentric approach to it. He was convinced not only that logic was a method of understanding the question, it was the only method: "I believe that no one can fully understand these things unless they have stayed up all night studying philosophy, and dialectic most of all."[4] His use of logic to examine this area was disturbing to many theologians. For some believers it is the ineffable mystery of the Trinity that makes it a satisfying article of belief. Attempts to explain it are no more than attacks on religious faith. But Abelard was proud of his treatise and is at pains to let us know that, among the students, it was a critical success:

> It was generally agreed that the questions were peculiarly difficult and the importance of the problem was matched by the subtlety of my solution. (Abelard, Autobiography)

He is equally convinced that it was the success of his work that pre-
cipitated the attack that was about to be launched against him. He
continues:

> *When it became apparent that God had granted me the gift for*
> *interpreting the Scriptures as well as secular literature, the num-*
> *bers in my schools began to increase for both subjects, while else-*
> *where they diminished rapidly. This roused the envy and hatred*
> *of the other heads of schools against me; they set out to disparage*
> *me in whatever way they could.* (Abelard, Autobiography)

The other heads of schools that he mentions were Alberic of
Reims and Lotulf of Lombardy, the two students of Anselm of
Laon who had been so incensed at Abelard's attack on their master
some eight years earlier. As masters themselves, they had now risen to
a position where they could make trouble:

> *They were able to influence their archbishop, Ralph, to take*
> *action against me and, along with Conon, bishop of Palestrina,*
> *who held the office of papal legate in France at the time, to con-*
> *vene an assembly, which they called a council, in the city of Sois-*
> *sons, where I was to be invited to come, bringing my treatise on*
> *the Trinity.* (Abelard, Autobiography)

Abelard was being summoned to what was effectively a trial for
heresy. The Council of Soissons, an important ecclesiastical town to
the northeast of Paris, took place in 1121. Alberic and Lotulf had
assumed the role of counsel for the prosecution. Their case was not
altogether a straightforward one. The anger against Abelard was
generated by a deep disapproval of his audacity in using logic at all
in discussing the Trinity. This, however, was not heresy as such. To
make such a charge stick it would be necessary to show that his
approach had led him into error; that was more difficult. The logic
of Abelard's treatise was intended for advanced philosophy students.

Ordinary clerics, no matter how senior, were unlikely to have the training needed to understand it fully.

His opponents were reduced to examining his writings in search of individual statements that appeared to contradict accepted doc-trine. They seem to have chosen to concentrate on an attempt to show that Abelard's very specific allocation of roles to the persons of the Trinity had committed him to the view that the Father was more powerful than the Holy Spirit. To this day it is not certain if such an accusation could have been proven. Whatever case there was would be technical and difficult to win, especially if the defense was being conducted by Abelard, who was almost certainly the world's best living logician.

Aware perhaps that they were on shaky ground, Alberic and Lotulf started, according to Abelard, to spread the (entirely false) story that he had taught that there was more than one God:

> Before I could make my appearance, my two rivals spread such evil rumors about me amongst the clerics and people that I and the few pupils who had accompanied me narrowly escaped being stoned by the people on the first day we arrived for having preached and written (so they had been told) that there were three Gods. (Abelard, Autobiography)

It may seem strange that the righteous anger of the people could be stirred up to the point of violence by theological transgression, but this was, in fact, not uncommon. There is even evidence that such mob violence was regarded as a form of natural justice by the author-ities. Since heresy charges were difficult to prove and no formal legal framework had yet been worked out for dealing with them, popular outrage offered a simpler solution. Abelard's teacher Roscelin had himself nearly been lynched during a visit to England in 1118 when the story of his heresy became current. Four years before that, two men called Clement and Everard of Bucy, near Soissons, had actual-ly been burned by a mob outside the city because they were believed to have set up communities outside the church and taught heresies. They were not established scholars, let alone onetime masters of schools, and therefore did not have the option to defend themselves in front of a council. Abelard must have been mindful of the incident.

Abelard tells us that as soon as he arrived in Soissons he went straight to the papal legate with a copy of his book "for him to read and form an opinion." He says he declared himself ready to make amends if he had written anything wrong but was told to take it to the archbishop so that, as he puts it, his enemies could judge him.

The council went into session for a number of days but Abelard says they were unable to find any objectionable statements in his book. He tells us that he attempted to influence opinion by speaking publicly about the Trinity every day before the council met, "and all who heard me were full of praise both for my exposition and for my interpretation." He also had a satisfying moment when Alberic finally found in the book a sentence that, he was convinced, was heretical. Abelard was able to point out to him that that particular sentence was actually a quotation from the preeminent father of the church, St. Augustine. Alberic and his followers had to retreat in disarray. The prosecution was not going well. Geoffrey, bishop of Chartres, is quoted by Abelard as speaking out to warn the council against ill-considered, precipitate action:

> "If you injure him through prejudice you must know that even if your judgement is deserved you will offend many people, and large numbers will rally to his defense; especially as in this treatise before us we can see nothing that deserves any public condemnation." (Geoffrey of Chartres, quoted in Abelard, Autobiography)

Even though the quote actually seems a little too humble and favorable to Abelard to be completely credible, the point that without hard evidence a conviction was liable to make the prosecutors look ridiculous was surely a good one. Geoffrey went on to recommend a solution for a problem that had always been favored by governments

and civil servants: he suggested that the question be referred to another committee:

> *His further advice was that my abbot, Adam, who was present,*
> *should take me back to my monastery, the abbey of St.-Denis,*
> *and there a large number of more learned men should be assem-*
> *bled to go into the case thoroughly and decide what was to be done.*
> (Abelard, Autobiography)

Abelard may be displaying an almost unconscious insight into the
workings of committees when he describes how this proposal was
received: "The papal legate agreed with this last suggestion, and so did
everybody else." It must, however, have been obvious to Abelard's
opponents that it would be all too easy for nothing to happen as a result
of this decision. They tried another line of attack and went to see the
papal legate in private. The legate, who was, in Abelard's words, "not
as much of a scholar as he should have been," was eventually persuaded to issue a condemnation of Abelard anyway.

Geoffrey, bishop of Chartres, was sent to break the news. He
reassured Abelard that in reality right was on his side, that he was an
unfortunate victim of unworthy emotions:

> *He said I could be confident that such violence so clearly*
> *prompted by jealousy would discredit them and benefit me, and*
> *told me not to worry about being confined in a monastery as he*
> *knew that the papal legate was only acting under pressure, and*
> *would set me free within a few days of his leaving Soissons. So*
> *he gave me what comfort he could, both of us shedding tears.*
> (Abelard, Autobiography)

In this emotional scene, and throughout his account of the Council
of Soissons, Abelard represents Geoffrey as a nice person who was
basically sympathetic to Abelard's plight but powerless to help him.
We, however, have some information that was not then available to

Abelard. Much later in his life, after the autobiography had been finished, Geoffrey was to appear again in Abelard's second heresy trial. There is every reason to believe that on that occasion, far from being a friend, he was very much on the side of the prosecution. Even from Abelard's account of this meeting with him at Soissons one might be led to suspect that Geoffrey was there not so much to comfort Abelard as to pacify him and prepare him to accept without fuss the humiliating final decision of the council:

> *I was then summoned before the council. Without any question-ing or discussion they compelled me to throw my book on the fire with my own hands, and so it was burned.* (Abelard, Autobiography)

The burning of a book is a symbolic act that carries as much emotional charge nowadays as it did in Abelard's time. The intention was clearly to discredit Abelard and to issue a public warning. There does not, however, seem to have been a concerted campaign to destroy copies of the book and indeed only a few years later Abelard was to issue an expanded version of it, containing much of the same text, under the provocatively confident title *Theologia Christiana*.

The condemnation of Abelard at Soissons was, even on its own terms, grossly unfair. One person, according to Abelard, did speak out at the time. Thierry, the master of the school of Chartres, who is well known for his learning in other contexts, shouted out demanding a retrial and, according to Abelard, exclaimed, "today in his mercy God acquits an innocent man." Thierry was warned by the archbishop to be quiet.

The fact that open dissent was possible at all indicates the complexity of the world of the Council of Soissons. Diverse factions were struggling for power, using whatever political tricks were available to get it. Abelard lost the fight on this occasion because so many elements were against him. That was to a large extent the result of his own ineptitude: if he had not antagonized Alberic and Lotulf when they were students in Laon, if he had kept his own abbot on his side, the whole episode might have been avoided. He was defeated because of behind-the-scenes chicanery, but the fact that it was felt necessary to use such tactics shows that rational argument was a potentially powerful force. There was as yet no monolithic church or state capable of crushing all dissent before it. Abelard was able to fight his corner, as he always did, with an almost simpleminded faith in the power of logical argument. That faith, even when defeated, was a still vital factor in the development of the tradition of critical inquiry, which is surely the most significant gift that the Western tradition has made to the world.

Just as Geoffrey of Chartres had predicted, Abelard was confined briefly in the nearby monastery of St.-Médard but soon released. The papal legate did not pursue the matter and so the episode of the Council of Soissons came to a conclusion with no further restrictions being placed upon him. He was sent back to his abbey of St.-Denis where, he reminds us, most of the monks already hated him.

He introduces the next part of the story with the words, "a few months later the chance came for the monks of St.-Denis to work for my downfall." In fact it would have been more accurate if he had said "a few months later I handed them the opportunity to work for my downfall." Once again Abelard's eagerness to clear a piece of muddled thinking by the application of logic was to have disastrous consequences for him.

The monastery of St.-Denis owed part of its prestige to what Kenneth Clark once called "a typical medieval muddle."[5] Over the years different people with the same name had been confused with each other. The historical St. Denis was an early bishop of Paris, whose Latin name was Dionysius. He was martyred in the year 270, according to legend beheaded on the hill that is now known as Montmartre. Over the years he came to be considered the patron saint of France. The abbey of St.-Denis was later founded on the place where he was buried. His remains were an object of veneration by pilgrims and therefore a source of income as well as prestige.

Thus far the story is straightforward. Complications arose when he became confused with another Dionysius, who is mentioned in the Acts of the Apostles. This Dionysius was converted to Christianity by St. Paul himself and then, according to legend, became the first bishop of Athens. Although they were separated in time by at least 200 years, the medieval conception of ancient history was flexible enough for them to be held by most people (especially the monks of St. Denis) to be one and the same person.* The identification of the abbey's patron saint with a character who was mentioned in the Bible and who had actually met St. Paul contributed to the position of St. Denis as the most important monastery in France.

When Abelard was able to return to the extensive library of the main monastery, he began to study *The History of the English Church and People* by the great eighth-century scholar from Durham known as the Venerable Bede. Abelard spotted that Bede's account of history was inconsistent with the beliefs of the monks. Bede said that Dionysius had not been bishop of Athens at all but bishop of Corinth.† Abelard was quick to share this information with his brother monks:

> *I showed my discovery, by way of a joke, to some of the brothers who were standing by, as evidence from Bede, which was against us. They were very much annoyed and said that Bede was a complete liar and they had a more truthful witness in their own Abbot Hilduin, who had spent a long time in Greece investigating matters.* (Abelard, Autobiography)

---

* In fact the confusion was made even greater by the addition of yet another Dionysius, the author of some rather obscure mystical writings. Although these books were, as is now thought, written in the sixth century the tradition had grown up that they were the work of the Dionysius who had been converted by St. Paul. These works of the so-called Pseudo-Dionysius were, because of the emphasis on the spiritual properties of light, influential in the development of Gothic architecture, which happened during Abelard's lifetime.

† The bishop of Corinth was, in fact, yet another Dionysius who lived about 150 years after St. Paul.

Hilduin had been abbot of St.-Denis 400 years earlier. The fact that he had felt the need to travel to Greece in order to investigate mat-ters rather indicates that this was a long-standing issue about which monks at the abbey were liable to be sensitive. It concerned, after all, not just the status of the abbey but also its capacity to generate income. The monks put Abelard to an instant loyalty test and asked him point blank whom he believed, Bede or Hilduin. Anyone read-ing the mood of the monks might have tried a diplomatic response to the effect that since Hilduin had actually been to Greece, he probably knew what he was talking about. Abelard, however, was handi-capped by his love of the truth:

> *I replied that the authority of Bede, whose writings are accepted by the entire Latin church, carried more weight with me.*
> (Abelard, Autobiography)

Having now affirmed that in his opinion the monks' status was based on an error, Abelard should not have been surprised when they "began to cry out that now I had revealed myself as the enemy of the monastery, and was moreover a traitor to the whole country in seek-ing to deny the glory that was its special pride."

Even Abelard by now had grasped that the situation was becom-ing dangerous, so he made an attempt to calm them:

> *I said that it did not much matter whether he was the bishop of Athens or came from somewhere else, seeing that he had won so bright a crown in the eyes of God.* (Abelard, Autobiography)

His intentions were good, but angry people are seldom pacified by being told that the issue over which they are getting heated does not really matter. The monks went immediately to complain to Abbot Adam, who, given the prevailing mood in the monastery, probably had little choice but to listen to them and act. He prepared to send

Abelard to the king on a charge of treason. Abelard was evidently both outraged and scared:

> *I was so horrified by their wickedness and in such deep despair after having borne the blows of fortune so long feeling that the whole world had conspired against me, that with the help of a few brothers who took pity on me I secretly fled in the night.*
> (Abelard, Autobiography)

In order to be safe he left France entirely and went to the priory of St. Ayoul in the town of Provins, just inside the county of Champagne. Abelard was, he tells us, slightly acquainted with the Count of Champagne, Thibaud II. Thibaud was himself very well connected. He was married to Adela, the daughter of William the Conqueror, and was the nephew of Henry I of England.* Since France was at this time almost permanently at war with England, relations with Louis were not good enough to make Thibaud inclined to hand Abelard back even if he had been asked.

Abelard at this time seems to have conceived the ambition to set up his own monastery in the county of Champagne. This might have suited Count Thibaud quite well. He already had Bernard's increasingly successful monastery of Clairvaux in his territory and he might have welcomed another house headed by a celebrity. They added to the prestige of the county and attracted both people and money. Monasteries were frequently located in beautiful, tranquil spots but they were seldom completely cut off from the secular world of travel and commerce. A balance had to be struck between cloistered seclusion and access to benefactors. Champagne was an ideal location for religious houses: it was full of unspoiled countryside yet

---

* Thibaud was very nearly to become king of England on the death of Henry in 1135. He was actually offered the crown but was at the last minute outmaneuvered by Henry's other nephew, Stephen.

was also a very wealthy area situated on the crossing of the trade routes linking newly rich areas of France.

When Adam, abbot of St.-Denis, paid a visit to Champagne Abelard asked Thibaud to petition him first to forgive Abelard for absconding and second to give him permission to set up on his own:

> *I approached the count and begged him to intercede for me with the abbot and obtain his pardon and permission to live a monastic life wherever a suitable place could be found. The abbot and those with him took counsel on the matter so as to give the count their answer on the same day, before they left.* (Abelard, Autobiography)

Even though Abelard was a nuisance, he was not without his uses for St.-Denis. He was famous and his presence gave them unquestionable intellectual respectability. What is more, for him to have joined another order would have been an insult to France's greatest monastery. Abbot Adam probably did not believe that Abelard would restrict himself to setting up a small hermitage on his own and so refused permission. He also increased the pressure on Abelard to return to St.-Denis:

> *They threatened me with excommunication if I did not return quickly, and absolutely forbade the prior of St.-Ayoul with whom I had taken refuge to keep me any longer, under penalty of sharing my excommunication.* (Abelard, Autobiography)

Excommunication was a serious threat. It would have put Abelard outside the law in church circles and certainly put a stop to any teaching. On the other hand, a return to St.-Denis in his present circumstances would almost certainly have the same consequences. He was in a no-win situation. But then he had a rare stroke of luck: shortly after returning to St.-Denis, on February 19, 1122, Abbot Adam died.

NINE

"Not strong enough to dig, too proud to beg"

1122–1129

*In the very lairs of wild beasts and lurking places of robbers, where the name of
God was never heard, you built a sanctuary to God and dedicated a shrine
in the name of the Holy Spirit.*

Heloise, First Letter

BBOT ADAM was replaced by Abbot Suger, a
man destined to become one of the major political
figures of the age. He had himself been educated at
the abbey of St. Denis, at the same time as the future
king Louis VI. Suger worked hard to consolidate
the traditional role of the abbot as royal adviser until he eventually
became the king's deputy, standing in for him when he was away at
the crusades. Suger started by reforming the practices at St. Denis to
such an extent that he even won the approval of Bernard of Clairvaux. Under his management the abbey was destined to gain even
more wealth and power than it already had. Its attainment, under
Suger, of its status as the abbey most associated with French royalty is
considered by some to be a contributing factor in the emergence of
Paris as the capital of France.

Abelard tells us that Suger was unwilling at first to grant him the
right to set up his own house but that "a certain Stephen, the King's
Seneschal" intervened on his behalf. This, of course, was Abelard's
patron, Stephen de Garlande.* With the help of his influence,

---

* The rather coy reference to him as "a certain Stephen" mirrors the reference he makes to

Abelard was given permission – confirmed in the presence of the king – to quit St. Denis. The only condition was that he should not act to the detriment of the prestige of St. Denis by putting himself under the authority of another abbey.

> *And so I took myself off to a lonely spot I had known before in the territory of Troyes, and there, on a piece of land given to me, by leave of the local bishop, I built a sort of oratory of reeds and thatch and dedicated it in the name of the Holy Trinity. Here I could stay hidden alone but for one of my clerics, and truly cry out to the Lord, "Lo I escaped far away and found refuge in the wilderness."*[1] (Abelard, Autobiography)

He seems to have seen his hermitage (initially there were so few people that it really did not count as a monastery) as a resting place of personal significance, the monastic equivalent of a home of one's own. The location that Abelard had chosen was in pleasant wooded countryside, next to the little river Ardusson, which joins the Seine at Nogent. The town of Troyes, seat of the local bishop, was 40km away. Nothing is left of the house from Abelard's day; even the exact position of the reed and thatch oratory that he mentions is a matter of speculation. The existing buildings date from the eighteenth century, when the convent was well enough funded to be rebuilt. The only remnants from the twelfth century relate to the supply of water: a channel diverting part of the river through monastery land and a carved stone wellhead, but these are most likely to be from the time when Heloise was abbess.

The surrounding countryside is fertile, arable land. Presumably at this time it was still being cleared for farming in response to the growth of the population. It was from neighboring farmers, as well

---

a "certain church" in which he and Heloise were married, giving credence to the idea that this took place in the Chapel of St. Aignan, which was attached to Stephen's house.

as his influential contacts, that Abelard needed financial support. This was difficult for him; he was a scholar, temperamentally unsuited to wheedling money out of landowners. He describes himself as "not strong enough to dig, too proud to beg."[2] He seems to have been uncomfortably aware of his own limitations as a fundraiser: he later rather ungraciously remarks that it was easier for Heloise to make a success of her convent because she was a woman and therefore attracted more sympathy.

The name he chose was unique – the Paraclete. The word is Greek, meaning "one who assists" or "helper." In classical times it also meant legal helper or advocate, but in the Bible it is used with a very specific meaning. The word occurs only a few times in the New Testament but each time it refers to the Holy Spirit in its role as spiritual helper or comforter (*consolator* in Latin), which is how it is usually translated. Christ tells his disciples in Luke's gospel that the Paraclete will remain with them after his death to bring them the comfort of religious faith. We are told that the Paraclete resides within the redeemed soul and that it provided the disciples not only with strength, but with the inspiration to proclaim their belief. It is evident from the way in which Abelard writes about it that he too saw the Paraclete as something within himself. The house that he named after it was for him an outward expression of that – a kind of external manifestation of an inner kernel of divine inspiration:

> *Because I had come there as a fugitive and in the depths of my despair had been granted some comfort by the grace of God I named it the Paraclete in memory of this gift.* (Abelard, Autobiography)

There must also have been, inevitably for Abelard, an element of provocation in the choice of a name that refers to the Trinity, the study of which had led only recently to his condemnation. His attachment to the Paraclete, however, is primarily a personal and emotional one. He is upset when he leaves it and, almost as if it were his child, he is even more upset when he thinks it is uncared for. It would not be long before he would be expressing to Heloise his desire to be buried there.

The personal nature of his relationship with the Paraclete makes relatively credible Abelard's claim that his original intention was to found a small hermitage, not a monastery at all. That phase of the Paraclete's existence was, however, destined to be short-lived. Students flocked to him once again, asking to be taught. He confesses that he was having such trouble in raising funds that he was obliged to break his vows and start to run a school for money. The takings, he is careful to point out, went to the school, not to himself:

> *Since I was not strong enough to dig, and too proud to beg, I returned to the skill that I knew, and made use of my tongue instead of working with my hands. For their part, my pupils provided all I needed unasked, food, clothing, work on the land as well as building expenses, so that I should not be kept from my studies by domestic cares of any kind.* (Abelard, Autobiography)

This description of a philosopher with time to get on with his work while diligent students provide him with everything he needs might well have represented ideal working conditions for Abelard, or for any academic. During this period he did indeed write one of his most important works, *Theologia Christiana,* an expanded version of the book he had been forced to burn at Soissons.

Events in Paris, however, were about to change Abelard's fortunes once again. It had been thanks to his patron, Stephen de Garlande, that he now had his own monastery rather than being on trial for treason, but Stephen now found himself in trouble. In 1123, shortly after the accession of Suger as abbot of St.-Denis, a new bishop of Paris, Stephen of Senlis, had come to power. He was a supporter of the reformers and an enemy of Stephen de Garlande, whose personal wealth and temporal power he considered a mockery of his position as archdeacon of Notre-Dame.

He started a campaign against Stephen that would result eventually in his removal from office. Garlande's power had earned him many enemies. As one chronicle puts it, he had started to rule the king rather than serve him. A letter exists, for example, from Bernard of Clairvaux to Abbot Suger stating that, although Bernard knows that Stephen is a friend of his, he really ought to help in curtailing his influence.

The details of the incident are not clear, but it seems that in 1127 a legal dispute had been engineered with Stephen de Garlande. The conflict had escalated and eventually the decision went against him, resulting in his loss of the post of seneschal. He seems to have panicked at this and staged a revolt, supported by Thibaud of Champagne. The attempted coup (if that is indeed what it was) failed. Stephen de Garlande was disgraced and his lands were confiscated. The house on the Ile de la Cité was destroyed (only the chapel was spared) and the vines on the slopes that led up from the left bank to the abbey of Ste.-Geneviève were uprooted.

There is also some uncorroborated evidence that things were not going perfectly for Abelard at the Paraclete at this time. An English poet called Hilary of Orléans, who was apparently a student there, records in a short poem an incident from student life. A breach of discipline on the part of the students (we are not told what) results in Abelard banning them from sleeping on the Paraclete grounds. They are obliged, therefore, to live in the local village and walk in every day. They stage a revolt in order to persuade Abelard to relent. The poem ends at this point, so we do not know whether he did so. Hilary's account does confirm Abelard's picture of the Paraclete as a place thronged with students. It is also possible that his hasty decision to exclude recalcitrant students from the grounds may have been the result of his intimate feelings for the Paraclete. He might well have been a little disturbed, even in the best of times, about rowdy students spoiling the atmosphere of his special place.

An overreaction to a breach of discipline is also a not uncommon symptom of stress. If Abelard had already heard about the fall of

Stephen de Garlande it might well have made him anxious, even though he was safe from direct attack since the county of Champagne supported the Garlande faction. The defeat of the Garlandes might well have put the reformers in an aggressively triumphant mood and Abelard does indeed confirm that he was very concerned about the activities of those he calls his "former enemies":

> *They went up and down the country slandering me shamelessly in their preaching as much as they could, and for a while brought me into considerable disrepute in the eyes of the ecclesiastical as well as of the secular authorities.* (Abelard, Autobiography)

His recent experience at Soissons would have given him good reason to fear another attack. This anxiety built up until he was "in such a state that I only had to hear of a meeting of clerics to believe that they were plotting against me." He even considered deserting the Christian world for Muslim Spain:

> *I thought of quitting the realm of Christendom and going over to the heathen there to live a quiet Christian life amongst the enemies of Christ at the cost of what tribute was asked. I told myself that they would receive me more kindly for having no suspicion that I was a Christian on account of the charges against me and they would therefore believe I could more easily be won over to their pagan beliefs.* (Abelard, Autobiography)

There is, of course, an element of irony in this remark: "If people think I am not a Christian then, very well, I will leave Christendom." It was probably not a serious threat. Although contemporaries of Abelard did translate the Koran and there were Muslim scholars who were soon to become respected in Europe, in his own writings he does not express any particular interest in Islam either as a faith or as a culture.

As it happened, he didn't need to leave Christendom. Instead, he was given the opportunity to move to the distant land of Brittany. He was invited to become abbot of an ancient monastery on the Atlantic coast at a place called St./Gildas/de/Rhuys. This was a prestigious post: the abbot of St./Gildas had political duties in the court of the Count of Brittany as well as religious ones. It seems likely that the invitation originated with the count, Conan III, possibly supported by his mother, Ermengarde, who is known to have had a strong inter/est in religious matters and corresponded with the eminent clerics of the day, including Bernard of Clairvaux. Abelard may have been brought in as a "celebrity abbot" to increase the intellectual respectabil/ity of Brittany. Perhaps he was influenced by the implied flattery of such an offer as well as being glad to distance himself from his oppo/nents. Looking back, though, as he wrote the autobiography, he viewed the decision to leave the Paraclete only with regret:

> ... an opportunity was offered to me that I believed would bring me some respite from the plots against me; but in taking it I fell among Christians and monks who were far more savage and wicked than the heathen ... God knows, I should never have accepted the offer had I not hoped to find some escape from the attacks that, as I said, I had perpetually to endure. (Abelard, Autobiography)

St./Gildas/de/Rhuys is in the modern *département* of Morbihan, which means in Breton "inland sea." This refers to a large body of water connected to the Atlantic Ocean by a narrow channel through which a fierce tide tears back and forth twice a day. The monastery stands on a rocky cliff, close to this channel. On the other side – not far by boat but a day's journey by land as one circles the inland sea – are the standing stones of Carnac. These remnants of the remote megalithic past fascinate the modern visitor but Abelard would almost certainly have seen in them further evidence of the innate pagan savagery of the Bretons. The very wildness that today makes the area an attractive place for a holiday would for him have marked it out as the edge of the universe, something as far from the cathedral school of Paris as it would be possible to imagine. It should have been obvious that Abelard and the Bretons were not going to get on:

> The country was wild and the language unknown* to me, the natives were brutal and barbarous, the monks were beyond control and led a dissolute life that was well known to all. Like a man who rushes at a precipice in terror at the sword hanging over him and at the very moment he escapes one death, meets another, I willfully took myself from one danger to another and there by the fearful roar of the waves of the ocean at the far ends of the earth where I could flee no farther, I used to repeat in my prayers the words of the psalmist: "From the end of the earth I have called to thee when my heart was in anguish."³
> (Abelard, Autobiography)

The monks and lay population were unspeakable and the local aristocracy was no better:

> In addition the abbey had long been subject to a certain powerful lord in the country who had taken advantage of the disorder in the monastery to appropriate all its adjoining lands for his own use, and was exacting heavier taxes from the monks than he would have done from Jews subject to tribute. (Abelard, Autobiography)

The reference to the extortion of money from Jews is interesting. It was standard practice at this time for the state to impose special taxes on the business activities of Jews. Europe was in the process of devel-

---

* As he was born in Brittany this may seem puzzling. There are two possible explanations. Either he had not learned the Breton language at all because, as he is careful to point out, he grew up only on the very edge of Brittany and his father was not a Breton, or he had learned a dialect significantly different from that of the monks.

oping the repellently anti-Semitic mentality that it was so disastrously to maintain for centuries to come, but it was not yet inherent in the culture. During the first crusade Jews had been attacked in eastern Europe but there had been no such incidents in Paris. A synagogue and a Jewish market stood in the middle of the Ile de la Cité, so Abelard would have had the opportunity to meet Jews and even to talk theology with rabbis, as many Christian medieval theologians did. He put this experience to use in a book called *Dialogue Between a Philosopher, a Christian, and a Jew.* In this work the philosopher, who of course represents Abelard, quizzes each of his interlocutors about the nature of his faith. The Jew explains his religion as practice: people of his faith show their devotion to God by observance of their dietary and other laws. This understanding of religion is, of course, the opposite of Abelard's. For him, good or evil, piety or impiety, are to be judged on the basis of intention rather than action. Nonetheless, although the philosopher does argue against him, the Jew is represented by Abelard as a devout and sincere person who presents his case convincingly. The philosopher is aware that Jews are subject to persecution and his Jewish interlocutor gives the willingness of his people to suffer attacks as a result of their faith as an indicator of their piety. Neither Abelard nor Heloise (who refers to Jews in a similar context in one of her letters) ever shows the contempt or viciousness towards Jews that has subsequently so marred the history of Christian civilization.

In Brittany Abelard was close to his family. We know from the records of the cathedral that his brother Porcarius had become a canon at Nantes. Abelard and Heloise's son, Astralabe, who had been brought up by his uncle, was now about ten years old (the year of his birth, like almost all dates relating to the affair, being known only to within a couple of years). He was to go into the church and would one day also become a canon at Nantes, so it is quite possible that he had already commenced his studies there under the aegis of his uncle.

It is impossible to imagine that Abelard was not in touch with his son. In fact there is even a work of his that gives some insight into what passed between them. It is the rather odd poem, known as the *Carmen ad Astralabium,* or "Song (Poem) for Astralabe," the only extant version of which seems to be a hastily written early draft of the work — well overlength at 1,000-plus lines — on which he probably worked during his time at St.-Gildas. It is not known whether Abelard ever finished it. In the version that has come down to us at least (there are several copies but none dates from earlier than a few decades after his death), it is repetitive, unstructured, and boring — something no writer would want others to see. Nonetheless it is inter-esting to have even an imperfect knowledge of what Abelard wrote when he yielded to the quite natural temptation to try to pass on his accumulated wisdom to the succeeding generation. For all its imper-fections it does offer a glimpse of Abelard's preoccupations as well as his relationship with his son.

The poem begins with a line that, along with the very existence of the poem itself, is strong evidence for Abelard's continuing love for his son:[4]

> *Astralabe, my son, the delight of your father's life,*
> *I have a few words for your instruction.*

Heloise is mentioned only once, as holding the belief that there are some sins that are so pleasant that it is impossible to repent of them. She says exactly this, of course, in her letters. We also know from the letters that she kept her true feelings a secret from most people, lead-ing to the conclusion that only Abelard could have had the knowl-edge to write these lines:

> *This is the constant lamentation of our Heloise*
> *that she often makes to me and to herself:*
> *"If, unless I repent of my early sins,*
> *I cannot be saved, there is no hope for me:*

still so sweet are the joys of the sins we committed
that even remembered they pleasure me, these sins that pleased
me all too much."

The reference to "our Heloise" gives a credible and rather charming picture of a family unit. A father shares with his son the weary — but ultimately affectionate — acceptance of the mother's foibles. It is not known whether Astralabe ever saw the poem or at what age Abelard would have intended him to see it, but an adolescent boy's embarrass-ment at such a reference to his parents' carnal bliss is probably best not imagined.

Much of the advice that he gives to Astralabe would not be out of place in an end-of-term address at a school: be honest, play the game, avoid the temptations of easy pleasure:

> *May you care more for learning than for teaching:*
> *for with your teaching you profit others, but your learning is for*
> *yourself.*
>
> *Stop studying when you have nothing more to learn,*
> *but never think of stopping until then.*
>
> *Everyone can be free from crime*
> *but not everyone can be free from flaws.*
>
> *As a wise mind should not be deceived, so a good mind should not*
> *deceive; to be deceived is a flaw, to deceive is a crime.*

He makes frequent references to the dangerous power of insincere words. At Soissons and subsequently in his life, rhetoric showed itself to be a more effective weapon even than his logic. He could analyze arguments in minute detail but others were better able to sway the decisions of councils. It is not surprising, therefore, that flattery and the cynical misuse of language should have repelled him:

> *While the tongue is a small part of the body, it is a major fire,*
> *fewer people have perished by the sword than by the tongue.*

> *The flatterer appeases the stupid man, the detractor appeases his*
> *enemy; the pious ear repels them right away.*

On the subject of sex he gives some mixed signals. At one point
he gives advice that Heloise's Uncle Fulbert might have wished he
had taken in respect of his own niece:

> *If you have a daughter, guard her night and day*
> *so that she may not cast you into perpetual disgrace.*

But he is not without a word of sympathy for the women he must at
least have seen on the Rue St-Denis:

> *The humble prostitute is better than the arrogantly chaste lady.*

He also expresses views that, one might guess, would be typical of
his age and not untypical of men of any age:

> *There is nothing better than a good woman and nothing worse*
> *than a bad one.*

Quite extraordinarily, in the midst of exhortations to chastity there
are these lines, which add up to "if you can't be good, be careful":

> *If you cannot live chastely, do not despise living discreetly;*
> *Popular opinion is more powerful than life itself for you.*

He reserves a special distaste for difficult women from the nobility.

> *An arrogant woman is worse than a woman of the streets.*
> *It is possible to please the one, but there is no way to please the*
> *other.*

She is the fire burning down the house;
any real fire you can imagine is less than this flame.

There are several remarks along these lines in the poem and it has been suggested that they are references to Ermengarde, the mother of Count Conan, who, although she may have been responsible for Abelard's original appointment, might subsequently have fallen out with him. It is certainly credible that Abelard would not get on with a willful aristocrat who had originally employed him effectively as a pet theologian. If this were the case she might well have encouraged the monks in their increasing insubordination, metaphorically, as he puts it, "burning down the house" of St. Gildas.

The Cistercians also come in for criticism. They were a new, strict order who were effectively Bernard of Clairvaux's private corps of evangelists, fighting for the reform movement. It is easy to imagine that they came over as self-satisfied in their piety and arrogant in their assurance that their faith needed no scrutiny, least of all from Abelard's logic. While traditional Benedictines wore black, Cistercians were distinguishable by their habits of undyed wool. This explains Abelard's reference to them as sheep. Here, as with other references, one gets the feeling that his dislike of them went beyond a simple doctrinal disagreement:

You do not want to win the favor of the people by your clothing;
the fleece of a sheep cannot deceive the farsighted.
They do not get confused about what is a sheepskin and what is
the pelt of a fox.
You will not be made holy by your dress; you may be made proud.

Perhaps Abelard felt he had to warn Astralabe against pride. It is not uncommon to wish to save one's child from the very faults that one has oneself. Perhaps he wanted to warn him specifically against joining the Cistercians – they were expanding all over Europe and making inroads into Brittany at the time. If that is the case, the strategy did not work: Astralabe was eventually to become abbot of a Cistercian house at Hauterive in Switzerland, but only after the death of his father.

The "Song for Astralabe" ends but it does not conclude. After over 1,000 lines packed with too many and too similar aphorisms it is still hard to see quite what message the young Astralabe would have been expected to take away with him. Abelard was a skilled writer and it is possible that he could have produced a memorable work after several revisions. On the other hand, perhaps he realized the project of summarizing the totality of one's wisdom as a single work is destined always to fail.

As relations with those around him in Brittany worsened, Abelard's regret at leaving the Paraclete began to turn into guilt: "I often used to groan and tell myself that I deserved my present sufferings for deserting the Paraclete, the Comforter." He was evidently most worried by the thought of it being neglected. It would be dangerous to make too much of the observation, but it is remarkable that Abelard never talks in such terms of the loss of Heloise as he does of his separation from the Comforter:

> I was in deep despair when I remembered what I had fled from and considered what I had met with now; my former troubles were as nothing in retrospect. What tormented me most of all was the thought that in abandoning my oratory I had been unable to make proper provision for celebrating the Divine Office, since the place was so poor that it could barely provide for the needs of one man. (Abelard, Autobiography)

Abelard saw what happened next as providential, an example of the Comforter intervening directly in his life:

> But then the true Paraclete himself brought me true comfort in my great distress, and provided for the oratory as was fitting, for it was his own. (Abelard, Autobiography)

He is right that there is something almost miraculous about what was about to take place. That a chain of events should lead to the Para-clete finding a suitable custodian in the shape of Heloise does seem to be a rather neat solution on the part of Providence. She was, at this time, still at the convent of Argenteuil, where she had become a nun following Abelard's castration. Despite her having taken her vows more out of obedience to her lover than any genuine calling, her nat-ural talents had served her well and she had risen to become prioress, second in command to the abbess herself. She had no reason to leave Argenteuil. More surprising even than her move was the fact that it was occasioned by an instance of just the kind of duplicity and self-interest that usually defeated Abelard. His own description of how it happened is very brief:

> It happened that my abbot of St.-Denis by some means took
> possession of the abbey of Argenteuil where Heloise — now my
> sister in Christ rather than my wife — had taken the veil.
> (Abelard, Autobiography)

Modern research has given us a much more vivid account of Abbot Suger's takeover of the convent of Argenteuil. It was part of the broader campaign to enhance the power of St.-Denis. Argenteuil was attractive to him because, not only did it bring wealth to his abbey, it also gave him a point of access to the river Seine.

In 1129 Suger made his bid for Argenteuil. The convent was independent and apparently flourishing so he needed to produce a very plausible case. His argument was in two parts. The first was a familiar one: he announced that Argenteuil had become corrupt and sexually depraved and for that reason should be closed down. Just as in the case of the convent of St.-Eloi, shut down for exactly the same reason just over twenty years before, we do not have enough evidence to decide whether there was any truth in this charge. We do know for certain, of course, that Abelard and Heloise had once made love in the refectory, which would certainly have been good supportive evi-

dence had Suger known about it. Some historians have also suggested that because Heloise, in her later letters, displays a sound understanding of the mechanisms whereby a nun might become corrupted
she must herself have witnessed it. But that would surely be to under-
estimate her imaginative capacities.

These charges, if they were believed, would be enough to close
Argenteuil but they did not make the case for St.-Denis taking it
over. To do that Suger used a document that he presented to a convocation headed by a papal legate in the abbey church of St.-Germain-
des-Prés.* The document, which was apparently 300 years old, was
a charter declaring that Argenteuil had been given to St.-Denis by
the then king, Louis the Pious, the son of the emperor Charlemagne.
It was written in a recognizably antique style and was signed by the
king and various bishops who were known to have been his contemporaries. The council was impressed by Suger's case, found in his
favor, and decreed that Argenteuil from now on belonged to St.-
Denis.

Suger's original charter no longer exists, but later copies of it have
survived. The language and style of the document are certainly
authentic. That is because every part of it is an exact copy of another document that was in the library of St.-Denis. It was only twenty
years ago that the scholar Thomas Waldman found that for nearly
every part of the charter he could identify a passage of another document that was the same, word for word. This cannot be a coincidence; somebody had copied passages from genuine documents and
put them together – in modern parlance "cut and pasted" them – to
produce a very convincing forgery. Like Abelard before him, Suger
had been making good use of the famous scriptorium of St.-Denis.

Suger's subsequent behavior suggests that he himself might
have felt uncomfortable about obtaining Argenteuil by deception.
He almost obsessively collected signed edicts from those in authority,

---

* The tower of this church, along with the chapel of St.-Aignan, are the only two buildings still standing from the time of Abelard.

confirming the transfer. The papal legate Matthew of Albano had signed at the council. Suger then collected the signatures, each on a separate document, of the bishop of Paris, the king, and the pope. When, a few months later, the pope died, Suger made sure that he also had a new declaration signed by his successor. In successive written accounts of the events he lays more and more stress on the authenticity of the documents until in an autobiographical account he manages to imply that he had known the truth about Argenteuil all his life, or at least from an early moment when "in the very impressionable age of my adolescence, I used to leaf through the ancient charters of the abbey's possessions kept in its chests."[5]

If anyone at the time had doubts about Suger's case they kept them to themselves. Monks were indeed installed at Argenteuil and the house as well as at eight dependent institutions and the rents of their lands (which he took the opportunity to increase) passed into the hand of St.Denis. The monks who replaced the nuns were obliged to follow an ultrastrict regime: they never ate meat and fasted three times a week, doing penance, perhaps, for another man's sins.

As for the nuns, who were now homeless, a group of them formed their own community and went to a house in Malnoüe in Brie,* under the leadership of their abbess. The rest, who seem to have elected Heloise as their leader, were offered accommodation by Abelard:

> *I realized that this was an opportunity sent me by the Lord for providing for my oratory and so I invited her, along with some other nuns from the same convent who would not leave her, to come to the Paraclete; and once they had gathered there I handed it over to them as a gift, and also everything that went with it.*
> (Abelard, Autobiography)

---

* For seventyfive years they tried to have the decision reversed by legal means – hardly the action of women who believed their community to have been guilty of depravity. In the 1160s they even persuaded Maurice de Sully, bishop of Paris, of the justice of their case. Unfortunately at the time his own power was being disputed and he was not able to help them.

It was not quite so simple as Abelard makes it sound. It was not clear, for example, that Abelard had the right just to give the Paraclete to anybody he chose, especially not to a nun who was by implication disgraced. Once again, however, luck favored Heloise's move. It happened that the new pope, Innocent II, was in France trying to get support in a dispute with a rival candidate. Abelard attended a council in the city of Morigny and, since the pope was trying to please as many people as possible, he was able to obtain papal approval for his gift.

Heloise and the nuns moved to the Paraclete and began the task of building up and running the convent.

> *Their life was full of hardship at first and for a while they suffered the greatest deprivation, but soon God, whom they served devoutly, in his mercy brought them comfort: he showed himself a true Paraclete to them too in making the local people sympathetic and kindly disposed toward them. Indeed I fancy that their worldly goods were multiplied more in a single year than mine would have been in a hundred, had I remained there, for a woman, being the weaker sex, is the more pitiable in a state of need, easily rousing human sympathy, and her virtue is more pleasing to God as it is to man.* (Abelard, Autobiography)

Abelard tells us that he visited the nuns "to see how I could help them." He also preached to them. But, in the two years or so before their correspondence restarted, we also know – because Heloise reminds him of it so passionately – that Abelard did not provide her with what she calls the "healing balm of friendship" for which she longed.

This lack of emotional contact, together with his misconception of her as a good nun, are the first things she tries to remedy in subsequent letters. Her presence at the Paraclete becomes part of her argument: his obligations toward the Comforter, she tells him, should now be transferred to her:

> *For after God you are the sole founder of this place, the sole builder of this oratory, the sole creator of this community. Everything here is your own creation.* (Heloise, First Letter)

Over succeeding years she would attempt to reestablish their spiritual closeness. The Paraclete would be part of this process. If she had not had the additional link with some special inner part of Abelard that her place at the Comforter gave her, Heloise's task would have been even more difficult.

TEN

"You are greater than heaven, greater than the world"

1132

The monks beset me with demands for their needs, though there was no common
allowance for me to distribute, but each one of them provided for himself, his
concubine, and his sons and daughters from his own purse. They took delight in
distressing me over this, and they also stole and carried off what they could, so that when
I had reached the end of my resources I should be forced to abandon my attempt at
enforcing discipline or leave them altogether.

Abelard, Autobiography

T THE MONASTERY OF ST./GILDAS the
situation had deteriorated. What had started as
mutual incomprehension had evidently now
become open hostility. Abelard, who had dared to
criticize the great royal monastery of St./Denis for
its laxity, was unlikely ever to settle down with monks who were open
about their families. Perhaps the monks who took delight in tormenting him were also aware that his heart was not in the business of
managing a monastery. Abelard's attempt to instill discipline by
threatening excommunication (which in this case meant expulsion
from the monastery) was almost certainly already too late:

*Sometimes I tried to put a stop to their lawless insubordination
by excommunication, and compelled those of them I most feared*

to promise me either on their honor or on oath taken before the rest that they would leave the abbey altogether and trouble me no more. (Abelard, Autobiography)

He was reduced, in other words, to begging and threatening the recalcitrant monks, not in order to make them behave themselves, but just to make them go away. He is describing an irreparable break-down of discipline. As in all his dealings with authority he seems to exhibit what might nowadays be described as poor management skills. His wit and intelligence were of no use here except to mark him out as an outsider, an awkward intellectual with pretentious Parisian ways.

But Abelard cannot be blamed entirely for the problem. It seems that St./Gildas was not a unique case. There are records of similar events in the monastery of St./Saviour near Redon, in Brittany. In 1126 the duke, Conan III, had himself admitted that he could no longer control the monastery because of what he called "the accu-mulated perfidy of the Bretons." His solution was to shift the prob-lem elsewhere: he asked that the monastery be put under the direct control of the pope.

According to Abelard the situation at St./Gildas became even worse. He begins to tell a story of repeated physical attacks against him by the monks, even though he was, in the language of monasti-cism, their father:

> *The hostility of my sons here is far more relentless and danger-ous than that of my enemies, for I have them always with me and must be forever on my guard against their treachery. How many times have they tried to poison me — as happened to St. Benedict. I guarded as well as I could against their daily assaults by pro-viding my own food and drink; they tried to destroy me during the very act of sacrament by putting poison in the chalice.* (Abelard, Autobiography)

For monks to try to murder their abbot by poisoning the sacramental wine (which is considered, during communion, to be the blood of Christ) must rank as one of the most serious crimes it is possible to commit in a monastery.*

In addition to Abelard's being literally handed a poisoned chalice, the attempts on his life continued (according to him) outside the monastery, even at times when he might have considered himself safe. He tells us that there was even an attack during a trip to Nantes to visit the Count of Brittany, who was apparently a family friend.

> *On another day when I had gone into Nantes to visit the count who was ill and was staying there in the home of one of my brothers in the flesh, they tried to poison me by the hand of one of the servants accompanying me, supposing no doubt that I should be less on my guard against a plot of that kind. By God's intervention it happened that I did not touch any of the food prepared for me. But one of the monks I had brought from the abbey who knew nothing of their intentions ate it and dropped dead; and the servant who had dared to do this fled in terror as much through consciousness of his guilt as because of the evidence of his crime.*
> (Abelard, Autobiography)

This episode leading to the death of a monk who was presumably one of Abelard's loyal companions must have been disturbing not just for Abelard but for his brother Porcarius. He is presumably the "brother in the flesh" whom Abelard mentions; we know from the cathedral records that he was a canon in Nantes at the time. Abelard does not say, but it seems likely that the attack occurred in Porcarius's house. We can only imagine the effect the news of the incident had

---

* In the Middle Ages only the celebrant drank the wine. This remark therefore suggests that Abelard had been ordained a priest – only priests may celebrate the mass. Most, but not all, monks become priests. The fact that Abelard had done so perhaps argues an increasing seriousness in his commitment to religion or even an attempt to give himself a role at Heloise's Paraclete.

on Abelard's son, Astralabe, who was by then about sixteen years old. Abelard does not refer to their reactions. He goes on to recount how he had become effectively a fugitive in his own monastery:

> *From then on their villainy was known to all, and I began to make no secret of the fact that I was avoiding their snares as well as I could; I even removed myself from the abbey and lived in small cells with a few companions.* (Abelard, Autobiography)

He finishes this episode, and brings his autobiography to a close, with the conflict unresolved. As he brings the account of his life up to date he starts to write for the first time in the present tense:

> *I am still in danger and every day imagine a sword hanging over my head, so that at meals I dare scarcely breathe.* (Abelard, Autobiography)

The troubles of Abelard at St.-Gildas make startling reading: monks with wives and children; attacks and attempted murder; the manslaughter of one of Abelard's companions; the abbot of a respected monastery being obliged to live in hiding. The story, however, lacks something. It is less compelling than any of the rest of the autobiography. Missing from this episode is what scriptwriters sometimes call the backstory, the events that led up to it and give it context but that cannot be determined from the action itself. There are just too many questions left unanswered. What did the count have to say when he heard that an attempt had been made on the life of a senior cleric whom he himself had appointed? There were many monks and Abelard was only one; if they were determined to kill him, why didn't they succeed? If, as has been suggested, the enmity of the duke's mother, Ermengarde, was behind the revolt, there is all the more reason to ask why a woman of her importance didn't manage to have him killed if that is what she wanted. What was the real motive of the rebel monks? Did his family not try to do something about his plight? Even the most gifted scholars seem so far to have been unable to come up with plausible answers to all these questions.

It has been suggested that Abelard may have been undergoing some sort of mental breakdown at this time that might have led him to exaggerate and even to imagine things. That would be consistent with his story that earlier in his career he had been obliged to return to Brittany for an extended rest – perhaps he was after all prone to this kind of episode. He might even have been suffering from some phys-ical ailment, the symptoms of which were the paranoia and delusions that we are tempted to detect in his story. But the letters that he wrote during this period show no signs of irrationality. It has also been sug-gested that he may be exaggerating his plight in order to justify his later decision to abscond from St.-Gildas for good. His account might, on the other hand, be factually correct in every detail. It is impossible to tell.

What is not in doubt is that he was genuinely in a state of desper-ation about his life when he came to the end of the autobiography. His current predicament is the climax of his tale of misfortune: a professional career all but destroyed by the jealousy of his fellow aca-demics; lust that enticed him into a disastrous love affair that ended in his castration; exile to a land of homicidal monks. The point has undoubtedly been made to the unknown friend who needed encour-agement – there are others worse off than you:

> *Dearly beloved brother in Christ, close friend and long-standing companion, this is the story of my misfortunes that have dogged me almost since I left the cradle; let the fact that I have written it with your affliction and the injury you have suffered in mind suffice to enable you to think of your trouble as little or nothing in comparison with mine, and to bear it with more patience when you can see it in proportion.* (Abelard, Autobiography)

The fact that, as Heloise says, "You wrote your friend a long letter of consolation prompted no doubt by his misfortunes, but really telling of your own" makes it easy to believe that the autobiography always was something more than just a favor to a chum. It is an exercise in self-analysis. Abelard is now in his late forties and trying to make sense of his life. He has tried to see where he has gone wrong, why things haven't worked out as well as they should have for someone of his undeniable talent. He has tried to produce a narrative that explains the mechanisms that have caused the events that have shaped his life so far. The answers he offers — pride, lust, a fierce Breton temper, and the ever-present jealousy of others — are both an explanation and a judgment.

When he finished he presumably sent the letter to his friend as intended. It is not certain how Heloise came upon a copy. The monk may have sent it on to her for some reason, but it seems more likely that Abelard sent it himself. It would not be unnatural for him to want Heloise to read his explanation for his actions. In his next letter he is forceful in his request for her to pray for him in his misery so he evidently wanted her to know also of his plight at St.-Gildas. He might even have sent it to her just for information. It may well not have occurred to him that Heloise might be displeased that he had chosen to address this lengthy story to another monk rather than to her. He would perhaps have reasoned that she came out quite well in the story, being represented at the end as a devout and respected abbess, happy at last.

His belief that Heloise was, on balance, at peace was so wildly erroneous that it is reasonable to ask what kind of contact there had been between them since their taking holy orders. We know that he had visited the Paraclete a number of times since Heloise and the nuns from Argenteuil had taken it over, but we have no idea of the circumstances of the meetings. Abelard was, as he says in the autobiography, sensitive to accusations that he had returned to his old lustful ways, so perhaps we can assume that he arranged never to be alone with her. Even in a public meeting with many people present, though, it is hard not to wonder what may have passed between them.

They must have faced each other at some moment. He must have looked at her; they must have exchanged some greeting; they must have listened to each other talking, even if it was only to a third person. Heloise might have reasonably expected a flicker of non-verbal contact even if she cannot have hoped for her man to read in her eyes the full extent of her dissatisfaction. If he was determined to believe that she was happy perhaps he did behave with nothing but punctilious formality whenever they were together, giving Heloise no covert acknowledgment of their shared experience. She would surely have keenly felt the absence of "the healing balm of comfort" that can come even from something as simple as a glance.

As she sat alone in the Paraclete writing the first of her letters, she would be reacting to the pain of that apparent rejection. She was hurt not because she had not met Abelard for some years but because she had. To have read his letter, written to somebody else, would have doubtless increased that feeling. She does acknowledge the tragic content of his autobiography – "No one I think could read or hear it dry-eyed"– but the letter she writes in reply does not offer sympathy. She complains that she is never given "a word from you to give me comfort while you are here." What she begs for more than anything, with that repeated word *obsecro,* is personal contact:

> *I beg you then listen to what I ask – you will see that it is a small favor that you can easily grant. While I am denied your presence, give me at least through your words some sweet semblance of yourself.* (Heloise, First Letter)

We do not know how long she had to wait between writing the final "farewell my only love" of her letter, folding and dispatching it, and receiving a reply from Abelard. There is always a little insecurity that follows the sending of a letter, a slight feeling of being, as one waits, in the power of the recipient. This would have been all the more acute for Heloise because she was hoping that a twelve-year silence would be broken.

Abelard's reply – his first letter to Heloise since the daily exchanges of the newly discovered "early letters" – opens with a simple formula: "To Heloise, his dearly beloved sister in Christ, (from) Abelard her brother in Christ." The time of indescribable fragrances and fresh branches of love has passed. He evidently feels that they should be communicating as members of religious orders, loving each other "in Christ." It might well have seemed to him that since they were a monk and a nun they had no choice. The letter, however, is not cold in tone. His affection both for Heloise and for the sisters of the Paraclete is obvious. He begins by answering her question, "Why have you not communicated with me and tried to comfort me?"

> *If since our conversion from the world to God I have not yet written you any comfort or advice it must not be attributed to indifference on my part but to your own good sense, in which I have always had such confidence that I did not think anything was needed.* (Abelard, First Letter)

The remark is undoubtedly well meant but it does miss the point. Not only does it show that Abelard has not yet understood that Heloise is not happy but it also shows a failure to understand what it is that she asked for in her first letter. The comfort that she seeks is not something that can be substituted by her own good sense. Again, typically for this philosopher, he does not always think deeply about other people's feelings.

Abelard then turns the subject back to himself, understandable perhaps for someone who is in fear for his life. He asks Heloise to pray for him. In common with all his contemporaries, Abelard had no doubts about the efficacy of prayer. He quotes Moses, Jeremiah, the Book of Judges, and the Psalms to show specifically how prayers from a wife can help a husband. He reminds her of the special prayer for his well-being that the nuns of the Paraclete used to say at the end of each of the services of the *officium* whenever he visited them. They ended with the words, "O God, who through thy servant hast been pleased to gather together thy handmaidens in thy name, we beseech thee to grant both to him and to us that we persevere in thy will." He suggests that in his absence they recite an updated version in which the final line is changed to "we beseech thee to protect him in all adversity and restore him in safety to thy handmaidens."

He wants them to pray not merely for his safety but that he should come back to the Paraclete. There are some indications that Abelard was effectively after a job there; in later letters he seems to offer himself as resident spiritual adviser and priest to the convent. It would not be unusual for a convent to have a resident male priest; nuns after all always needed the presence of a man to administer the sacrament. If that is what he is asking for, Heloise never responds to the suggestion.

Whatever his intentions, it is clear from what he writes that he has warm feelings for the Paraclete and for the sisters there. Not only does he ask to be buried there but he is very specific about the reasons for choosing a convent as his last resting place:

> *I do not believe that there is any place more fitting for Christian burial among the faithful than one amongst women dedicated to Christ. Women were concerned for the tomb of our Lord Jesus Christ; they came ahead and followed after, bringing precious ointments, keeping close watch around the tomb.* (Abelard, First Letter)

Quite apart from the way in which Abelard manages, quite unaffectedly, to compare himself with Christ, his concern with the role of women is interesting. The image of a group of devout and chaste women tending and caring for one's grave is very appealing. One might also suggest that this was very close to the kind of attention he did in fact get whenever he visited the Paraclete. It would be hard not to like a convent whose nuns had doubtless been instructed by their abbess as to his great merit and who said prayers specifically for him eight times a day. Nonetheless, Abelard's attitude toward women here seems in marked contrast to his earlier tone in the autobiography where he, for example, condescendingly selects Heloise, "being not bad in beauty," for his bed. Abelard is beginning to show a genuine liking for women that is unusual in medieval writing. He finishes with a final request for the prayers of the nuns:

> *Finally, I ask this of you above all else: at present you are over-anxious about the danger to my body, but your chief concern must be for the salvation of my soul.* (Abelard, First Letter)

Abelard's letter is not unkind or insensitive but it still does not respond to Heloise's fundamental point that she is not happy. Nor does it go anywhere toward satisfying her emotional needs.

The letter that Heloise was to send in reply would alone be enough to make her famous. The previous letter followed a pattern dictated by convention, but there are no models for the next letter. It leaves no room for doubt about what is happening in Heloise's mind. If Abelard still believed that she was happy this would shock him out of it.

The effect that the letter had on him is evident in the first paragraph of his reply. He becomes a little formal and adopts the slightly pedantic manner that all good teachers find themselves eventually obliged to use. He begins by summarizing the structure of what she has said in her letter and setting out his plan:

> *The whole of your last letter is given up to a recital of your misery over the wrongs you suffer, and these, I note, are on four counts . . . I have decided to answer you on each point in turn, not so much in self-justification as for your own enlightenment and encouragement, so that you will more willingly grant my own requests when you understand that they have a basis of reason.*
> (Abelard, Second Letter)

The first of Heloise's four points seems at first sight to be a trivial quibble. She objects to Abelard's salutation. What he had written was: "To Heloise, his dearly beloved sister in Christ, (from) Abelard her brother in Christ."

"I am surprised, my only love," she says, "that contrary to custom in letter writing and, indeed, to the natural order, you have thought fit to put my name before yours in the greeting that heads your letter." This is a technical infringement of the rules of letter writing as composed in 1008 by Alberic of Monte Cassino: the name Heloise comes before the name Abelard whereas men's names should properly always precede women's.

It is reasonable to question what is going on here. Can this really be the most important thing that Heloise, a woman by her own admission suffering agonies of regret and misery, can say to Abelard, a man whose life is in imminent danger? The explanation comes when we remember the couple's fascination with the beginnings of letters. As the early letters show, inventing new and exotic salutations was almost a daily game for them. By referring to his greeting Heloise is covertly reminding Abelard of something that is of great importance to them and that others do not know about. She reinforces this feeling of intimacy by slipping a "my only love" into the same sentence. The remark also draws attention to her own salutation: "To her only one after Christ, (from) she who is his alone in Christ." In contrast to Abelard's, Heloise's greeting, while acknowledging that they are in holy orders and committed to Christ, manages also to get in another "only one" as well as including the assertion that she is his alone. She has neatly combined references to her own romantic love with their religious life without offending against either one. It is a summary of what Heloise wanted – the reconciliation of religion and the life of a lover. No wonder she employs a device to make Abelard think about it.

Her next point is not a clever conceit. It is motivated by genuine anguish at the thought of his death:

> We were also greatly surprised when, instead of bringing us the
> healing balm of comfort, you increased our desolation and made

the tears flow, which you should have dried. For which of us could remain dry-eyed on hearing the words you wrote toward the end of your letter: "If the Lord shall deliver me into the hands of my enemies so that they overcome and kill me"?
(Heloise, Second Letter)

As she has already done repeatedly and eloquently, she assures him of her love and of the consequences for her of being without him:

You ask, my dear love, if you chance to die when absent from us, to have your body brought to our burial ground so that you may reap a fuller harvest from the prayers we shall offer in constant memory of you. But how can you suppose that our memory of you could ever fade? Besides, what time will there be then that will be fitting for prayer, when extreme distress will allow us no peace? (Heloise, Second Letter)

There can be little doubt that Heloise would have been, as she said, thrown into the deepest torment by the loss of Abelard. Surely, however, this is not quite an appropriate response to someone who believes that he may be murdered at any minute. It is almost as if she is saying something like, "Shut up about being about to be murdered, it really upsets me." Some people might think that a more sympathetic response might have been to offer to appeal to somebody on his behalf, or perhaps to offer him shelter if he needed it. Heloise does neither of these things. Perhaps she is making allowances for what she considers to be exaggerations in Abelard's account of his own plight. Or perhaps there is actually a tussle going on, in the midst of this serious subject, about quite whom this conversation is about.

Abelard's defense on this issue is to point out that she told him in her first letter to write with (and he quotes accurately) "news of the perils in which you are still storm-tossed." He adds that the sign of true friendship is to share trouble: "there is no wider distinction between true friends and false than the fact that the former share adversity, the latter only prosperity." There seems to be no doubt about his sincerity either. He has every reason to think about his death, he says: "I am so critically placed in danger and daily despair of life that it is proper for me to take thought of the welfare of my soul. Nor would you if you truly love me, take exception to my fore‑thought." He even talks about being happier dead: "I cannot see why you should prefer me to live on in great misery rather than be happi‑er in death."

Heloise continued presumably to pray for him but she never grants him the sympathy he asks for. If that was indeed because she felt he must be exaggerating, subsequent events supported her view. Abelard was not after all murdered by the monks of St.‑Gildas.

Abelard refers to Heloise's third point in a way that makes it clear that this is not the first time he has heard it:

> *Third, you went on to your old perpetual complaint against God concerning the manner of our entry into religious life.* (Abelard, Second Letter)

This sounds a little like, "Heloise, darling, please don't start!" Since we know that they have not discussed personal matters since that time it follows that he must have last heard the old perpetual complaint in the days immediately after the castration, before they had entered monasteries. Since then he has persuaded himself, with no reference to her, that she no longer has these feelings. Heloise's purpose is to dis‑abuse him of this idea. She expresses herself with force:

> *O God – if I dare say it – cruel to me in everything! O merci‑less mercy! O Fortune who is only ill‑fortune, who has already spent on me so many of the shafts she uses that she has none left with which to vent her anger on others.* (Heloise, Second Letter)

She is surprisingly free in her criticism of God. Heloise has, she points out, lost everything – her lover and her secular life – and been obliged to become a nun in obedience to Abelard. All this happened through no fault of her own. It was all so unfair – "all the laws of equity in our case were reversed" – because, by the time the disaster occurred they had made amends: they were already married, not for-nicating as they had been previously. In fact they were not even living together.

> *While we enjoyed the pleasures of an uneasy love and abandoned ourselves to fornication (if I may use an ugly but expressive word) we were spared God's severity. But when we amended our unlawful conduct by what was lawful, and atoned for the shame of fornication by an honorable marriage, then the Lord in his anger laid his hand heavily upon us and would not permit a chaste union when he had long tolerated an unchaste one.*
>
> (Heloise, Second Letter)

"At least," she says, "I can thank God for this: the tempter did not prevail on me to do wrong with my own consent." She is alluding to the moral philosophy that was familiar to both of them: she did not sin in the downfall of Abelard because she did not consent to evil, which is Abelard's definition of sin. Earlier on, however, at the time of the affair she did yield to carnal desires. She does therefore have some sins to expiate, as she says: "too many earlier sins were commit-ted to allow me to be wholly free from guilt." She does wish to repent:

> *The sequel is a fitting punishment for my former sins, and an evil beginning must be expected to come to a bad end. For this above all may I have strength to do proper penance.* (Heloise, Second Letter)

The greatest surprise of her letter is the next remark. She announces that she cannot do proper penance for her sins, not because she does not have the strength but because she does not have the conviction. She cannot regret what she has done. This is not something she is pleased about — she describes herself later as a suffering soul crying out in her wretchedness — but it is something about which she has no choice.

Heloise and Abelard were both certain of the primary importance of a person's intention in any evaluation of right and wrong. They had studied and discussed it together. Perhaps the idea even came originally from Heloise. Now she is putting it into practice. She has studied her feelings for twelve years now and she knows that she does not have the inner will, the "intention," that would allow her to make "proper penance." The passage in which Heloise explains this to Abelard is startling in its immediacy. Intellectually she may regret her feelings but her description of them is so carefully observed that it reads like a celebration. With the reference to her "unhappy soul" removed, her words could almost be the lyrics of a song. It would be hard to find anywhere a better description of what it is like to be erotically in love:

> *In my case the pleasures of lovers that we shared have been too sweet — they can never displease me, and can scarcely be banished from my thoughts. Wherever I turn they are always there before my eyes, bringing with them awakened longings and fantasies which will not even let me sleep. Even during the celebration of the mass, when our prayers should be purer, lewd visions of those pleasures take such a hold upon my unhappy soul that my thoughts are on their wantonness instead of on prayers. I should be groaning over the sins I have committed, but I can only sigh for what I have lost. Everything we did and also the times and places are stamped on my heart along with your image, so that I live through it all again with you. Even in sleep I know no respite. Sometimes my thoughts are betrayed in a movement of my body, or they break out in an unguarded word.* (Heloise, Second Letter)

Abelard begins his reply to her outburst about the cruelty of God by admitting that he had believed she was over what he considers to be her bitterness:

> *I had thought that this bitterness of heart at what was so clear an act of divine mercy had long since disappeared. The more dangerous such bitterness is to you in wearing out body and soul alike, the more pitiful and distressing it is to me.* (Abelard, Second Letter)

Apart from warning her about the dangers of dwelling on these thoughts, his reply to her point is to urge her to recognize that the only route to happiness is to accept God's will. Abelard's argument is that God has in fact been good to both of them. By removing the possibility of any more lustful behavior he has led them to the superior life of monasticism. He reminds her of the pit of lust into which they had descended: the episode when they had sex in the convent refectory; the deceit of Uncle Fulbert; their blasphemous disguising of Heloise as a nun. Now God has economically brought two people to salvation (or in Heloise's case, potential salvation) with a single act:

> *He made use of evil itself and mercifully set aside our impiety, so that by a wholly justified wound in a single part of my body he might heal two souls. Compare our danger and manner of deliverance, compare the sickness and the medicine. Examine the cause, our deserts, and marvel at the effect, his pity.* (Abelard, Second Letter)

Abelard's advice to Heloise, the route by which he believes she may rid herself of her misery, involves the contemplation of suffering. In Christianity human beings can be saved only by the agency of the real human sufferings of Christ. Abelard tries to direct Heloise's thoughts toward the sufferings of their savior rather than their own.

Are you not moved to tears or remorse by the only begotten Son of God who, for you and for all mankind, in his innocence was seized by the hands of impious men, dragged along and scourged, blind-folded, mocked at, buffeted, spat upon, crowned with thorns, final-ly hanged between thieves on the cross? Think of him always, sister, as your true spouse and the spouse of all the church. He bought you not with his wealth but with himself. He bought and redeemed you with his own blood. (Abelard, Second Letter)

Passages like this may appear counterproductive, likely further to distress a person in torment, rather than save them. It would be easy to dismiss Abelard's assertions that all had been for the best as a (quite understandable) mechanism for his psychological survival in the face of irredeemable misery, an extreme form of whistling in the dark. Equally, his imploring Heloise fully to accept her religion can be seen as an extension of this, a (less laudable) desire to repress her, effectively to castrate her, as a kind of compensation for his own fate. It would be hard to deny that there were such elements in Abelard's attitude. But one mind can hold many thoughts and this is not a com-plete description of what Abelard is offering.

He is saying more than just "sit there and suffer." God, in his theology, is more often an agent of love than of vengeance. In his letter he includes for her a prayer he has written for God's mercy, asking Him to "come as redeemer not as avenger; gracious rather than just; the merciful father not the stern lord." The redemption that he is urging Heloise to accept is effected through the sacrifice of Christ but is a route to joy, not to suffering. The ultimate aim of religion, as seen by Abelard, is a kind of joyous spiritual homecom-ing, a return to a condition where all previous suffering no longer matters. Bliss not misery. In one of his hymns he describes this state:

The rest and the refreshing,
The joy that is therein,

Let those who know it answer
Who in that bliss have part,
If any word can utter
The fullness of the heart.[1]

If Abelard had really wanted to abandon Heloise to a life of spiritual imprisonment his letter would have been much colder. He could effectively have told her that she was now the bride of Christ and it was up to her to seek salvation from him. But he does not; even if he appeared cold during their previous meetings he is now plainly concerned about her welfare and conscious of the importance of their relationship:

> *Come too, my inseparable companion, and join me in thanksgiv-*
> *ing, you who were made my partner both in guilt and in grace.*
> *For the Lord is not unmindful also of your own salvation, indeed,*
> *he has you much in mind.* (Abelard, Second Letter)

Abelard emphasizes that the effect of God's sacrifice is to save human beings not by crushing but by elevating them. He makes this idea specific for Heloise in a statement that seems extraordinarily modern:

> *You are greater than heaven, greater than the world, for the*
> *Creator of the world himself became the price for you. What*
> *does he seek in you except yourself?* (Abelard, Second Letter)

These are not the words of someone whose aim is repression. But Heloise does not want to make the final leap into religious salvation. She recognizes that she has sinned but she cannot repent and she has no intention of repudiating her love of Abelard. She does not want to go for first prize in the race for virtue. She seems to be effectively offering to make a compromise with God.

14. The Paraclete church in about 1770. The chapel pictured is much later than Abelard and Heloise but it is probably situated on the site of his original oratory.

15. In a fifteenth-century manuscript, Bernard of Clairvaux (now with his saint's halo, or nimbus) is pictured holding the abbey of Clairvaux, which he founded and from which he took his name.

16. *The tower of the church of the abbey of St.⁓Germain⁓des⁓Prés is one of very few buildings in Paris that survive from Abelard's time. It was here that Abbot Suger arrived in the spring of 1129, carrying a forged document "proving" that the convent of Argenteuil belonged to him.*

17. *Bernard of Clairvaux (top) and (below) his assistant William of St.⁓Thierry, whose letter to Bernard was the foundation of the case against Abelard at the Council of Sens in 1142. The capital B is for Bernard, in a twelfth⁓century edition of his biography.*

18. *The ambulatory at the eastern end of the abbey church of St.-Denis. This was commissioned by Abbot Suger when the marriage of Prince Louis to Eleanor of Aquitaine had provided him with a political triumph. It is considered by architectural historians to be the first building in the gothic style. Its ribbed, pointed vaulting and elegant columns would have seemed startlingly modern to those who first saw them.*

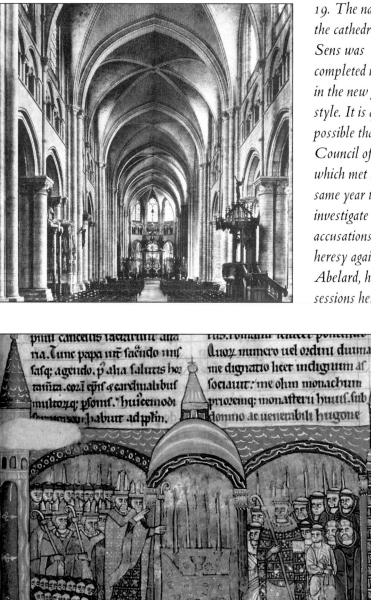

19. The nave of the cathedral at Sens was completed in 1140 in the new gothic style. It is quite possible that the Council of Sens, which met in the same year to investigate accusations of heresy against Abelard, held its sessions here.

20. An archbishop and bishops assemble in the midst of the monks for the dedication of the great church at Cluny Abbey, known as Cluny III. The building was new when Abelard arrived there.

21. *The abbey of Cluny as it was at the time when Abelard stayed there. It was a vast, self-contained community, a symbol of old monasticism in a changing world.*

22. *Much of the medieval abbey of Cluny remained up to the time of the French Revolution as this eighteenth-century illustration shows. Today there is nothing of the great church but one of its four towers.*

23. *The memorial to Abelard and Heloise that was erected in the church at the Paraclete in 1621. This drawing was made just before the French Revolution by Auguste Lenoir, the man who was later to be responsible for moving the couple's remains to Paris.*

24. *The gothic tomb built for the couple in 1817 in the new cemetery of Père Lachaise. It is being contemplated by one of the many pairs of lovers who have visited it since.*

25. *The effigy of Heloise lies beside that of Abelard under the canopy. The remains of flowers that have been thrown over the railings by admirers are almost always to be seen strewn around the tomb.*

I do not seek a crown of victory; it is sufficient for me to avoid danger, and this is safer than engaging in war. Any corner of heaven in which God shall place me will satisfy me. No one will envy another there, and what each one has will suffice. (Heloise, Second Letter)

Despite her sins she is confident that she will be given a place in heaven but she is content to accept an undistinguished one in order to retain her love. To this end she begs Abelard to desist from praising her for her piety. She is resigned to a future preserving as best she can a little of her religion and all of her love.

Abelard has presented his case well but all of his arguments were, of course, perfectly well known to Heloise. She has thought her position through over and over again for twelve years and even the man she loves cannot persuade her to change her mind. By the time Abelard finishes his second letter to her with "Farewell in Christ, bride of Christ; in Christ farewell and live in Christ" the couple have talked themselves into an intellectual and emotional deadlock. If she wants to make any progress now toward her ideal of the perfect friendship, Heloise must try a different strategy.

ELEVEN
Return to Paris

1132–1137

It is for you then, master, while you live, to lay down for us what Rule we are to follow for all time, for after God you are the founder of this place, through God you are the creator of our community, with God you should be the director of our religious life.

Heloise, Third Letter

 ELOISE'S NEXT LETTER opens with a terse, four-word salutation:

Domino specialiter, sua singulariter.

The words *specialiter* and *singulariter* are part of the technical language of medieval philosophy and opinions vary as to what exactly the greeting means. It is probably most fully translated along the lines of:

[From Heloise], *the Lord's by virtue of belonging to a certain group, his* [that is, Abelard's] *as an individual.**

The opening is so unusual that it is tempting to speculate that once again Heloise may be using her salutation as a kind of manifesto. Perhaps she is drawing Abelard's attention to the distinction between

---

* It has also been rendered, significantly differently, as "[To] him who is especially her lord, [from] she who is uniquely his." But this does not seem to fit so well with the context, or with the significance that the words would have for the couple as technical terms.

the individual Heloise who is Abelard's (and who, we know from her previous letters, is going to remain Abelard's) and Heloise the nun, a member of a group. This seems a very complicated way of saying something relatively simple, and it is. But by using the vocabulary of philosophy about the two most important, but opposing, aspects of her life, Heloise may want to remind Abelard of her need to reconcile them.

Each of Heloise's previous two letters had presented Abelard with something that he was not expecting. The first had confronted him with the unpalatable fact that Heloise was not happy; the second had told him that she had, in another technical phrase from medieval philosophy, "no intention" of repenting her love and giving herself entirely to God. The surprise in this letter comes in the next sentence. Heloise casts it in terms of her continued obedience to him. Abelard has told her not to dwell on her bitterness; very well, she will not:

> *I would not want to give cause for finding me disobedient in anything, so I have set the bridle of your injunction on the words that issue from my unbounded grief; thus in writing at least I may moderate what it is difficult or rather impossible to forestall in speech.* (Heloise, Third Letter)

She is now resolved to stop writing about her emotions. The unique channel, through which we have heard the ideas and the feelings of a remarkable woman who lived 900 years ago, is closing:

> *I will therefore hold my hand from writing words that I cannot hold my tongue from speaking; would that a grieving heart would be as ready to obey as a writer's hand.* (Heloise, Third Letter)

She will no longer put down her feelings. The loss is history's — it is felt by anyone who has come into contact with Heloise in the intervening nine centuries. Encounters with people in the past who have the skill and passion sincerely to communicate their feelings are too rare not to be regretted when they end. For Abelard, even though he asked her not to go on about "her old perpetual complaint," the announcement must have been a surprise. But Heloise was not given to making flippant threats that were later rescinded, and was true to her word.

This absence of any further indication of her emotions is sometimes referred to by historians as "the silence of Heloise." Some scholars have in the past treated the decision to stop writing as an invitation to imagine the sequel for themselves, as if it were the dots (…) with which a sentence trails away, or a slow fade-out in a film. It has been suggested that Heloise underwent some sort of conversion whereby she dropped her complaint against God and became the model abbess that Abelard had described in his autobiography. This view, however, is not credible: if Heloise was going to change her mind she would surely have carried on writing about it. The point of stopping writing about her thoughts is that, because she knows she is not going to change her mind, further conversation on the subject is pointless.

Far from being a fade-out, the silence of Heloise is a freeze frame — a device that takes the last instant of a scene and holds it much longer than expected, allowing us to contemplate it and fix it in our minds. The image that is frozen in this case is of Heloise at the end of her previous letter: confident at having reasoned out her position, strong enough to resist not only Abelard but even God, calmly secure in the expectation of her modest corner of heaven.

The decision to stop speaking provides a dramatic moment, for which Heloise has a taste. She created one when, after the castration, she took the veil in obedience to Abelard, despite the protests of her friends, and another when she defied convention and refused to marry Abelard. But good narratives do not normally end on dramatic moments; they use them to make a story progress, not bring it to a close. Heloise, sure enough, begins her next sentence with a phrase that is frequently used in stories to recover from the deceptive feint of a false ending: "And yet . . ."

> *And yet you have it in your power to remedy my grief, even if you cannot remove it. As one nail drives out another hammered in, a new thought expels an old, when the mind is intent on other things and forced to dismiss or interrupt its recollection of the past.* (Heloise, Third Letter)

Despite the dramatic announcement, Heloise is not ending the conversation; she is suggesting a change of subject. It is a painful and difficult transition, like driving out a nail, but not the end of the story. She wants to find an area about which the couple can communicate without reaching deadlock and without increasing her pain. She also chooses, of course, a subject that will ensure Abelard's continuing interest. She knows that his belief in the power of philosophy will never leave him. He believes, with the optimism of his age, that all problems will one day be solved through logical reasoning and study, probably by him. She therefore shifts from telling him what she feels to asking him what he thinks:

> *And so all we handmaids of Christ, who are your daughters in Christ, come as supplicants to demand of your paternal interest two things that we see to be very necessary for ourselves. One is that you teach us how the order of nuns began and what authori-ty there is for our profession. The other that you will prescribe some rule for us and write it down, a rule that shall be suitable for women.* (Heloise, Third Letter)

She wants to know the answers to questions that relate to the fundamental problem of how nuns can fit into the tradition of monasticism. There were at the time, of course, many ancient con-vents that seemed to have managed to run themselves somehow for hundreds of years. Heloise, however, makes the point that the great

St. Benedict, who wrote the "rule" that is effectively the manual for Western monasticism, did not specifically consider the role of women and therefore left many unresolved questions that it is up to Abelard to answer. She was to be so successful in persuading Abelard to apply himself to this area of study that he eventually produced what the historian Michael Clanchy calls "the most sub⁄ stantial writings of the twelfth century on women's place in Chris⁄ tianity."[2]

Heloise continues with examples of the kind of question that is on her mind. The first thing she talks about is that the rule of St. Benedict is very specific about what clothing should be worn by a monk. The provisions of his rule in this area can, she says, be a prob⁄ lem for women:

> How can women be concerned with what is written there about cowls, drawers, or scapulars? Or indeed with tunics or woolen garments worn next to the skin, when the monthly purgings of their superfluous humors must avoid such things? (Heloise, Third Letter)

During their periods — which in the Middle Ages were indeed regarded, as Heloise describes, as the outflow of an excessive amount of one of the four constituent fluids of the body, or humors — women at this time commonly wore a cotton undergarment that could be washed. The scratchy woolen garment prescribed by St. Benedict, presumably for reasons of austerity, presented difficulties. Wool is not amenable to frequent washing, and monastic habits would certainly not have been washed as often as once a month. This problem is of obvious practical importance and it does indeed relate to the fact that St. Benedict was less than sensitive to the spe⁄ cific needs of women. However, one might reasonably also ask whether this really is the first question that needs to be asked by somebody who is deeply concerned with the future of women in Christianity. Nuns had solved the practical problem perfectly well —

as she herself knew because she grew up in a convent — and the point that they may have been technically failing to follow the rule must surely be a minor one.

Just as in the case of Heloise's apparently trivial interest in the technicalities of how to begin a letter, one might suggest that she is almost teasingly drawing Abelard's attention to the intimacy of their shared past. Unlike many monks, Abelard would have had some experience of menstruation. Even to this day men often find women's "monthly purging of their superfluous humors" strangely disturb-ing, a distasteful challenge to their model of womankind and how they relate to it. Perhaps by mentioning it at all she is both reminding him of their erstwhile closeness and at the same time embarrassing him with the intention of provoking him into action — using her apparent weakness as a strength.

Her next question doesn't altogether leave this area of possibly shared experience:

> *What about the abbot's table, set apart for him with pilgrims and guests? Which is more fitting for the religious life: for an abbess never to offer hospitality to men, or for her to eat with men she has allowed in? It is all too easy for the souls of men and women to be destroyed if they live together in one place, and especially at a table, where gluttony and drunkenness are rife, and wine, which leads to lechery, is drunk with enjoyment.* (Heloise, Third Letter)

The problem here is that, according to St. Benedict, hospitality was one of the duties of the head of a monastery. Pilgrims and visiting dignitaries had to be entertained by the abbot. There is doubtless an issue for a convent of preserving proper decorum here, but Heloise does seem to warm to her subject in a way that makes one suspect that she might be recalling, or trying to get Abelard to recall, some specif-ic incidents that the couple might have remembered. She quotes from the Roman poet Ovid's book *The Art of Love* about the dangers of drunken meals:

That is the time when girls bewitch men's hearts,
And Venus in the wine adds to the fire.[3]

To those who might object to the apparent relative unimportance of the points she has raised she has an answer. She immediately quotes the apostle James to point out that all rules must be obeyed equally, "For if a man keeps the whole of the law but for one single point, he is guilty of breaking all of it."[4]

Heloise will continue her dialogue with Abelard, but from now on it will be, at least in the form that we have any record of it, a series of questions. Most of them will have no apparent reference to their affair. They begin with issues about nuns and the place of women in religion but they move into broader areas. Heloise will ask about God's will, the nature of sin, and about the origin of right and wrong. The questions are often challenging and witty, sometimes very technical; they are frequently amazingly far reaching in their scope.

Questions are more than requests for information; they are methods of directing the responses of the person questioned. Heloise has closed the window on her intimate emotional inner world in order to concentrate on steering Abelard's area of inquiry. By asking about the conflict between the rules of monasticism and things that are the commonplaces of the secular world Heloise has perhaps already shown that she is not abandoning her search for a friendship that combines romantic and erotic love with spirituality and religion.

Abelard's own life also changed rapidly as the dialogue between the lovers began to enter its new phase. Records show that in 1132 Stephen de Garlande, his old patron, had recovered from his disgrace enough to be restored to the politically important post of chancellor, second in rank only to the seneschal who commanded the king's army. The previous chancellor, who was the nephew of the powerful Abbot Suger, had for some reason been removed from the post. It is not certain quite why this happened. It may be that the number of competent people of the right social standing in France was actually so small that the king had little choice at the time than to reinstate Stephen. Whatever the reason, this change of fortunes had a predictable effect on the career of Abelard.

With Stephen again able at least to offer the use of Ste.-Geneviève as a place at which to reopen his school, Abelard evidently decided to leave St.-Gildas. This was definitely against the rules: an abbot is responsible for the welfare of his monastery; he is like the captain of a vessel. Abelard was jumping ship. It does not seem to have worried him that he had only recently been writing to Heloise to remind her of the duties of a nun, urging her to forget her own feelings and do her duty. With the autobiography now finished and sent to its various recipients we no longer have a firsthand account of Abelard's actions so we do not know the exact circumstances of his departure. Perhaps he was even reduced to a clandestine flight at night, avoiding the various monks and hostile lords that might waylay him. Some of them might have been glad to see the back of him, it is true, but others might have tried to take advantage of a final opportunity to kill him. Other forces, possibly those allied with Count Conan III, who had at one time seen him as a celebrity abbot who would bring credit to the area, might still try to prevent him from leaving and disgracing the monastery. At St.-Gildas itself there is a local tradition that he actually had to leave the monastery by way of the privy. This would have been little more than a chute that led through the outer wall. Whether or not it is true, the picture of flight and loss of dignity has a kind of symbolic veracity – a famous philosopher, so far out of sympathy with the authorities and with those around him that he was forced to make a run for it.

Abelard did indeed set up his school again at Ste.-Geneviève. He seems to have been in good form in the lecture theater. There is a firsthand account of him from the English churchman John of Salisbury. John was to go on to have an international career in the church, traveling back and forth across the Alps, as he proudly boasts, ten times before eventually becoming bishop of Chartres. He visited Paris in his midtwenties and enrolled in the school of Abelard, whom he calls by his two other nicknames, Palatinus Peripateticus.*

> *I attached myself to the school of Palatinus Peripateticus who then presided on the hill of Ste.⁄Geneviève; that is to say not under the licence of the bishop of Paris, the doctor illustrious admired by all. There at his feet, I received the first elements of dialectica, and according to the measure of my poor under⁄ standing I received with all the avidity of my soul everything that came from his mouth.* (John of Salisbury, Metalogicon)[5]

It is interesting that John bothers to point out that the Ste.⁄Geneviève is outside the limits of jurisdiction of the bishop. Was he perhaps aware that, since Abelard had deserted his post at St.⁄Gildas, he would not have been allowed to open a school within the cathedral precincts? Only his patron, Stephen de Garlande, could give him the protection he needed to start teaching again.

Abelard's situation in Paris – a sort of abbot on the run – was cer⁄ tainly awkward. His supporters probably felt it rather suited him, but to his detractors it made him an easy target. Bernard of Clairvaux, in a letter to the bishops of France, mocks him as "an abbot without monks and a monk without a rule"; there is, he continues, "nothing of the monk about him except the name and the habit."[6]

Nor was the position of his patron, Stephen, as secure as it once had been. Although he was back as chancellor he was never to regain the even more powerful job of seneschal. He had now only a fraction of the power he once wielded. His authority was to be even further

---

* Abelard liked the epithet "peripatetic." At the beginning of the autobiography he proudly tells us that he traveled France "like a true peripatetic philosopher." The reason for the appeal of the name was that in ancient Athens the followers of Aristotle were known as Peripatetics. Abelard seems to think that this was because they traveled around the country but the modern opinion is that it was because they, like many academics to this day, liked to expound their ideas while pacing up and down. "Palatinus" comes from the wordplay between "man from le Pallet" and "man from the palace."

weakened as a result of the intensifying struggle between the reformers and their opponents.

It began when the bishop of Paris attempted to have the canons of
Notre-Dame cathedral, who were minor clergy, replaced by strictly
reformist Augustinian canons (the order that William of Champeaux, Abelard's opponent, had joined at St.-Victor). Had this happened it would have been a coup for the opponents of the king. The
cathedral of France's greatest city would have been instantaneously
converted into a center for the reform movement. Louis VI managed
to block the move and then began to pursue a vendetta against the
bishop. A series of rows erupted that were overtly sectarian.

Once again events centered on the expulsion of nuns from a convent. Reformers wished to take over the convent of Chelles to the east
of Paris and install a community of monks. Stephen de Garlande led
the faction that opposed this. Rows turned into riots that culminated
in a murder in which Stephen himself was implicated. One Thomas,
prior of St.-Victor, a reformist, was stabbed and died in the arms of
his brothers within sight of Stephen's castle of Gournay-sur-Marne.
The perpetrators of the crime turned out to hold land on Stephen's
estate. For a time Louis seems to have tried to protect Stephen by
taking no action — two letters from the pope in Rome survive asking
why the incident has not yet even been investigated.

Eventually, however, the king was prevailed upon to act. As punishment, Stephen's abbey of Ste.-Geneviève was placed under inter-
dict. This was a sort of excommunication for institutions rather than
for people. Interdicted monasteries were not allowed to continue their
religious functions: they were not allowed to celebrate the mass; they
were not even allowed to ring bells. The interdiction probably did
not prevent Abelard from teaching there but it must have turned the
abbey into something like a ghost monastery, unable to fulfill its primary function. It was also a very public display of the weakening of
the power of Stephen de Garlande.

The truth was that there was no longer room for Stephen in the
higher echelons of French politics. Abbot Suger was now controlling

the administration of the king's temporal power. He would continue to display enormous political skill in maneuvering both reformers and royalty to the advantage of the state and himself. Eventually he would become regent of France, deputizing for the king while Louis VII was away fighting the second crusade.

Suger's political style seems also to have dovetailed very effectively with that of Bernard of Clairvaux, leaving even less room for Stephen de Garlande on the political stage. Bernard had become the de facto leader of the reform movement. He maintained control by virtue of his ability to influence rulers and sway crowds. He had started his takeover of the emerging Cistercian order as soon as he became a monk by simply arriving with a band of followers, many of whom were his relatives, at the abbey of Cîteaux and demanding to be let in. His powers of persuasion were put to great effect, building up the numbers of the new order. Parents were even advised to keep their sons away if they did not want to have them talked into joining up. The Cistercians under Bernard caught a wave of public enthusiasm. The order expanded rapidly and was evidently so attractive that monks from less modern orders longed to be Cistercians. At York thirteen monks left their monastery and petitioned the archbishop to be allowed to found their own Cistercian house. He gave them the land that was later to become the site of Fountains Abbey and Bernard himself dispatched his most trusted master of works to supervise the building. This was such an impressive start that the dean and one of the canons of York Minster decided to join them.

During Bernard's lifetime Cistercian abbeys were founded all over Europe. Anyone who has visited one of the many abbeys that survive will have been struck by how beautiful they are. Almost without exception, they are still places of great calm. The acoustics in Cistercian churches make them ideal locations for concerts of medieval music. This enduring atmosphere of devotion is certainly one of the reasons for the popular success of the Cistercians. What Abelard, in a rather curmudgeonly way, considered to be overosten tatious false piety many people plainly saw as a genuine pathway to inner peace.

The Cistercians were a well-organized international order, run with a near-perfect balance of rule from the center and delegated power. With an expanding international organization behind him, Bernard was able to exert his influence all over Europe. He wrote voluminously to heads of state and church; letter after letter condemning where necessary, cajoling and offering deals more frequently. There was hardly a political event of any importance during his adult life in which he was not in some way involved. His success was a triumph of the art of networking that made him not just the head of the reform movement but also probably the most influential man of the twelfth century.

The greatest triumph of Suger's political skill came in the year 1137. He engineered a marriage between Prince Louis, the future Louis VII, and Eleanor, heiress of Aquitaine to the South, thereby securing an alliance with that province. This move was a masterpiece of diplomacy as it almost doubled the wealth of France at a stroke. It also confirmed permanently Suger's position close to the king.* The wedding of young Louis to Eleanor of Aquitaine took place in Bordeaux. It was a major social and diplomatic affair attended by all the leading French political figures including, of course, Bernard. Suger also celebrated his victory by commencing work on the rebuilding of the eastern end of the church of his own abbey of St.-Denis in the new Gothic style. It is a structure of far-reaching narrow ribs and walls pierced with stained-glass windows of the most extraordinary color. It remains to this day one of the miracles of medieval architecture.

---

* In fact the plan was not destined to work in the long term. The remarkable Eleanor of Aquitaine's career was going to be too much for one monarch. After accompanying Louis VII on the second crusade and several other adventures, she left him for the man who was about to become King Henry II of England. The alliance between Aquitaine and France was then at an end. Suger's great project had come to nothing.

Suger, in his later writings, supplemented the construction work he had supervised with a great deal of theorizing about the link between God and the light that his stylistic innovations allowed to permeate the new building. The theory of light and divinity came from the mystical writings of a sixth-century Syrian monk, known to history as the Pseudo-Dionysius, who was another part of the confu-sion that surrounded the identity of St.-Denis, which Abelard had attempted to clarify during his unhappy stay at the abbey.*

With Suger and Bernard between them triumphantly presiding over a newly enlarged France there was probably no room for Stephen de Garlande. When the old king died less than a month after the wedding of his son to Eleanor of Aquitaine, the matter was settled. Whatever residual feeling of sentiment that might have remained between Stephen and the old king was now of no use to him. On the accession of Louis VII Stephen was obliged to retire. He went into a monastery. His power seems to have been so dimin-ished that he was not even given a choice of abbey: he entered not Ste.-Geneviève, of which he had been dean for twenty years, but St.-Victor, the Augustinian house that had been the stronghold of Abelard's adversary William of Champeaux.

Presumably Stephen had once sat in his monastery at the top of the hill contemplating with satisfaction the trouble that his philoso-pher Abelard was causing for William of Champeaux, just down the hill in St.-Victor. Now he himself was down the hill, living out the rest of his life as a regular canon, expected to follow the rule of St. Benedict with reformist zeal. The abbey of St.-Victor eventually took over Ste.-Geneviève along with its lands, including the slopes on which Stephen's vines used to grow.

---

* Historians have since pointed out that the references in Suger to the Pseudo-Dionysius work relate only to the introduction. There is no evidence that Suger had actually read the whole thing. To be fair to the abbot it should be pointed out that the book in question is a spectacularly impenetrable work of mystical obfuscation.

Nothing now remains of the abbey of St. Victor, where Stephen himself was buried. The necrology — the list of people who should be commemorated in the monastery's prayers — does, however, survive. Among the names of the great and the good who have helped the monastery are, rather surprisingly, those of Abelard and Heloise. This is odd, considering that Abelard was such an implacable opponent of the school of St. Victor's eminent founder. One cannot help but wonder whether Stephen had used his political skills within the monastery for the last time to ensure that at least his famous protégé should be recognized and celebrated in what he was once happy to refer to as the enemy camp.

John of Salisbury, in the account of his visit to Paris, is apparently surprised as well as regretful that Abelard left teaching in the year 1137, but it must have been obvious to those who were not recently arrived from across the Channel that the end of Stephen's career would also be the end of Abelard's, at least as a philosopher in the schools. Although Abelard continued writing and was to produce a large body of work with Heloise in connection with the Paraclete, he was never again to teach philosophy in a school.

Abelard had the good fortune to end his public career still at the peak of his abilities, still impressing and delighting his students. He was still arguably, as Michael Clanchy memorably calls him, "the most famous man in the world."[7] He was to leave behind him a comprehensive corpus of books on logic, theology, and ethics, amounting to about a million words in all. Some of his books have been lost, but the key works survive — *Sic et Non,* the book of contradictions and problems for philosophers to solve; the *Dialectica,* his book on logic that draws on his conflict with William of Champeaux; *Ethica,* the book on moral philosophy that outlines the theory of intentionalism and contains his controversial remarks about the innocence of newborn babies; even the book that he was forced to burn at Soissons, *Theologia Summi Boni,* survives not only in the version that was condemned but also reworked as the *Theologia Christiana,* which he rewrote in defiance of the ban. A generation of philosophers was influenced by Abelard; his contribution can be detected in the ideas and references of the thinkers who immediately followed him. (We know also, for instance, that Pope Celestine II, who succeeded Innocent II just after Abelard died, had copies of his works.)

Abelard was cheated of a truly substantial place in the history of ideas by an unforeseen turn of circumstances. Shortly after his death copies of previously unknown works on philosophy by Aristotle began to arrive in Europe. Abelard and his fellow philosophers had had only direct access to a very small part of Aristotle's writings. Some of his works had been lost in the 1,300 years since his death, but many others had just not yet been translated into Latin from the original Greek (which very few people in Europe could read). They did exist, however, and were being studied by Islamic scholars.

This situation had worked quite well for Abelard and his contemporaries. On the important question of Universals, for instance, they were able to read only an elementary introduction to Aristotle's main work on the subject by a later philosopher called Porphyry. Since his treatment was simplified, he had left some tantalizing questions unanswered. This lack of a real authoritative statement turned out to be a useful stimulus. Abelard and other thinkers had had the confidence to try to fill in the gaps. When, after Abelard's death, Latin versions of the previously unknown works by Aristotle began slowly to become available they were, of course, leapt on with enthusiasm. Abelard's work began to look a little old-fashioned. A hundred years after his death his influence had apparently declined radically, superseded by that of a man who had lived a thousand years earlier but of whom medieval scholars were so respectful that they simply called him "The Philosopher."

Abelard once did – almost prophetically – complain in a lecture that, although it might be possible to write a work as great as that of Aristotle, it would never be respected in the same way because it was not by the great man. Even so, those who have studied Abelard's work in detail have seldom come away with anything but respect for his achievement. Bertrand Russell, for instance, a man not pre-disposed to admiring those with religious backgrounds, says of Abelard's theory of Universals that "most modern discussions of the problem of Universals have not got much further."[8]

We know that, after he left Paris in 1137, Abelard continued to write, but we do not know where he was until 1140 when he arrived in the town of Sens to answer charges of heresy. Since he seems to have been obliged to leave the city, he must have gone somewhere else.

TWELVE

The Comforter

In wishing to depict the beauty of the soul and describe the perfection of the bride of Christ, in which you may discover your own beauty or blemish, I propose to instruct your way of life through the many documents of the holy Fathers.

Abelard, Fifth Letter

HERE IS NO EVIDENCE that Abelard spent any time at the Paraclete during the three years that elapsed between his departure from Paris and his next appearance in the historical record in 1140. On the other hand, there is no proof that he did not, and there are substantial reasons to believe that there was a great deal of contact between him and Heloise during this period. Abelard was to produce a large body of writing, ranging from hymns to treatises on philosophy, most of which are known to have been written for use at the Paraclete. This cannot have been achieved without, at the very least, consultation between him and Abbess Heloise. It does seem likely, therefore, that during the "lost years" of 1137 to 1140 the couple met frequently, or even that Abelard stayed for some time at the convent that he had named the Comforter. The work that was done in this period must count as a final joint project of the lovers. We can also see from some of this writing that Abelard, the overconfident master of the schools who had described Heloise as "not bad in looks" and had been so sure of his ability to seduce her, underwent a significant change.

Even before he had left St./Gildas for Paris, Abelard had already contributed not just to the well/being of the nuns of the Paraclete but to the cause of women in general. His response to Heloise's request "that you teach us how the order of nuns began and what authority there is for our profession" is much more than just a history of nuns. He makes an eloquent and well/argued general case for the signif/ icance of women in the history of Christianity that stands out as a counterbalance to the misogyny that became increasingly pro/ nounced in the century that followed his death.

It was in the next letter, however, that he began to assist Heloise with the development of the Paraclete. In her letter she had expand/ ed at some length on her request "that you will prescribe some rule for us and write it down, a rule that shall be suitable for women." Having touched on the difficulties raised by menstruation and the dangers incurred by letting women socialize with men, she had given an analysis of St. Benedict's Rule, the original constitution for a Christian monastery, which had been written in the sixth century. She had argued against a too strict adherence to it. She had listed many examples of circumstances – sickness, inclement climate, the frailty of age – in which a reasonable person might allow slight infringements. She argued in favor of flexibility over matters that do not have obvious moral importance:

> *I would like to see the same dispensation granted in our own times, with a similar modification regarding matters that fall between good and evil and are called indifferent, so that our vows would not compel what cannot now be gained by persuasion.*
> (Heloise, Third Letter)

In fact she had listed so many exceptions that her letter begins to read like a critique of rules in general rather than a request for more of them. This is, of course, consistent with the ethical viewpoint that Heloise shared with Abelard. For them, intentions rather than actions were the criteria for deciding whether something was good or evil. As she put it, "true Christians are totally occupied with the inner man rather than outward works." Following a rule, therefore, cannot make even the most devout nun good unless her intention is good. Although she was herself eloquent about the needs of her convent there was no doubting Heloise's desire to involve Abelard: "It is for you then, master, to lay down for us what rule we are to follow for all time."

Abelard did indeed provide an outline of a set of regulations for the convent in his next letter. He begins by sketching the daily routine of the house, specifying where the nuns should go after each of the services of the *officium*. He then discusses administration at some length. He suggests that it is better for the abbess to be a mature woman who has been married rather than a virgin who has spent her whole life in convents. She does not have to be an intellectual, he adds, but, "if she is not lettered, let her know that she should accustom herself not to philosophical studies nor dialectical disputations but to teaching of life and performance of works."[1]

He lists seven officers who are responsible for the day-to-day running of the convent —infirmarian (responsible for health), cellaress (food and drink), portress (security and routine contact with the outside world), wardrober (clothing, bedding, and footwear), chantress (religious services and liturgy), sacristan (care of religious paraphernalia, chalices, etc.), and, of course, abbess. Again, they do not need to be scholars, or even literate. In fact, with the exception of the abbess and the chantress, who are concerned with liturgical matters, he would prefer them not to be. Those who are literate could spend their time more profitably in the scriptorium. The logic of this is obvious, but the danger is that intelligent people might find themselves being given orders by less intelligent ones, which would inevitably cause problems. Had he considered it in the light of his own experience Abelard would surely have been acutely aware of the dangers of such a situation. He also spends some time making the point that the head of a monastery must remain close to the monks and never neglect them. This is a little rich considering that, when he wrote it, he himself was on the point of absconding from St. Gildas. (He, no doubt, would have argued that the monks there had by their bad behavior placed themselves beyond the limits of any regula/tions.)

Abelard goes on to give guidelines for personal hygiene and diet. He specifies that the nuns should wear undergarments (although he does not discuss their "monthly purging of humors"). As for dietary rules, he follows Heloise in her dislike of specifics, "do not deny the weaker sex any use of food but forbid the abuse of it." It is greed and self/indulgence that must be avoided, he argues, not any particular food. On the question of wine, after a lengthy discussion he decides to restrict the nuns in general to wine with a 25 percent dilution of water. He allows the consumption of undiluted wine only as a med/icine for the sick.

The most radical thing Abelard suggests is that the Paraclete should have added to it an accompanying house of monks whose abbot should be in charge of the dual community as a whole. It has been suggested, quite credibly, that Abelard was doing no more in this than trying to create a job for himself. Once again, however, the system he advocates has not been thought through. Although the abbot would be in overall charge, every monk would be obliged to swear his allegiance to the nuns, to "bind themselves by oath to the sisters not to consent to their oppression in any form." The sentiment is completely laudable but Abelard has in fact produced a formula that would result in the monks having hopelessly split loyalties. In the event of a dispute between abbess and abbot, whom were they to sup/port? Abelard was a great and original thinker but he just did not seem to have a knack for management. Neither Heloise nor any of her successors acted on the suggestion.

Abelard's letter concerning a rule for the convent gives the im/pression of being a series of notes that could well have come out of discussions between him and Heloise. There is another book written at this time, however, that is specifically framed as a conversation between them. Known as the *Problems of Heloise,* it comprises a series of forty-two questions said to have been posed by Heloise, each of which is followed by an answer from Abelard. The work is prefaced by a letter from Heloise asking for Abelard's special guidance, in which she reiterates his doctrine that it is abhorrent to try to practice religion without understanding: "How can we read the Bible and glide over difficult passages, just thinking that they are divinely inspired?"

The questions she asks are all, as one might expect, intelligent and challenging. Frequently, what seems at first sight to be a naive inquiry turns out to be one that has very profound consequences. The Bible, she points out, tells us there is more joy in heaven over one sinner who repents than over ninety-nine just persons who do not need to repent. "Why," Heloise asks, "should that be so? Surely it is better never to have sinned than to have to be brought back from sin by an act of contrition?" Abelard replies that what she says is correct, it *is* better. But the Bible doesn't say that one is morally better than the other, merely that there is more joy in heaven over it. Some of the questions are provocative in the way that one might expect from a bright stu-dent: "Does Christ's challenge to those who were preparing to stone a woman to death for adultery, "Let him who is without sin cast the first stone," mean that nobody who isn't perfect has the right to punish anybody, ever?"; "The Lord says, 'don't swear by your head because you can't change a single hair of it.' If you could change it, would it be all right to swear?" Abelard's answers consistently show erudition, insight, and good sense. It seems to have been his idea to attribute the questions to Heloise and not that of some later interpo-lator. The fact that he mentioned her when he did not have to (in other works he just poses questions to himself) suggests that he really was intending to commemorate her contribution to the book. Again it seems most likely that this collaboration would have taken place during face-to-face encounters rather than by letter.

Another reason to believe that Abelard visited the Paraclete after he left Paris is that he obviously loved the place. When he was exiled in St.-Gildas and it was unoccupied he was in genuine distress:

"what tormented me most of all was the thought that in abandoning my oratory I had been unable to make proper provision for celebrating the Divine Office." When Heloise took it over he had even more reason to love it, due not only to her presence but also to that of the nuns, who became very important to him. He expresses the explicit wish, for example, to be buried among them. The combined charm of the sisters of the Paraclete might, one suspects, have played its part in forming the generalized support of women that he shows in the letters. He also had family reasons for feeling close to the Paraclete, and indeed for visiting it. From the necrology — the book that records the days on which friends and members of the convent have special masses said for them — we know that two of his nieces, Agnes and Agatha (the daughters presumably of one of the brothers who was not a canon at Nantes), became nuns there.

Abelard and Heloise were by now a mature couple; she was in her midforties, he in his late fifties. The passion of their early life could be expected (even in their case) to have diminished. In the best relationships desperate ardor is eventually replaced by humor and the comfort of shared experience. This was certainly a possibility for Abelard and Heloise as they walked in the grounds of the Paraclete, discussing plans for expansion or visiting the site of the new church that was under construction at this time. They would have had plenty to talk about. Did their conversation ever return to the subject of Heloise, her unsuitability as an abbess and her need for love and comfort from Abelard? These were the areas of discussion on which Heloise had shut the door in her third letter.

The couple could have kept their conversation clear of these areas. They could have spent hours talking earnestly about philosophy, theology, and the future of the Paraclete, while all the time avoiding topics that related to the unresolved aspect of their lives. To have done so would hardly have made them exceptional among those in long-term relationships. Heloise, however, had left herself a loophole in the text of her third letter. She says, "I will therefore hold my hand from writing words that I cannot hold my tongue from speaking."

Far from intending to avoid the subject it sounds almost as if she was planning to raise it at their next meeting. Perhaps there were, after all, the emotional outbursts that Heloise says she is incapable of holding back, scenes of recrimination as the couple walked together on the edge of the uncultivated woodland far from the convent buildings. Whatever passed between them did not prevent Heloise from drawing Abelard even closer to the convent that they both loved. She had already persuaded him to give his time and energy to the project. Perhaps, however, her greatest achievement was to harness the very aspect of Abelard that had made her first love him: his ability as a songwriter.

At Heloise's request, Abelard wrote the words and music (although the music for all but two of them is lost) for 133 hymns for use at the Paraclete. Abelard had complained of the many monasteries where hymns were sung but not understood and where many festivals were not even properly marked with suitable hymns. It is typical of his self-confidence that he felt able to rectify the situation by single-handedly producing hymns for the entire year.

The hymns were without doubt the greatest influence that Abelard was to have on the life of the Paraclete. For the members of the community they mapped out the year in terms of feasts and festivals, and the day in terms of the eight services of the *officium*. Their repetition and familiarity was in itself a kind of meditation. The pattern linking the hymns with the seasons was a reminder of the convent's place in the universal cycles that govern existence: day and night, good and evil, life and death. He is proud of his triumph of clear thinking and even celebrates the fact that, in his view, the final flowering of religion will be a state of comprehension when all mystery is resolved:

> *Mystical symbols now throw off all secrecy*
> *Truth is apparent no longer in mystery*
>
> (Abelard, Hymn for Sunday, Lauds)[2]

The subjects of the hymns include a selection of saints. He makes sure that he has included the patrons of the monasteries where he has served: St. Denis and St. Gildas. Gildas was a Welshman who came to Brittany in the sixth century to bring light to the heathen Bretons. Abelard sympathizes with his exile in a "desolate land where there had lived a belligerent race." As well as celebrating themes for the major festivals of the church – birth at Christmas, death and rebirth at Easter – the hymns also pick out themes appropriate to the time of year and the time of day as well as inviting contemplation of the virtues of chastity and poverty and obedience appropriate to nuns.

One hymn in particular expresses very well the monastic ideal of poverty. The nuns of the Paraclete rejected the wealth of the world in favor of a life of simplicity in a rural setting. Although this can be construed as a pointless act of isolationism – cutting oneself off from the reality of life – those who choose it claim that their simplicity and isolation brings them closer to reality on a universal scale. The idea is not impossible to understand, even if one does not choose to pursue it oneself. Abelard expresses this thought in one of the early hymns with a quite uncharacteristic simplicity.

> *Remember worshiper for you*
> *Was made the earth from which you grew*
>
> *By sun alone can man be warm*
> *Who lacks the fire in winter's storm*
> *The poor man in the darkness of the night*
> *Yet has the moon and stars for his delight*
>
> *In bed of oak the rich man lies*
> *The poor the meadow satisfies*
> *For here in melody the birds are spent*
> *And here each flower adds its separate scent*

Rich man, you spend your wealth too fast
In building that which will not last
You paint the ceiling with a sun on high
And fill with pictured stars the seeming sky

Below the roof of real sky
The poor man sleeps in heaven's eye
The real sun, the constellations there
The lord has painted as the poor man's share

                    (Abelard, Hymn for Wednesday, Matins)

The first cycle of hymns begins with a series intended for singing at the early morning office in the first light of dawn. It celebrates the origin of the world:

Lord Creator full of grace
Who holds all matter in its place
Creation by your glory stays;
The world you keep resounds your praise.

                    (Abelard, Hymn for Sunday, Matins)

Abelard and Heloise demonstrated an interest in cosmology throughout their lives: their early love letters are filled with references to the stars and, of course, they named their child after an instrument that models the movements of the heavens. It is not so surprising, therefore, that a book on cosmology that Abelard produced at this time should have been written, according to the introduction, at Heloise's "instigation and persistent urging."

The *Hexaemeron,* a Greek title that might be freely translated as "The Six Days of Creation" is a commentary and analysis of the biblical account of God's creation of the universe. In it, Abelard expresses effectively the deep pleasure that can be derived from the contemplation of the nature of the physical world, both then and now. He calls it elsewhere "the ineffable sweetness of harmonic modulation."[3] The intention of his book, however, is to do something that is not a possibility for the scientists of our own age: to link the physical nature of the universe with ideas of good and evil. He concerns himself with God's intention in creating the world. Abelard raises a question which, in its modern form, still puzzles physicists: "What made the universe come into existence?" The medieval version of this is, of course, "Why did God create the world?" Abelard dismisses as illogical any idea that it was a spontaneous decision, even a whim, on the part of the creator. The idea of the created universe must have been part of God for eternity, he argues. This is not the end of the story, however. The material world was actually brought into being, he argues, not as a result of God's innate nature but by an act of love. To deny this element of the creation, he claims, is to deny God's rationality. Love is a factor that crops up repeatedly in medieval thought in a way that is lacking in its modern counterparts.

At the other end of the scale, human love – "strong as death for those who know the Lord"[4] – is also mentioned frequently in the hymns. It is not hard to find examples that, one can imagine, had a special, personal meaning for the couple while ostensibly celebrating the relationship of nuns to God:

> *Rising as the morning light she walks on high*
> *Bound to Him, her heavenly spouse, in marriage tie*
> *Here on earth betrothed to him she made her vow*
> *There she lives, his wife, and in his presence now.*
> *As nuptial rites in faith are bound*
> *Eternal marriage joys are found.*
>
> (Abelard, Hymns of the Virgins, Lauds)

The "eternal marriage" that this hymn mentions is a theme that occurs quite often in Christianity. For all its apparent disapproval of marriage and sexual union, the image of the meeting of lovers is frequently to be found among the metaphors, allusions, and images with which spiritual ideas are expressed. The main biblical source for such imagery is the book of the Old Testament known as the Song of Songs, or sometimes the Song of Solomon. This book is an erotic love poem full of the most sensuous and striking imagery: breasts like young roes that feed among the lilies . . . lips like a thread of scarlet . . . teeth like a flock of sheep that are even shorn . . . hair like a flock of goats . . . the joints of thy thighs like jewels, the work of the hands of a cunning workman.[5] The connections of this work with religion are not obvious at first glance but the book has nonetheless remained a staple of both Jewish and Christian theology. The clue to its Christian interpretation comes in that other great favorite of the Middle Ages, the Apocalypse. The vision of the end of the world, also known as the Revelation of St. John the Divine, ends with an account of the final fulfillment of God's purpose. The world is destroyed and replaced by a new creation. The writer sees a new heaven and a new earth "coming down from God out of heaven, prepared as a bride adorned for her husband."[6] The union of lovers – of bride and husband – represents, therefore, the ultimate fulfillment of religion. It can also stand for the union of the soul to God, of the human mind to the word of God, and Christ to the church. The bliss of union with a lover, the return home, are all metaphors for the joy of religion.

The eternal marriage was also part of the hymn that the nuns at the Paraclete sang on Easter Sunday every year. It was called the *Epithalamica,* a Greek word for marriage song, written in the form of a short drama: the story of a bride who loses her groom and then refinds him. This immediate symbolic meaning is, of course, the crucifixion and resurrection of Christ. But the story of death and rebirth, especially associated with the renewal of spring, is in fact even older than Christianity. Perhaps it has always stood for the hope that the world of pain and death might be transformed by some spiritual process into peace and happiness.

In the *Epithalamica* a chorus of women wedding guests is found asking the bride to tell them of her expected joy. The bride replies with a description of her joy in terms of spring, "the bristling winter is now past, the heavy rains are over and gone; lovely springtide has opened the earth."[7] The drama of the situation is provided when the bride goes to look for her groom and he is not there. She looks for him, "by night I go forth seeking him; hither and thither I run in my seeking." Eventually she finds him and after the pain of separation there is the joy of reunion:

> *Pain brought on a sleepless night,*
> *Pain made overpowering by love;*
> *Desire made unbearable by waiting,*
> *Till Lover comes to visit the beloved.*

The sequence was not, of course, intended to be acted out on a stage like a play; it was "performed" by a static choir as part of a religious service. Nevertheless the sequence has the elements of plot, dialogue, and character that qualify it as a dramatic work. Its introduction in the middle of the mass must indeed have had the desired effect of heightening the listeners' emotional response to the events being commemorated. Another manuscript from this period has survived, not directly associated with the Paraclete, that contains the text of two similar short sequences. They both feature Mary Magdalene; one deals with women anointing the body of Christ after his death, and the other with the discovery of his resurrection.

Constant Mews, the scholar who positively identified the new letters as being by Abelard and Heloise, believes that these two sequences, along with the *Epithalamica,* were in fact written by Heloise. His case rests on a stylistic analysis of the works. Despite the fact that the two sequences about the Magdalene have no immediate connection with the Paraclete, they are certainly very similar to the *Epithalamica* in style and even have some lines in common. It is the versification that makes Mews believe that they may all be by Heloise. He notes that, unlike the poems in the group that Abelard wrote, the *Epithalamica* makes great use of rhyme. It is clear from their other writings that rhyme is a poetical device that Heloise favored but that Abelard did not. His poems tend to avoid too much rhyme in order to make them sound classical. Heloise, on the other hand, cannot resist using little half-rhyming phrases even within the prose of her letters (she promises, for example, "to always repay you and in all ways obey you," *tibi rependere et in omnibus obedire*). It is also true that the existing manuscript of the *Epithalamica* is quite separate from those containing the other poems that were written for the Paraclete, suggesting that it never was part of the bundles of hymns that Abelard delivered to the convent. That also would be consistent with Heloise having written it.

Abelard himself also seems to have started experimenting with the art of dramatization. He wrote a series of poems called the Laments (*Planctus*). These take the form of a series of poetic mono-logues, spoken by characters from the Bible who have suffered ex-treme bereavement or separation. In the lament for the death of his loyal friend Jonathan, for example, King David expresses the extent of his own distress by contemplating his own death:

> *Low in thy grave with thee*
> *Happy to lie,*
> *Since there's no greater thing left Love to do;*
> *And to live after thee*
> *Is but to die,*
> *For with but half a soul what can life do?*
> (Abelard, Lament of David for Jonathan)[8]

The Laments are unusual subject matter for Abelard. They do not involve logic or abstract argument; they are meditations on emo-tion and kinship. In this work we apparently see the emergence of a changed Abelard. It is almost as if, at this relatively late stage in his life, he had started to take an interest in aspects of experience that the combative master of the schools of Notre-Dame-de-Paris would never have considered. Not only has he become a significant cham-pion of the rights of women in religious orders but he has started to apply his intellect to questions of feelings. That is not to say, of course, that Abelard did not previously have feelings – he writes about his love, for instance, in the new letters – but it is only in the Laments that he begins to dramatize (and therefore at some significant level to analyze) the feelings of others regarding the universal experiences of love, pain, and separation.

Again we cannot say with certainty that Heloise had any influence on Abelard over these compositions. It is possible that she simply "took delivery" of a cycle of poems from him without any previous discussion. It seems much more credible, however, that – just as with the Problems and with the hymns – the Laments and their subject matter would have been discussed during Abelard's visits to the Paraclete. If we accept this it is not so farfetched to see Heloise's influence in Abelard's new areas of interest.

In the absence of documents such as the autobiography or the personal letters relating to this period there are, of course, severe limits to what conclusions can be drawn about the interactions (if interactions there were) between the couple. It seems quite credible, however, that, taken together, the rule for the nuns, the *Problems of Heloise,* the *Hexaemeron,* and the hymns constitute a joint body of work through which Abelard and Heloise both nurtured the growing Paraclete. It has been suggested that the convent became in a way the child of their intellectual union, just as Astralabe was the child of their physical union.

The society in which these events were happening was undergoing rapid change. The convent that they were building was, in a way, a symbol of resistance against a radical transformation that was being forced on monasticism in the twelfth century. The overall trend of the time, encouraged by the reforming faction, was increasingly to exclude women from religion. The Cistercian order, for example, had no women's houses and no intention of founding any. The replacement of women's convents with male monasteries, as had happened with St.-Eloi and Argenteuil, became commonplace. Double houses, where convent and monastery acted as a pair (in the way that Abelard had suggested for the Paraclete), were routinely disbanded.

The general situation of women was to worsen steadily over the next two centuries. Already, at exactly the time that Abelard was writing for the Paraclete, in Rome the doctrinal conference known as the second Lateran Council was condemning all nuns who lived by any rule other than those laid down by established fathers of the church. They were in fact condemning Heloise and Abelard's project of a religious order tailored to the needs of women as, in their words, likely to lead to "shameful depravity." Had Heloise been born just two decades later it would have already been much more difficult for her to assume her role as abbess of the Paraclete.

The same council also banned nuns from singing in choirs alongside monks. It also reiterated yet again the rules regarding strict celibacy for the minor clergy. This was plainly proving difficult to enforce. Women's status is, of course, further reduced by the imposition of strict celibacy on male clerics: not only does it reinforce the idea that women are vehicles of evil but it also literally removes them from the locus of male decision-making. In the secular world also the marginalization of women is well documented. As commerce increased, trades such as weaving, which had once been a woman's occupation, became a source of income and were therefore taken over by men. Women found themselves excluded from the new key industries. Paradoxically, even the increased use of languages other than Latin for scholarly purposes militated against women. Once Heloise, for example, had mastered Latin she had proved herself exceptional and therefore worthy of attention. As Latin declined and ceased to be an exclusive key to the world of letters, women no longer had even that method of attaining access to the world of scholarship. Not one of the new universities that were founded in the second half of the twelfth century accepted women as staff or as students.

To those who knew her, or even those who had just heard about the Paraclete, Heloise might well have stood as a welcome example of someone who had managed to resist these regrettable trends. Long after her death the story of the highly educated woman, whom one late-medieval poet describes as "very wise Heloise,"[9] would surely have been an inspiration to any woman who aspired to intellectual greatness. The fact that she also managed to enlist Abelard's whole-hearted support in her project makes it all the more important. The couple's collaboration over the Paraclete must have been, for those who knew about it, an example of the possibility of true friendship between a man and a woman. As one commentator has recently put it, they had given male–female friendship a legitimacy.[10] How far Heloise herself saw the final stage of her relationship with Abelard as the success of her quest for the perfect combination of love and friendship is less easy to know. We can only guess whether or not the lives they shared at this period did indeed begin to provide the comfort of friendship for which she had begged in her letters.

We can imagine that the years following Abelard's final departure from Paris were quite happy and productive for him. He was paying frequent visits to the convent that he loved; he was working with Heloise on varied projects that were new and challenging enough to maintain his interest. It was in many ways the perfect final phase of the career of an eminent thinker. But it was not the final phase; his life was to be transformed once more. The impetus for change was to come, as it had once done for Heloise, from a letter that was not addressed to him.

He saw, or perhaps he just heard about, a letter that had been sent to Bernard of Clairvaux. It was a formal accusation of Abelard, calling him a heretic, even describing him as evil. It had been prepared for Bernard by one of his followers, William of St.-Thierry. It might have been sensible for Abelard to ignore it. Bernard and his associates opposed the application of logical analysis to religion; it was inevitable, therefore, that they would oppose him. But Abelard was not one to avoid a fight. He always tended to see his life in military terms; even when describing his philosophical disputes he would lapse into the language of sieges, attack, and combat. He did not ignore the letter. He saw it instead as a call to what is traditionally the final phase of the career of an eminent fighter – the last battle.

THIRTEEN

The Council of Sens

Abbot Bernard abhorred the Masters who used human reason and insisted on relying too much on secular wisdom, and also, if ever anything was said to him condemning something that was out of harmony with the Christian faith, he lent a ready ear to it.

Otto of Freising, The Deeds of Friederich Barbarossa[1]

ERNARD OF CLAIRVAUX had his reasons for wishing to discredit Abelard but he did not, at first, want the public confrontation that occurred at the Council of Sens. That was something on which Abelard had insisted. The archbishop of Sens had been persuaded that it was a good thing and Bernard had reluctantly agreed.

Bernard was not skilled at dialectics or debate. He did not even pretend that he was, describing himself a child in these matters compared with Abelard, the experienced warrior. Bernard's powers of persuasion were almost irresistible, but he was accustomed to having people listen to him and then eventually agree, not to fighting his corner. It was his persuasiveness that had filled the monasteries of the Cistercian order with enough new recruits to triple its size. Later he would stand on a hill in southern Burgundy and speak with such passion that he persuaded the Burgundians and the French to give their support to the military expedition in the Middle East known as the second crusade.

He was capable of intense religious feeling, which he endeavored to pass on to others with an almost childlike passion. His faith manifested itself throughout his life in periods of self-denial and rigorous fasting. His behavior today would certainly be classified as that of someone with an eating disorder: biographers tell of rigorous fasts followed, when they were broken, by episodes of vomiting. We are also told that in his youth he used to plunge into icy water in order to curb his carnal passions. He was always acutely aware of the corrupting potential of sensuality. He even considered the decorative arts capable of distracting the soul and leading it into depravity. He was very disturbed by the weird gargoyles and demons that decorated the (by that time slightly out of fashion) Romanesque style of architecture. He felt they would distract from the purity of the religious experience. "Why," he asked in an affectation of bewilderment, "are there filthy apes there, wild lions and monstrous centaurs, half-men, and striped tigers?" Cistercian churches are always identifiable as austere places of spiritual contemplation with simple lines and undecorated capitals. His belief in simple, unsophisticated faith is expressed in one of his most famous and oft-quoted remarks, "From wood and stones you will learn more than you can from any master."[2]

Abelard would have reacted with horror to the idea of religion as unthinking contemplation. To him all things, including faith, had to be subject to reason. Life was a puzzle that would ultimately be solved by study and rational inquiry – "by doubting we come to inquiry; by inquiry we come to truth." Abelard actually believed that unthinking faith was wrong; it was to him a sin to say a prayer without understanding it.

Bernard saw Abelard's desire to use logic to pick apart the meaning of religion as a threat to the most precious thing any human being could experience:

> *The faith of simple folk is laughed at, the mysteries of God forced open, the deepest things bandied about in discussion without any reverence . . . the Easter Lamb either boiled or torn to pieces and eaten raw just as a beast would eat it, quite against the command of God.* (Bernard of Clairvaux, Letter 327)

His concern was that if Abelard's approach prevailed, the light of reason might destroy the mystery of faith. The spiritual element of the human experience might just be analyzed away — "the Easter Lamb boiled and eaten." His objection to Abelard was, as much as any specific doctrinal infringement, that he had the arrogance to believe that the mystery of religion could be understood at all. Abelard, he complained, treated the word of God as if it were just another philosophical text. He showed a contemptuous refusal meekly to accept the wisdom of God. His sin was pride.

> *He prefers the inventions of the philosophers and his own nov-elties to the doctrine and faith of the Catholic fathers. He proves himself a heretic not so much by his error, as by his pertinacious defense of error. He is a man who goes beyond due measure, making void the virtue of Christ's cross by the cleverness of his words.* (Bernard of Clairvaux, Letter 193)

Bernard's fears for the long-term future of religion have, of course, proved to be absolutely justified. The effect of the progress of ratio-nalism over the centuries that separate us from him has been to mar-ginalize the spiritual side of experience so effectively that it has all but disappeared from the domain of respectable human discourse. How big a change there has been can be seen if we remember that, at the time, Bernard's preoccupations were considered central to his society and to the people around him. In our age, however, Bernard's reflec-tions on the contemplation of wood and stones sound like the doc-trine of some obscure outlandish "new age" sect.

Whether we prefer to regard this sidelining of the spiritual as a tragedy or as progress, it would be very unfair to hold Abelard responsible for it. He was ultimately just as spiritually motivated as Bernard. He was not opposed to religious faith; far from it, he had just written two lengthy letters to Heloise recommending that she, like him, should devote herself to it more completely. The conflict between Abelard and Bernard was not a question of faith versus reason; it would be fairer to call it faith with reason versus faith without reason. In his rhetoric, Bernard tried to represent their argument as a titanic clash of ideas on the result of which hung the very future of Christendom. It is clear from the letters of his contemporaries, however, that many of them felt it was no more than a very regrettable clash of personalities.

It does seem that Abelard irritated Bernard. In a letter written in preparation for the council in which he draws attention to Abelard's jeering blasphemies, he warns, "just listen to his guffaws!"[3] There are few things more irritating than the laugh of someone we consider shallow and trivializing. Bernard, as we can tell from his writings, was seldom at ease with laughter or humor of any kind. Perhaps that is typical of someone who places great reliance on simple faith – uncritical sincerity is a natural target for a well-aimed joke. Bernard, in his treatises on correct monastic behavior, specifically identifies "inappropriate mirth" along with curiosity and lightheartedness as steps that lead inevitably toward the sins of vanity and pride.

Bernard had in fact already had one row with Abelard. It was over a very slight matter of biblical interpretation but Abelard had chosen to take it very seriously. In 1138 Bernard seems to have visited the Paraclete in order to check the orthodoxy of its practices. This was just part of the process of ratifying Heloise as abbess and the visit seems to have gone well – Heloise always managed to get on with Bernard. One criticism that he made, however, was that they were using an unorthodox version of the Lord's Prayer. The prayer, which begins with the words "Our father," owes its importance to Christianity to the fact that it is the only one that Christ himself is reported to have spoken. Different gospel accounts of Christ's life give slightly different versions it. At the Paraclete they were using the version from St. Matthew's gospel rather than the one from St. Luke's, which was favored by most monasteries. This wasn't a heresy – both versions are, after all, from the Gospels – it was just a slightly unusual practice. The argument was over the phrase "give us this day our daily bread." In the Latin version, St. Luke calls the bread *quotidianus,* "daily," but in Matthew the word is *supersubstantialis,* which means something like "life sustaining."

Heloise seems to have passed Bernard's comment on to Abelard for reply. The letter that he wrote to Bernard on the subject survives. It shows him warming to the issue – it was his home territory; his book *Sic et Non* is about exactly this kind of problem. He launches a spirited defense of the Paraclete, full of quotations and references. The version in St. Matthew is the right one to use, he says, because only St. Matthew was actually there when Christ first said the prayer. The Greeks, he says, also recite the St. Matthew version because it uses the Greek word *epiousios** for "daily," which he claims is the correct word. He lists several other, more arcane, reasons why Luke is not to be trusted, before finishing up with a list of six minor infringements of orthodox practice that – he happens to know – are in use at Bernard's own monastery at Clairvaux. He does generously say that he is not condemning Clairvaux for these practices, merely pointing out that unorthodoxy can be found everywhere.

Abelard's lack of diplomatic sensitivity never ceases to amaze. The letter was written at a time when not only had he just absconded from St. Gildas but he was also without a political patron, yet in this letter he goes out of his way gratuitously to offend one of the most powerful churchmen in the world. His letter cannot fail to have left Bernard frustrated and even more distrustful of "modern masters who place too much reliance on reason."

The move against Abelard started within twelve months of this incident in 1139. It took the form of a letter addressed to Bernard from his assistant, one William of St. Thierry. William had been present at Abelard's earlier condemnation in Soissons. He says that he had loved Abelard at first but had eventually seen the errors in his

---

* Abelard was just quoting the Greek to impress. If he had read the complete passage from both Luke and Matthew in the original he would have seen that the whole argument in fact arises from only the inconsistencies of the Latin translation. The phrase is exactly the same (*artos epiousios*) in both Greek gospels.

teaching. There is no more passionate opponent than one who feels he has been duped; perhaps it was even his own errors he was attacking rather than Abelard's.

The letter of accusation, which was quite possibly written at Bernard's request, contains a great deal of rhetoric about Abelard's bad attitude and even his inherent evil. Its more substantial accusation takes the form of a list of the apparently heretical ideas that William has found in Abelard's writings. It is this list that, slightly expanded, was to form Bernard of Clairvaux's "charge sheet" when he made his attack on Abelard at the Council of Sens. The statements on the list are not exactly quotations; they are expressions of ideas that, it is claimed, are to be found in Abelard's works. There was evidently a certain amount of confusion about some of the statements, which was probably inevitable given the difficulty of finding definitive copies of a person's books in an age without printing. Some of the ideas are hard to find in any of Abelard's works. There are also some references to ideas contained in a book called *The Sentences*. Later Abelard would point out meekly that he had never written a book with that title. The charges are not completely trumped up, however: many of the ideas are easily found and obviously are things that Abelard had asserted.

The list divides broadly into two categories. First are statements taken from Abelard's theory of the Trinity, the logical quagmire surrounding the three aspects of God – Father, Son, and Holy Spirit – which had been the key subject under discussion at Abelard's previous heresy investigation. The suspect propositions on the list are, for example, "That the Father has full power, the Son a certain amount of power, and the Holy Spirit no power,"[4] "That the Holy Spirit is not of the same substance as the Father and the Son," and "That the Holy Spirit is the same as the 'world soul.'" These propositions refer to issues that appear arcane and complicated, hardly less so then than now. Although the nature of the Trinity was important to medieval theology, not everybody could find their way easily around the abstractions and logical pitfalls that surrounded it. Abelard was, however, the acknowledged expert on the Trinity and a brilliant debater. He would be able to defend his position with relative ease.

The second set of questionable propositions relates to Abelard's ideas of sin and redemption. These ideas come from the theory of the intentionality of sin that seems to have been worked out with Heloise during their time together in Paris. Among the propositions is the one that states: "Those who crucified Christ did not sin." Even Abelard, when making this statement, had taken the precaution of couching it in a hypothetical way, "to those who might ask this we might be able to answer . . ." Again there would be a number of logical lines of defense that Abelard could take over this question: to say that they did not sin does not mean that their act wasn't evil; even Christ says "forgive them for they know not what they do"; how could those who were ignorant of it be guilty of sin? At the very least, it is a puzzle to be reasoned out, not an excuse for immediate censure.

That Abelard could have defended himself is certain. Whether or not he really was a heretic is far less clear. Even today there is debate about whether his ideas do not lead inevitably to conclusions that would place him outside the limits of the Catholic church. What is certain is that he was not critical of religion as a whole, or even of Christianity specifically in the way that a modern atheist might be. He did not consider himself a heretic. On the contrary, Abelard expected to be recognized as a significant champion of the Christian faith. The Council of Sens was an opportunity to make that case.

Bernard, remembering his previous experience, plainly did not want a public showdown. It was, however, important to him that Abelard be publicly shown to be subject to his judgment. There were considerations in this that went beyond feelings of personal disquiet and irritation. Bernard was concerned that Abelard might become the focus of insurrection. It is known that a man called Arnold of Brescia had come to study with Abelard in Paris. Arnold really was a dangerous subversive – he preached that the church ought not to hold material possessions. Despite repeated condemnations, he went on for another twenty years, espousing what would today be called revolutionary causes, until eventually he was execut⁄ed. There is no evidence that Abelard shared his radical views but it was known that Abelard had a following elsewhere in Rome. Two cardinals, Hyacinth Boboni and Guy of Castello, are known to have had copies of his works in their libraries. William of St.⁄Thierry in his letter had claimed that Abelard boasted of this, which seems entirely credible. These factors probably contributed to Bernard's feeling that failure publicly to censure Abelard might lead to a weak⁄ening of his own position in Rome.

Rather than precipitate a public confrontation, Bernard visited Abelard to discuss the accusations. We do not know where this dis⁄cussion took place – perhaps Bernard visited him at the Paraclete; it is not far from Clairvaux. Face⁄to⁄face the effect of logical argument is less devastating – a sharp logical point can often be overwhelmed by an effusion of platitudes and protestations of good intentions. Bernard's biographer gives an insight into this approach when he tells us that the abbot went to Abelard, requesting "with his accustomed goodness and kindness that the error should be corrected, rather than that its author should be confounded."[5] We know about this meeting only from Bernard's letters, so we do not know Abelard's reaction for certain, but it is very hard to imagine that any amount of goodness, kindness, or simple faith would ever go anywhere near denting Abelard's absolute conviction that, in matters of logic, he was right.

One of Bernard's biographies claims, however, that Abelard agreed with Bernard at the meeting.[6] That is not impossible to imag⁄ine. If one is, like Abelard, convinced of the absolute correctness of one's cause then it really does not matter what one says to someone whom one regards as an intellectual inferior. Bernard would have done a lot of talking and most of it would have appeared to Abelard to be ill thought out rhetoric. Abelard might well have agreed with him just to shut him up. This would also be consistent with his having, not much later, decided that agreeing with Bernard was a mistake and that he should try to engineer a chance to vindicate himself by requesting that the archbishop of Sens give him an opportunity to speak.

If Bernard knew that he had already browbeaten Abelard into agreement once, it would also explain why we find him protesting so strongly about the unfairness of the contest at the Council of Sens — he even refused at first to take part. He had already won, so why should he risk combat again in a field where he was not strong?

> *When all fly before him he challenges me, the weakest of all, to single combat. The archbishop of Sens, at his request, writes to me fixing a day . . . I refused, not only because I am a youth and he an experienced warrior, but also because I thought it unfitting that the ground of faith should be discussed by human reasoning when it is agreed that it rests on such a firm and sure foundation.*
>
> (Bernard of Clairvaux, Letter 189)

But Henry, archbishop of Sens, insisted, and Bernard had to agree. The convocation was fixed for June 3, 1140.

The meeting does not seem to have been called specifically for the discussion of Abelard's beliefs. There had been a planned showing of relics on this date. This was an important occasion in itself because relics were not then kept permanently on display. The earthly remains of saints represented a link with those who, beyond the grave, intervened in heavenly matters on behalf of men. To see the relics displayed was a chance to exploit that link and ask the saint for help.

The sense of occasion must, however, have been greatly added to by what can only be called the trial of Abelard. The new king, Louis VII, was there himself. There is no record of his making any contribution to the council — probably a wise decision. Henry, archbishop of Sens, was also there, as were six other bishops, among them Hugh of Auxerre, a relative of Bernard, who had been with him when he set up the monastery at Clairvaux, and Geoffrey of Chartres, who had apparently lent a sympathetic ear when Abelard was condemned at Soissons but had in fact persuaded him to burn his book. Thibaud, count of Champagne, was there. He had given Abelard shelter and permitted him to set up the Paraclete and was not only its patron but also the patron of Bernard's monastery at Clairvaux. There was a host of other officials, clerics, and politicians drawn from all over France but not one professional philosopher among them.

The town of Sens had something new to show off. They had just finished building the first Gothic cathedral in the world. Gothic was the new architectural style that Abbot Suger had pioneered in his renovations of St. Denis and of which Bernard approved, so long as there were no grotesque decorations. The cathedral of Sens had taken ten years to build. It soared into the air, a huge stone edifice composed of delicate ribs and columns. The beauty of its structure was visible to anyone who entered it. It was a sign of the aspirations of the new age, the heroic triumph of men in the service of God. Since it would undoubtedly have been inside the new building that the relics were being displayed, it is not unreasonable to guess that the disputation too was held there.

Standing in the new cathedral, it might well have seemed to Bernard of Clairvaux, who was, at fifty, ten years younger than Abelard, that modernity was on his side. The approach of Abelard and those like him might have appeared hopelessly old-fashioned. Thinkers who were fixated on pagan ancient philosophers and meandered through baffling abstract arguments might well have seemed no more than a minor back current in the inevitable tide of history. His alarm at the dangers of Abelard and his kind would be all the more genuine for his belief that, by rights, the future belonged to him and to the Cistercians.

We think of disputations and heresy trials as part of the Middle Ages, but in 1140 they were still not at all common and there were no set rules for conducting them. It would be a hundred years before the papacy formalized the approach to heresy by instituting the Inquisition. In the absence of agreed procedures or a formal constitution, Bernard himself took the role of chief prosecutor. The culmination of the proceedings was to be the vote of the full council on the issues that Bernard had put before them.

Bernard was an experienced political manipulator and he employed a move well known to all those who thrive in the world of committees. He did his best to ensure as much support as possible before the debate. John of Salisbury tells us that he brought all the bishops together for a meeting the night before. Berengar of Tours, a student and supporter of Abelard who also writes about the council, seems to imply that at this meeting the bishops were drunk. This is probably an exaggeration (Berengar is quite prone to them) but it points to the atmosphere of conviviality that probably did prevail as Bernard chatted to the bishops, calling a favor here, offering a quid pro quo deal there, perhaps reminding one of them of a peccadillo that had so far been overlooked. Had the bishops paused for an instant they might have reflected that the scene illustrated a fact that, in practical matters, transcended any consideration of faith or reason: Bernard had political power and Abelard did not.

At the council the next day, Archbishop Henry recalls, Bernard began by holding up a copy of Abelard's *Theologia Christiana* and promising to expose all those propositions that he had noted to be "absurd or even plainly heretical."* Bernard's letters give a flavor of the rhetorical flourishes with which he opened his case.

> *I know not what there is in the heavens above or in the earth*
> *beneath that he deigns to know nothing of: he puts his head in the*
> *clouds and scrutinizes the high things of God then he brings back*
> *to us unspeakable works that it is not lawful for a man to utter.*
> (Bernard of Clairvaux, Letter 190)

Bernard was undoubtedly impressive. A secondary effect of his language must have been to create an atmosphere totally unconducive to the kind of debate at which Abelard excelled. Bernard started to go

---

* Fortunately, neither William nor Bernard ever seems to have realized that the *Theologia Christiana* is in fact no more than a rewrite of the *Theologia* (possibly called *De Trinitate*), which Abelard had been obliged to burn at Soissons twenty years earlier.

through the list of questionable statements. It was more or less the same as the one that his assistant, William of St. Thierry, had prepared for him. There were, however, a few differences. The first proposition that he read out for the council to condemn must in particular have given rise to a ripple of puzzlement:

The shocking comparison of the Trinity with a brazen seal.

It was just odd. To compare one of the central mysteries of the Christian faith with a brass instrument for impressing patterns on sealing wax may not in itself be heretical, but it does seem pointless. Why would anyone say that?

Bernard's opening was a, possibly well-planned, *coup de théâtre*, perhaps even revenge for his defeat in the Lord's Prayer argument. There was no reason to begin with that particular proposition. There were some on the list that anyone could understand as questionable: "That the holy spirit had no power," for example; "That those who crucified Christ had not sinned" could also have been the basis of accessible discussion. The point of the brazen seal remark was to hold Abelard up to ridicule. How could anyone take him seriously if he said things like that?

Abelard had indeed compared the Holy Trinity to a brass seal. It was an idea he used to demonstrate the (highly orthodox) view that all the persons of the Trinity were separate yet equal parts of the same entity. The image occurs in a philosophical treatise intended for philosophers and students who would be familiar with ideas of substance and accident, genera and species, universals and particulars. The seal in Abelard's argument had three aspects: its matter, brass; its potential for sealing, "sealability"; and the actual act of sealing. He related these to the Father, Son, and Holy Spirit respectively and drew conclusions about their natures. Abelard was using his philosophical insight to clarify and strengthen a religious mystery. Apart from the slightly unusual choice of example it is hard to find anything heretical in this particular line of inquiry. It had probably worked very well on countless classes of eager students. As an argument it was clever, original, and effective – typical of Abelard at his best.* Taken out of context, however, in front of an assembly of nonphilosophers who were already hostile from the previous night's meeting, it was a disaster.

Bernard continued with the list of propositions. "That the Holy Spirit is not of Substance with the Father"; "That omnipotence belongs properly and specially to the Father"; "That Christ did not take flesh in order to free us from the devil"; "That God ought not to hinder evil"; "That we have contracted from Adam not guilt but its punishment"; "That a man is made neither better nor worse by his works."[7] Many of these raise issues that are, to this day, interesting. These were fruitful areas in which Abelard could practice his methods of doubt and inquiry but it must have been obvious that that was not going to be possible at the Council of Sens.

Abelard had almost certainly heard about the meeting of the previous night. He did have supporters in Sens. Although many of them were impassioned students with very little clout where it counted, they would at least have kept their eyes and ears open. As Bernard continued, Abelard could probably observe the bishops nodding sagely, happy to associate themselves with the great abbot, secure in the feeling of having their prejudices reinforced – there is nothing like hearing about the sins of others to make us feel good about ourselves. The bishops were not interested in theology. They would not think about the issues in the way that he would; they would seize on whatever idea was easiest to grasp. The ideas behind the brazen seal would have taken him hours to work through with a bright student; there was no hope of reaching these old men. Although he could see the

---

* The argument is in fact a sort of philosophically sophisticated version of St. Patrick's famous analogy of the shamrock. He had, about eight centuries earlier, compared the three persons of the Trinity to the three leaves of a shamrock – unity and diversity together in one object. His choice of this image is, of course, the reason why the shamrock later became the symbol of Patrick's adopted homeland of Ireland. Nobody, however, has ever accused St. Patrick of heresy because he compared the Holy Trinity with a plant.

truth clearly, he had no means of communicating it to them. He could amaze a class of students, he could write songs, he could delight Heloise, but he had never been able to persuade those in authority of anything. The council could bring him only pain.

At some point, as Bernard continued with the list of charges, Abelard interrupted him and demanded to speak. Geoffrey of Auxerre, one of Bernard's biographers, who was at the council, says that Abelard's "memory became very confused, his reason blacked out and his interior sense forsook him."[8] Others, including the archbishop, confirm that he was "taken aback" or that he had "lost confidence." Abelard managed to announce that he wished to appeal to the papal court in Rome and then walked out, refusing to listen any further.

Abelard had opted not to continue the fight. Whether it was because he was seriously ill, as has been suggested, or just tired, or because he had seen the futility of trying to persuade people who will not listen, we cannot tell. The council seems to have accepted his appeal, which is odd because it is not normal to appeal against a judgment that has not yet been given. Perhaps they felt that an appeal to the pope had to be taken seriously — Geoffrey of Chartres, who was a papal legate and therefore representing the pope's interests, was one of those present. Perhaps, on the other hand, some of them took pity on Abelard. Whatever the reason, Bernard was not happy with the decision: "he has appealed from judges he himself has chosen, a course that I do not think should be allowed,"[9] he said.

Abelard set off for Rome, intending to make his appeal in person. This for a man of sixty was presumably quite a major undertaking, even though some of those who supported him might well have elected to make the journey with him. He had, of course, met Pope Innocent II before, when he had argued for the transfer of the Paraclete to Heloise at the Council of Morigny. He also could rely on a hospitable reception from the two cardinals who possessed copies of his books.

The council seems to have continued to consider the case in his absence. They voted and duly condemned his works. But this was no

longer relevant, as Bernard realized perfectly well. He started a campaign of letter writing to try to ensure that the pope would in turn
condemn Abelard. He wrote to the pope, of course, and to Cardinal
Guy of Castello, one of the two who is known to have had a copy of
Abelard's *Theologia*. He warns them not to be taken in by Abelard
who, he claimed, was abetted by the subversive Arnold of Brescia.
Bernard casts his adversary in the role of the Philistine giant from the
Old Testament, making it clear that he is, beyond any doubt, a real
and present danger to decent civilization:

> *Goliath, advancing mighty in bearing, girt all round in his fine
> accoutrements of war and preceded by his armor bearer Arnold
> of Brescia. The pair of them are like two overlapping scales
> that prevent the air from opening. They have each drawn their
> bows and filled their quivers with arrows; now they lie in
> ambush ready to fire at unsuspecting hearts.* (Bernard of Clair-
> vaux, Letter 189)

Just in case the letters were not enough, Bernard also sent an assistant, Nicholas of Clairvaux, to Rome in order to back them up with
a personal testimony of the wickedness of Abelard.

Abelard had traveled south across France and into Burgundy,
where he stopped at the ancient and powerful monastery of Cluny.
The abbot, Peter the Venerable, later described his state as "weighted
down by the attacks of certain people who attach the name of heretic
to him." Abelard probably decided to rest there. The monastery of
Cluny was vast, almost like a city in itself, a self-sufficient community nestling among the wooded hills of southern Burgundy. It was the
home of 400 monks who were attended by thousands of lay brothers.
It owned and controlled land for miles around, comprising something approaching a self-contained state within the duchy of Burgundy. The Cluniac organization stretched all over Europe. It has
been estimated that 12,000 monks owed their allegiance to the
mother house. One account complains of the deafening noise within

the great church as hundreds of monks filled the side chapels, simultaneously saying masses for all their various benefactors. The Cluniac order was as ancient as the Cistercians were modern. It had been founded over 200 years earlier and it owed much of its success to the fact that its charter had given it direct allegiance to the pope, thereby allowing it to avoid interference from local nobles and bishops. It was, compared to the Cistercians, rather lax in its interpretation of the Rule of St. Benedict but it did have a deservedly good reputation both for the furtherance of scholarly study and for the practice of charity. Abelard was welcomed at Cluny. He was regarded as a celebrity. If, as one suspects, he was already ill he would have been secure in a place that could give him the best available medical attention.

In the meantime Nicholas of Clairvaux had reached Rome with Bernard's letters. His mission was evidently successful. The papal proclamation, which condemns Abelard for "pernicious doctrines and other perverse teachings contrary to the catholic faith" is dated July 16, 1140,[10] only six weeks after the Council of Sens. He was forbidden to teach or to travel and his books were ordered to be destroyed "wherever they might be found." Bernard's assistant, who had initiated the prosecution, William of St.-Thierry, writes gleefully of bonfires of books in the streets, but nobody else mentions them so it is assumed to be an exaggeration. We do know, however, that the cardinals who had copies of the *Theologia* kept them intact.

News of Abelard's condemnation must have reached Cluny very soon. Although the abbot and the monks were undoubtedly very nice about it, everybody concerned must have been aware that Peter Abelard, also known as Peter the Peripatetic, was now effectively under arrest.

FOURTEEN

"And so Master Peter ended his days"

1142

Just as nothing moves in the heavens that is equal to the sun
So the ends of the earth encompass nothing to match you.
While you live may you fare well, after death may you taste joy.

Heloise, Early Letters, 49

BELARD WAS A DIFFICULT MAN who frequently showed insufficient sensitivity to the feelings of those around him. It is quite plain, however, that many of those whom he encountered in his life were not entirely guiltless either. When we consider the vicious Fulbert who had him castrated, or Bernard the rabble-rouser who condemned him, or the, at the very least ill-disciplined, monks of St.-Gildas it is hard not to agree with the opinion he expresses in his autobiography that he was unlucky with those he met during his life. It seems fitting, therefore, that at the very end of it he should come into contact with a luminously kind and considerate man.

Peter of Montboissier, abbot of Cluny, was already by this time known as Peter the Venerable. His entire life seems to have been characterised by modesty, justice, and diplomatic skill. Wherever there was conflict he tried to find an equitable solution. He increased and broadened the charitable work of the Cluniacs throughout Christendom. He is known also to have defended the Jews against persecution. There is a story that, such was his modesty, he prayed repeatedly to die on Christmas Day so that in the midst of the yearly celebrations he would not be given special commemoration. Records show that his wish was apparently granted.

He had a gift for soothing differences of opinion even in what were potentially the most difficult clashes. It was inevitable, for example, that he should come into conflict with Bernard of Clairvaux: the Cluniacs and the Cistercians represented what were in some ways fundamentally opposed approaches to monasticism. Bernard and Peter clashed over specific issues relating to wealth and comfort in monasteries. Bernard even produced a paper on the subject that was little more than a very thinly disguised attack on the Cluniacs. Peter the Venerable's reply is a model of reasonableness, contrasting sharply with Bernard's customary rants:

> *What does it matter if men of the same purpose and profession come by a different path to the same country, if by a variety of ways to the same life, if by manifold roads to the same heavenly Jerusalem, the mother of us all . . . you will see that all those points that seem to be differently observed become one through charity . . . Therefore where there is no charity there is no humility, and where there is no humility there is no charity.* (Peter the Venerable, Letter to the Cluniacs and the Cistercians)[1]

Peter was the last of four long-lived and long-serving abbots whose combined administration lasted for nearly two centuries. Their lengthy periods of tenure provided a stability within the order unusual for any age. Under Peter, the abbey's great church, known to architectural historians as Cluny III, had just been completed. It was not built in the modern Gothic style of Sens cathedral but was the final flowering of the old style known as Romanesque. Built with round arches and solid pillars, it was decorated in corners with the fantastic sculptures of demons and devils that so upset the modernist Bernard of Clairvaux. The nave, at 187 meters, made it the largest church in the world. It held this record – despite the explosion of cathedral building that was about to overtake Europe – until 1612 when the new basilica at St. Peter's in Rome was built, following a design by Michelangelo, deliberately to be about 25 meters longer.

In contrast to the new cities that were built up of competing, diverse units all jostling together, Cluny as a community was a single entity, moving with a single purpose. Peter the Venerable accepted Abelard as a member of the monastery. He tells Heloise that he had insisted that he be given the status of a high-ranking senior monk even though he was new to the order. The abbot remarks that "his learning could be of benefit to our large community of brothers," so it may be that he had some official duties as a teacher. The ancient monastery quite possibly suited the aged and tired philosopher, providing him with the comforting warmth of an old college or a club.

Peter the Venerable tells the story of Abelard's last days in a letter to Heloise notable for its courtesy and affection. He is careful to point out that they are proud to have had Abelard with them:

> In the last years of his life Providence sent him to Cluny and in doing so enriched her in his person with a gift more precious than any gold or topaz. (Peter the Venerable, Letter to Heloise)[2]

To Heloise he refers to Abelard as "him who was yours, him who is often and ever to be named and honored as the servant and true philosopher of Christ." He also pours praise on her, comparing her to famous women from the Bible and history. He tells her that, even though he did not meet her, he had heard of her thirty years before as a young man when, even then, she was already famous for her scholarship and devotion to serious study.

Those who succeed best in hierarchic systems are those who can reassure their superiors that everything is in safe hands. Peter had that gift in great measure and he used it on Abelard's behalf by writing to the pope, asking for mercy. The letter is couched in the most level diplomatic terms, all the time praising and calming the pope. He recaps the situation and slips in a word to reassure His Holiness of Abelard's continuing implacable opposition to heresy:

Master Peter, well known I believe to your Holiness, passed by Cluny recently on his way from France.* We asked him where he was going. He replied that he was weighted down by the persecution of those who had accused him of heresy, a thing he abhorred, that he had appealed to papal authority and sought protection from it. We praised his intention and urged him to make his way to that refuge we all know. We told him that apostolic justice had never failed anyone, be he stranger or pilgrim, and would not be denied him, and assured him that if he had real need of mercy he would find it with you. (Peter the Venerable, Letter to Pope Innocent II)[3]

Peter continues the story with an account of a visit from the abbot of Cîteaux who was head of what was nominally the mother house of the Cistercian order and therefore technically Bernard's boss. Although he was eminent and respected, he came nowhere near to Bernard in real political power, but nevertheless was working with Peter the Venerable to find a way out of the conflict between Abelard and Bernard:

In the meantime the lord abbot of Cîteaux arrived, and spoke with us and with him about a reconciliation between him and Bernard of Clairvaux. We too did our best to restore peace, and urged him to go to Clairvaux with the abbot of Cîteaux. We further counseled him, if he had written or said anything offensive to orthodox ears, to take the advice of the abbot of Cîteaux and of other wise and worthy men, curb his language, and remove such expressions from his writing. (Peter the Venerable, Letter to Pope Innocent II)

It is hard to imagine so much conciliation and pacification really working on Abelard, but strangely it seems to have had an effect. Peter goes on to tell how Abelard did go to Clairvaux and was reconciled with Bernard:

He went and came back, and on his return told us that through the mediation of the abbot of Cîteaux he had made his peace with Bernard and that their previous differences were settled.
(Peter the Venerable, Letter to Pope Innocent II)

In Peter the Venerable's account of the reconciliation all difficulties melt away in the face of firm but fair talking. Peter is, of course, acting in Abelard's interests and saying all he can to make the pope rescind his condemnation. He does not, therefore, attempt any details of the meeting between Bernard and Abelard. Neither of them was a particularly forgiving man by nature and it is very difficult to imagine this encounter being genuinely suffused with the balm of reconciliation any more than the one that preceded the Council of Sens. It is much easier to conjure up a picture of mumbled words of forgiveness and apology given with bad grace while the elderly abbot of Cîteaux struggled to prevent a row from erupting before the meeting ended with a stiff-limbed and insincere kiss of peace. Bernard and Abelard had presumably each realized that neither of them could gain absolute victory in the fight and so they accepted a compromise.

Two documents by Abelard have survived that seem to relate to this meeting. They are each a different kind of retraction. The first, misleadingly titled the *Apologia contra Bernardum,* is a relatively combative set of answers to the charges, almost as if they were the notes for the defense statement that he never gave at Sens. The other document, called the *Confessio Universis,* is a much more conciliatory statement of faith, confirming the orthodoxy of Abelard's beliefs – that he believes in the equal power of the three persons of the Trinity, and so on. Bernard himself is coyly referred to as "our friend." This second document is in fact so supine in attitude, and so unlike Abelard, that some historians have suggested that he may have been being sarcastic. It is an interesting theory and it is quite possible to believe that Bernard would not have been terribly sensitive to sar-

---

* Cluny was, of course, not in France but in Burgundy.

casm. The document also bears some similarity to other *"confessiones"* written by other, later recipients of Bernard's zeal for rooting out heretics. Perhaps this document was to become the standard state-ment of orthodoxy that Bernard insisted that those he prosecuted must sign before they could be certified free of heresy – a kind of pro-forma list of beliefs on which all the right boxes had to be checked.

Abelard was now sixty and certainly ill (Peter the Venerable refers to his age and weakness). Perhaps he was quite glad to agree – presumably as part of the deal with Bernard – that he should contin-ue as a monk at Cluny and never return to lecture in Paris. Peter the Venerable again soothes the anxieties of the pope that there will not be any more problems from Abelard the teacher:

> *Meanwhile on our advice or rather, we believe, inspired by God, he decided to abandon the turmoil of the schools and teaching and to remain permanently in your house at Cluny. We thought this a proper decision in view of his age and weakness and his reli-gious calling and believed that his learning could be of benefit to our large community of brothers.* (Peter the Venerable, Letter to Pope Innocent II)

There is a third document dating from this time, preserved by Abelard's supportive student Berengar, which is also his final letter to Heloise. The *Confessio Heloisae* (Confession to Heloise) is very brief. It does not begin with a salutation but with a sentence of almost chilling urgency:

> *Heloise my sister once dear to me in the world now dearest to me in Christ, logic has made me hated in the world.* (Abelard, Con-fession to Heloise)

There is probably some truth in what he says, as an insight into the cause of his condemnation. It contains a broader truth also: that in the spectrum of possible approaches to life that ranges from cold insistence on the truth of pure logic at one end to the companionable give-and-take of affable conversation at the other, Abelard was always to be found at the end at which hostility was provoked.

The letter continues with a brief reaffirmation of the orthodoxy of his theory of the Trinity – "I believe in the Son co-equal with the Father in all things," and so on. He finishes with a statement of the solidity of his faith:

> *This then is the faith on which I rest, from which I draw my strength in hope. Safely anchored on it, I do not fear the barking of Scylla, I laugh at the whirlpool of Charybdis, and have no dread of the Sirens' deadly songs. The storm may rage but I am unshaken, though the winds may blow they leave me unmoved; for the rock of my foundation stands firm.* (Abelard, Confession to Heloise)

The (slightly forced?) references to Homer's *Odyssey* – Sirens, Scylla, and Charybdis – were presumably tailored to suit Heloise's taste for classical allusions. They would not have played so well with Bernard. The really memorable statement of Abelard's position on religion is, however, very straightforward:

> *I do not wish to be a philosopher if it means conflicting with Paul, nor to be an Aristotle if it cuts me off from Christ.*
> (Abelard, Confession to Heloise)

This is undoubtedly a positive affirmation of the priority of his religious faith. Few people who had read his letters to Heloise would seriously doubt its sincerity. It is not, though, a rejection of philosophy or of logic. Abelard does not want to be a philosopher if it takes him from St. Paul, but this conflict will never arise for him since it is fundamental to his beliefs that philosophy is not only compatible with religion but necessary to it. The logical conclusion is that Abelard will remain a philosopher.

Peter Abelard, now by contemporary standards an old man of

62, made one final journey on earth. He left the monastery of Cluny, accompanied presumably by an entourage of monks. Perhaps, in view of his illness, he was riding or in a cart, or even carried on a litter. The party left behind them the dark wooded hills that cradle Cluny and followed the ancient road that hugged the edge of the marshy valley of the little river Grosne. They continued through what is now the fine winegrowing country of the *Côte Challonais,* past a series of little churches whose architecture, though slightly rustic, showed by its style that they bore allegiance to the nearby mother house of Cluny. They crossed the broad river Saône at the town of Chalon and continued a little way out onto the plain until they came to St. Marcel, a small outlying house of the Cluniac order, about 50km from Cluny itself. It was in this much smaller monastery that Abelard was to spend the last days of his life.*

Peter the Venerable provides an explanation for this move. He says that it was for health reasons:

> *I sent him to Chalon to give him respite, since he was more troubled than usual from skin irritation and other physical ailments. I believed this would be a suitable place for him, near the city on the opposite bank of the Saône, because of its mild climate, which is about the best in our part of Burgundy.* (Peter the Venerable, Letter to Heloise)

There can be little doubt that Abelard was ill at this time, but once again it is possible to question the story that Peter the Venerable tells. Would one really leave Cluny in favor of St. Marcel for health reasons? St. Marcel is beside a river, on marshy ground – freezing

---

* The monastery has long since been disbanded but the church still exists. The present walls are probably in part the ones that Abelard saw, but the nave was rebuilt about fifty years after his time. The simple foliate capitals that were added then attest to a Cistercian influence of which Abelard would surely not have approved.

cold in winter and a source of disease in summer. Cluny is sheltered among hills, away from swamps. There is, apart from that, no appreciable difference in climate between them. Surely if Abelard needed treatment it would be sensible to remain at the main house of Cluny, where undoubtedly the better medical facilities would be provided.

It is possible to guess at another explanation for Abelard's final move. There is, after all, a discernible pattern in his movements throughout his life. After a certain time in any institution Abelard had always antagonized those around him to the extent that he was obliged to move, often to some outlying satellite house. This happened to him in the School of Notre-Dame in 1100, in Laon in 1114, in St.-Denis in 1117, St.-Gildas in 1130, and even, if we believe the story of the student revolt, in the Paraclete itself in 1127. In the Laments, among his last writings for the Paraclete, he does seem to have started to examine the emotional world of other people, but there is a limit to how much anybody can really change. Can it be that for one last time Abelard had pushed a logical argument too far, or made one provocative remark too many? Some people, perhaps including Peter the Venerable, would doubtless have found Abelard amusing and stimulating. But others might have felt threatened and disturbed, particularly if his cleverness were laced with the cussedness and even bitterness that sometimes comes with age. Perhaps a delegation had gone to Peter the Venerable complaining that, celebrity or not, Abelard's doubting and inquiring were disturbing the peace of the monastery. Peter the Venerable's reaction would have been to find a face-saving solution. What better than to remove him to a daughter house for the sake of his health?

Peter the Venerable does confirm, if not that Abelard remained difficult to the end, at least that he remained a philosopher. He tells Heloise that his reading was continuous and his conversation was always philosophical and scholarly. Peter confirmed to Heloise that, when the end of Abelard's life was near, the abbot of St.-Marcel prepared him for death with the ritual of the *viaticum*, literally "food for the journey," which is the name given to the prayers that provide spiritual sustenance for a departing soul. Even then Abelard continued to work:

> *He was engaged on such occupations when the visitor of the gospels came to find him, and found him awake, not asleep like so many; found him truly awake, and summoned him to the wedding of eternal life.* (Peter the Venerable, Letter to Heloise)

The idea of death as an invitation to a wedding feast is an appealing one. Perhaps Peter felt it was appropriate for Heloise because she was married, but it is even more appropriate for her because it recognizes that the object of a religious life is not ultimately prohibition and denial, but joy. In the hymns that were used in the Paraclete under Heloise this joy is referred to frequently – the joy of a wedding feast, the joy of finding a lover, the joy of homecoming.

Peter the Venerable, of course, finds the right words of comfort for Heloise:

> *And so Master Peter ended his days. He who was known all over the world for his unique mastery of knowledge. God cher-ishes him in his bosom, and keeps him there to be restored to you through his grace at the coming of the Lord.* (Peter the Venerable, Letter to Heloise)

Abelard's body was sent from St. Marcel to the Paraclete to be buried there, as he had requested. This again is an act of kindness on the part of Peter the Venerable; Abelard was a monk at Cluny and according to the rules should have been buried there. Peter, however, plainly recognized that Abelard's true home was at the Paraclete, just as he recognized the continuing importance of Heloise's love for him.

Perhaps Heloise wondered, as she whispered a final "farewell my only love" over his coffin, how long it would be before she would be, as Peter the Venerable had put it, "restored to him." In fact she had nearly a third of her life still to live.

Over the next twenty years Heloise would have been aware of the continuing development of medieval society. The formation of modern Europe continued with an explosion of cathedral building, a collective project of stone building unrivaled since the pyramids of Egypt. The continuation of the pursuit of the religious ideal in the Holy Land by military means, later known as the second crusade, was launched within six years of Abelard's death, under the encour- agement of Bernard of Clairvaux. The Cistercians themselves also continued to consolidate their power, contributing to the develop- ment of institutions as widely separated as the international corpora- tion and organized agriculture. Perhaps their strict discipline and attention to rules contributed also to a less welcome change that observers of the Middle Ages have identified. Some historians see a hardening of attitudes during this period. European civilization began to show the intolerance toward outsiders and foreigners that is one of its less attractive hallmarks. What had started almost as an outburst of irritation against alleged heretics such as Abelard coa- lesced into the systematic persecution of heretics, Cathars, Jews, and others. The desire to impose conformity and some imagined social purity that is the downside of the Western ideal had begun to show itself. It is not certain whether Heloise herself could have been aware of it but a process had been started that would result in the ideas that so preoccupied her – the contemplation of ideals of friendship and love – being moved much further down the agenda.

A large proportion of Heloise's last twenty years was spent in building up the Paraclete, carefully managing donors and liaising with landowners until, by the time of her death, the convent owned most of the valley of the Ardusson and had founded its own organi- zation with six daughter houses in France.

She kept in touch with Peter the Venerable. One of the hymns sung at the convent can be shown to come, not from Abelard, but from the practice of the monastery of Cluny – a tribute perhaps to her admiring friend the abbot. A further two letters between them survive. The first is from Heloise, thanking Peter for a visit to the Paraclete and reminding him that he promised to send a document of absolution to be hung over Abelard's tomb. Perhaps she was worried that he might be remembered as the heretic that Bernard tried to paint him. Peter did send a brief certificate in which he absolved him of all sins by his own authority. He also wrote a glow-ing epitaph for Abelard, which was intended for circulation to other Cluniac houses. In it he calls him "our Aristotle." He gives the monastery of Cluny credit for having brought Abelard back from the brink of heresy so that "at the end of a long life he had hope of being numbered among the good philosophers." Nowhere does he say that the pope ever rescinded his condemnation. With Abelard dead there would be less point in doing so, even if Peter the Venerable's soothing letter had had the intended effect on the pontiff.

In the same letter, Heloise also asks Peter for his help in getting a job for Astralabe. He was by then in his midtwenties and had estab-lished his career at the cathedral chapter of Nantes. It is natural not only that he might wish to broaden his experience by moving to a dif-ferent institution but also that his mother might try to find a position for him nearer to her convent:

> Remember also, in God's love, our Astralabe and yours, so that you may obtain for him some prebend either from the bishop of Paris or in some other diocese. (Heloise, Letter to Peter the Venerable)[4]

Peter replied, in the same letter in which he encloses the certificate of absolution, that he would try his best. He pointed out, however, that it was difficult for him to persuade bishops of anything. They were part of the national political network and would be reluctant to be seen to be doing favors for the abbot of Cluny, whose allegiance was directly to the pope. "But for your sake," he says, "I will do what I can as soon as I can." He did not succeed; Astralabe was not given a post by the bishop of Paris. He eventually moved to become abbot of the Cistercian abbey of Hauterive, far away in Switzerland.

In the library, the writings of Abelard for the convent — hymns, sermons, notes on the history of nuns, the philosophical questions and answers that he had produced with Heloise, and the treatise on the creation of the universe — would have been preserved and copied. Presumably the couple's intimate love letters were kept in a restricted section. The eight letters that make up the correspondence after the castration would be retrieved nearly 100 years later and published, to the fascination of the medieval world. The letters that Heloise had collected from the time of the affair would wait 300 years for Johannes de Vepria to anthologize them and a further 500 for Köntsgen and Mews to attribute them to the couple. Did Heloise want the letters to be discovered and published? It would not be unnatural for somebody in her position to hope that her story would be understood by people in the future.

Scholars have suggested that she might, during the long years following Abelard's death, have taken the opportunity to rewrite the letters, perhaps to change key points to make a more instructive or a more satisfying story. While it is, of course, possible that she did so, there would have been strong reasons for her not to. Abelard's letters were the most precious relic she had of their love. She would risk destroying a link with the past if she started to tamper with them. Relics are usually retained untouched. It is much more credible to imagine her returning to the letters and reading them over, partly no doubt to indulge herself with the bitter pleasure of nostalgia but partly also, perhaps, to continue to contemplate the puzzles that had occupied her since the first letters she wrote in Paris: the interplay between love and friendship, between desire and obligation in a relationship between a man and a woman.

Peter the Venerable, in his letters to Heloise, shows that he believes, as Abelard had once believed (before she corrected him), that she had "reformed" and transformed herself into the perfect nun by shedding her interest in romantic and physical love. He expresses this idea very graphically:

> *You trod underfoot what at the start you wore down by perse-*
> *verance through the grace of the Almighty — the head of the ser-*
> *pent, the old enemy who always lies in wait for women — and*
> *crushed it so that it will never dare to hiss against you again.*
> (Peter the Venerable, Letter to Heloise)

But Peter had not read Heloise's letters to Abelard. He did not know that she was, by her own admission, adept at playing the part of the perfect abbess while knowing within herself that it was a sham. She had deceived everybody, including Abelard, in the years before she had read his autobiography and was moved to write a reply. There is no reason to think she could not continue to do so.

Heloise herself has provided us with a picture of her mental state during the long period when she built up the convent of the Paraclete. It is the one that she herself offered to Abelard at the moment she decided to stop writing about her feelings — the account of her situa-tion that Abelard called "your old perpetual complaint." She had become a nun not out of conviction but out of an overwhelming, pas-sionate obedience to Abelard. She should be groaning with regret for their affair but the pleasures of the past were too sweet to repudiate. She could not alter her inner will — her "intention" — therefore she could not repent, therefore she could not really be a good nun:

> *I can win praise in the eyes of men but deserve none before God,*
> *who searches our hearts and loins and sees in our darkness, I am*
> *judged religious in a time when there is little in religion that is*
> *not hypocrisy.* (Heloise, Second Letter)

At the opposite extreme to the view of Heloise as a reformed character is the idea of Heloise trapped in a living hell, denied the physical and emotional relationship she craved, imprisoned by an unjust patriarchal system in which she did not believe. While she is undeniably unhappy about her fate – she herself is not slow to tell us of her distress – she is not at odds with the religion that is the foundation of medieval society. Heloise is not asking for the destruction of the elements of medieval life; she is searching for a different way to fit them together. She never despaired to the extent that she was incapable of action. From the moment when she began her letter in response to Abelard's autobiography she had been working. Her letters are all constructed with the intention of making Abelard respond to her by giving her comfort and helping to rebuild the friendship for which she longed. The fruit of Heloise's work was the body of writings and the hymns by Abelard, which now gave shape to the daily life of the convent. It is not completely fanciful to imagine that Heloise might have felt that she had managed to go some little way toward achieving the loving friendship that she desired. She might even have felt that the writings, which were at the same time a manifestation of their deep friendship and also a part of the very foundations of the convent, were a step toward the reconciliation of her love with religion that she had for so long been unable to attain.

The hymns in particular can sometimes be understood both as an expression of their love and of the religious intent of the Paraclete. There are, as we have seen, links within the allegorical framework of Christianity that connect the romantic love of couples with the experience of the divine. This connection was celebrated every Easter Sunday at the Paraclete when the nuns sang the hymn called the *Epithalamica,* which dramatizes the story of a bride who loses and then re-finds her bridegroom. The story is capable of more than one allegorical interpretation: Christ's death and resurrection is undoubtedly one; another is the eventual recognition by the soul of the comfort of true spiritual enlightenment; another is the return of the soul to God in death, to which Peter the Venerable alluded. But the hymn is also quite literally what it says: an account of the joy the two lovers experience in meeting after a separation. It is, of course, quite impossible ever to speak with absolute certainty about what another person is thinking, especially if nine centuries separate us from them, but on the other hand it is very hard to believe that either Abelard or Heloise could ever have heard the *Epithalamica* without recalling their own love.

The *Epithalamica* does not quite end with the bride's account of her own joy at the return of her lover. The chorus of young maidens attending the wedding go on to suggest the addition of a final part to the drama: the recitation of what they call a "psalm," the purpose of which is to "turn our mournful elegies into song." The psalm that they have in mind turns out to be a rather strange, exuberant, rhythmical chant, every line of which contains the words "This is the day!"– *Quam fecit Dominus, haec est dies!/ Quam expectavimus, haec est dies!/ Qua vere risimus, haec est dies! . . .*

> *This is the day the Lord made!*
> *This is the day we long awaited!*
> *This is the day that brings us laughter!*
> *This is the day that makes us free!*
> *This is the day our enemies scatter!*
> *This is the day the psalms foretold!*[5]

Constant Mews, the scholar who first verified that the early love letters were written by the couple, believes that it was in fact Heloise who wrote this poem along with the two short dramas about Mary Magdalene. His reasons for believing this are, as we have seen, mainly to do with the style of the verses.

But there is another reason for believing that these words are by Heloise: there is something of her character in the immediacy of the poem. It captures some of the intensity of a memory of a specific moment, just like the memories that she tells Abelard come back to her – "Everything we did and also the times and the places are stamped on my heart along with your image, so that I live through it all again with you." The *Epithalamica* goes out of its way to build up to and then to celebrate a particular instant of experience. It tries to halt the flow of time, pointing to a special day, perhaps even a special moment. Lovers often wish that their fleeting joy could be grasped and held forever. If the poem is indeed by Heloise it is easy to believe she might be remembering – alongside the religious, allegorical meaning appropriate to the convent – moments she had shared with Abelard when they laughed and made love together among their books behind closed doors in Paris, moments when the joy and closeness of friendship, physical pleasure, and some imperfectly perceived greater joy do indeed become one, just as Heloise had wanted:

This is the day that wakes the bridegroom!
This is the day that wakes the bride!
This is the day that restores all things!

This is the day, lovely spring!
This is the day, world's delight!
This is the day, newness of life!

This is the day the lord made! Amen

On Easter Sunday 1163, when she was in her late sixties, Abbess Heloise heard the *Epithalamica* for the last time. A few weeks later, on May 16, the necrology of the Paraclete records the passing of "the first abbess, the mother of our order." With an ambiguity that one can only hope was intentional, the nun who made the entry recorded not that Heloise died but that she "went joyfully to meet her Lord."

In the great church of Cluny a sequence of thirty masses was said for her on the orders of Peter the Venerable. At the Paraclete, on May 16 every year until the destruction of the convent in 1791, the nuns said their own special mass for the soul of Heloise.

EPILOGUE
Fame
<hr/>

The love, which had joined their spirits in life and which lives on through their most
tender and spiritual letters, has reunited their bodies in this tomb.

Catherine de la Rochefoucauld, Abbess of the Paraclete, 1701

(Epitaph in Père Lachaise Cemetery, Paris)

HE NUNS LAID HELOISE'S BODY to rest
beside Abelard's, in the crypt of their little church.
In doing so they were recognizing that the couple's
romantic love had been an integral part of the formation of the Paraclete. In the following centuries
the image of their love would keep their names alive long after all
memory of Abelard's philosophy, Heloise's writing, and the Paraclete
had faded.

The process of turning them into icons of love began relatively
quickly. As early as 1204, an anonymous writer had produced a
poignant account of the abbess's reunion with Abelard in death:
"when her dead body was carried to the opened tomb, her husband,
who had died long before her, raised his arms to receive her, and so
clasped her closely in his embrace."[1]

Their remains were to be moved five times after that; each time was
a step toward fame. In 1621, when the Paraclete was going through a
period of prosperity, a monument was built for them in the nave of the
refurbished church and their bodies were moved to a more prominent
place under the altar, most usually reserved for the relics of saints.

Two years after the French Revolution, in 1791, the Paraclete was disbanded and the following year the buildings of the convent were themselves sold "for public benefit." The bodies of Abelard and Heloise were removed to the church in the nearby town of Nogent-sur-Seine. There are records of visitors from all over Europe coming there to pay their respects to the couple, although in 1794 their grave was vandalized by revolutionary zealots.

Soon afterward the remains of Abelard and Heloise were returned to Paris, the city where it all began. The man responsible was an antiquarian called Alexandre Lenoir. He had been entrusted by the Assemblée Nationale to preserve the artifacts from the religious houses in France that had been abolished after the revolution. In 1800 he moved the remains of the couple, along with their monument, to a museum he had set up in a deserted convent in Paris that now houses the Ecole Nationale Supérieure des Beaux-Arts.*

In 1815 Lenoir was instructed by the government of the restored French king, Louis XVIII, to start returning the objects in his collection to their original locations. Abelard and Heloise, however, did not leave Paris. They instead became part of a scheme to popularize a cemetery. The large graveyard, known as Père Lachaise, had been opened ten years earlier in the northeastern outskirts of Paris to serve, not suburbanites, but the inhabitants of central Paris. It had not proved popular with those who lived in the fashionable *arrondissements,* however, and still remained mostly empty. The authorities developed a scheme to give the cemetery more cachet by installing the bodies of French celebrities. Abelard and Heloise, as both intellectuals and romantic icons, were perfect candidates.

The couple's remains were moved to Père Lachaise from Lenoir's museum in 1817. Their reward for helping the authorities was a magnificent monument in the Gothic Revival style. Full-size effigies of

---

* Lenoir was later to restore, and in some cases add, the remains of the many French kings and queens to their present resting place in the abbey of St.-Denis, completing thereby the final phase of abbot Suger's campaign to make it the official abbey of French royalty.

each of them lie on top of the tomb, their hands in attitudes of prayer; an elegant canopy rises above them. The inscription is a quotation, dated 1701, from Catherine de la Rochefoucauld, one of the most eminent later abbesses of the Paraclete.

The scheme of the authorities worked. Père Lachaise now holds the remains of hundreds of eminent citizens of France, as well as a few foreigners of whom Oscar Wilde and Jim Morrison, the singer with the Doors, are certainly the most visited. What is inside the tomb is uncertain. The last abbess of the Paraclete, Charlotte de Roucy, had told an inquirer in 1792 that the remains of Abelard were reduced to dust apart from the head. It is doubtful whether anything of them survives today.

The couple have not lacked representation in the arts since their deaths. Nine centuries' accumulation of books, poems, paintings, plays, operas, and films is so great that there are far too many to mention. The novel by Helen Waddell, *Peter Abelard,* which was published in 1933, should be noted for ensuring that a whole generation was aware of the story. Since then their fame has dipped rather than declined or disappeared. In the 1970s there was a spate of academic theories proposing that all or some of the letters were forgeries, which in turn probably inhibited popular reception of the story. Those ideas have now been almost entirely discredited and a new generation of historians is giving consideration to an enhanced assessment of Heloise's role in the story, particularly at the end. The effects of the "discovery" of the new letters have yet to work their way through the academic world. There is much to come.

Abelard and Heloise still have not entirely lost their place in the public imagination. If you visit their tomb today you are certain to see flowers that lovers and others have thrown over the railings to lie beside their final resting place. The activity will, however, probably not be so intense as it was in the nineteenth century when one visitor commented, "Go when you will, you will find somebody snuffling over that tomb."[2]

The visitor was right to be cynical, of course. A shrine dedicated to lovers in Paris is too easy a shot — sentimental and obvious. There is nothing special about falling in love — it is neither rare nor difficult. Heloise and Abelard are remarkable, not because they fell in love, but because they, each in their way, devoted their lives to the search for an understanding of human experience and the life of the spirit. Heloise's unique contribution was to insist on including her love in that understanding in a way that did not sentimentalize or compromise it. What we cannot tell is whether at the end of her life she felt that she had recaptured her love and that she and Abelard again shared the spiritual closeness of the past. If she did, that would indeed be a fitting ending to a great love story.

Notes

---

1   *"Darling"*

1. In the Latin of the manuscript in the Bibliothèque Nationale they are *Jerorius Crassa Labra, Ogerius Verberans Ferrum, Petrus Trahens Predam, Gaufridus Malus Monachus,* and *Raginaldus Plicat Vilanum.*

2. Aelred of Rievaulx, *De Spirituali Amicitia,* i, in Richard Southern, *Medieval Humanism and Other Essays* (London: Harper & Row, 1970).

2   *"At last I came to Paris"*

1. Heloise, First Letter.

2. Heloise, Early Letters, 43, 49, 112, 9.

3. Abelard, *Confessio Heloisae,* in Betty Radice, *The Letters of Abelard and Heloise* (London: Penguin, 1974).

4. Abelard, Autobiography, 58.

5. Robert-Henri Bautier, *"Paris au temps d'Abélard,"* in Jean Jolivet (ed.), *Abelard en son temps: actes du colloque* (Paris: Les Belles Lettres, 1981).

6. *Louis le Gros: annales de sa vie et de son règne 1108–1137,* ed. and tr. Achille Luchaire.

7. Guibert, *The Autobiography of Guibert, Abbot of Nogent-sous-Coucy,* tr. C. C. Swinton Bland (London: Routledge, 1925).

8. Orderic Vitalis, *Ecclesiastical History,* tr. Marjorie Chibnall (Oxford: Clarendon Press, 1969).

3   "By doubting we come to inquiry, by inquiry we come to truth"

1. John of Salisbury, *Metalogicon*, in tr. M.T. Clanchy, *Abelard: A Medieval Life* (Oxford: Blackwell 1997).
2. Abelard, *Sic et Non,* in James Harvey Robinson (ed.), *Readings in European History* (Boston: Ginn & Co., 1904–6).
3. Heloise, Early Letters, 16, 49.
4. Abbot Suger of St. Denis, *The Deeds of Louis the Fat,* tr. Richard Cusimano and John Moorhead (Washington, DC: Catholic Univ. of America Press, 1992); this quotation tr. in Constant J. Mews, *The Lost Letters of Abelard and Heloise: Perceptions of a Dialogue in Twelfth-Century France* (London: Macmillan, 1999).
5. Lindy Grant, *Abbot Suger of St. Denis* (London: 1988).
6. Harold Perkin, conversation with author, October 2002.

4   Master of the schools

1. Brenda Cook, "The Birth of Heloise: New Light on an Old Mystery?," in Henri Habrias (ed.), *Abélard à l'aube des universités* (Nantes: Univ. of Nantes, 2001).
2. F. C. Turlot, *Abaillard et Héloïse, avec un aperçu de XIIème siècle* (Paris: Janet et Cotelle, 1822).
3. C. Stephen Jaeger, *Ennobling Love: In Search of a Lost Sensibility* (Philadelphia: Univ. of Pennsylvania Press, 1999).
4. Ovid, *Metamorphoses,* tr. Mary Innes (London: Penguin, 1955), XIII, 89.

5   "Need I say more?"

1. Abelard, Early Letters, 50.
2. Peter the Venerable, Letter to Heloise, in Radice, *Letters*.
3. Heloise, Early Letters, 23.
4. Heloise, ibid., 25.
5. Abelard, ibid., 26.
6. Abelard, ibid., 41.

7. Abelard, ibid., 19.
8. Heloise, ibid., 45.
9. Heloise, ibid., 4.
10. Heloise, ibid., 81.
11. Abelard, ibid., 22.
12. Ibid.
13. Abelard, *Ethica* (Know Thyself).
14. Ibid.
15. Heloise, Early Letters, 98.
16. Constant Mews, interview with Rachel Kohn, ABC Radio (Australia), February 13, 2000.
17. Abelard, Early Letters, 6.
18. Heloise, ibid., 92.

6 *Love and marriage*

1. Abelard, Early Letters, 17.
2. Abelard, ibid., 33.
3. Abelard, Autobiography, 68.
4. Heloise, First Reply, 114.
5. Abelard, Early Letters, 28.
6. Abelard, ibid., 59.
7. Heloise, ibid., 60.
8. Abelard, ibid., 61.
9. Heloise, ibid., 76.
10. Heloise, ibid., 95.
11. Abelard, ibid., 99.
12. Walter Frölich (tr.), *The Letters of St. Anselm of Canterbury* (Kalamazoo: Cistercian Press, 1993).
13. Owen J. Blum (tr.), *The Letters of Peter Damian* (Washington, DC: Catholic Univ. of America Press, 1992).
14. 1 Cor. 7:28.
15. Clanchy, *Abelard,* 168.
16. Abelard, Third Letter, 149.

7   *"The story of my misfortunes"*
  1. Heloise, Second Letter.
  2. Heb. 12:14.
  3. Rom. 12:19.
  4. Otto of Freising, *The Deeds of Frederick Barbarossa,* tr. in Clanchy, *Abelard.*
  5. Matt. 19:12.
  6. Lucan, *Pharsalia,* tr. Jane Wilson Joyce (Ithaca: Cornell Univ. Press, 1993), 8. 94.
  7. Clanchy, *Abelard.*

8   *St.-Denis*
  1. Tr. in James Harvey Robinson (ed.), *Readings in European History* (Boston: Ginn & Co., 1904–6), 450–51.
  2. Clanchy, *Abelard.*
  3. Bernard of Clairvaux, Letter 77, tr. in Mews, *Lost Letters.*
  4. *Theologia Summi Boni,* tr. in Clanchy, *Abelard.*
  5. Kenneth Clark, *Civilization,* BBC TV, 1969.

9   *"Not strong enough to dig, too proud to beg"*
  1. Ps. 55:7.
  2. Luke 16:3.
  3. Ps. 161:2.
  4. All translations of the "Song for Astralabe" are from an unpublished typescript, ed. Brenda Cook, tr. Sylvania Barnard, 1993.
  5. Suger, *Liber de rebus in administratione sua gestis,* tr. in Thomas Waldman, "Abbot Suger and the Nuns of Argenteuil," *Traditio,* vol. 41 (1985), 239–72.

10   *"You are greater than heaven, greater than the world"*
  1. Abelard, "O Quanta, O Qualia," tr. in Radice, *Letters.*

11 *Return to Paris*

1. Peter von Moos, "Le silence d'Héloïse," in CNRS Colloques Internationales, *Pierre Abelard – Pierre le Venerable* (Paris: CNRS, 1975), 425–68.
2. Clanchy, *Abelard,* 223.
3. Ovid, *Ars Amatoria* I, 243–44, tr. in Radice, *Letters.*
4. James 2:10.
5. John of Salisbury, *Metalogicon,* tr. in Henry Adams, *Mont St.- Michel and Chartres* (London: Penguin, 1986).
6. Bernard of Clairvaux, Letter 193.
7. Clanchy, *Abelard,* 1.
8. Bertrand Russell, *History of Western Philosophy* (London: George Allen & Unwin, 1961), 430.

12 *The Comforter*

1. Abelard, Fourth Letter.
2. All translations of hymns in this chapter from Sister Jane Patricia, *The Hymns of Abelard in English Verse* (Lanham, MD: University Press of America, 1986) (adapted by author).
3. *Theologia Christiana.*
4. Hymn 121.
5. Song of Sg. 4.
6. Rev. 21:2.
7. *Epithalamica.* All translations in this chapter by Chrysogonus Waddell, "*Epithalamica,*" *Musical Quarterly* 72 (1986), 239–71.
8. Tr. Helen Waddell, in *Medieval Latin Lyrics* (London: Penguin, 1929).
9. François Villon (1431–63), "Ballade des dames de temps jadis." This is the poem that contains the famous line "où sont les neiges d'antan?"
10. Patrick McGuire, "Heloise and the Consolation of Friendship," in Bonnie Wheeler (ed.), *Listening to Heloise: The Voice of a Twelfth-Century Woman* (New York: St. Martin's Press, 2000), 303–22.

13   *The Council of Sens*
 1. Tr. in Clanchy, *Abelard.*
 2. Bernard of Clairvaux, Letter 106.
 3. Bernard of Clairvaux, Letter 190.
 4. Bernard of Clairvaux, Letter 337.
 5. Geoffrey of Auxerre, *Life of St. Bernard,* tr. Clanchy in *Abelard.*
 6. *Vita Prima S. Bernardi,* quoted in A. Victor Murray, *Abelard and St. Bernard* (Manchester: Manchester Univ. Press, 1967), 37.
 7. Bernard of Clairvaux, Letter 337.
 8. Geoffrey of Auxerre, *Life of St. Bernard,* tr. Clanchy in *Abelard.*
 9. Bernard of Clairvaux, Letter 189.
 10. Letter of Innocent II, tr. Clanchy, *Abelard.*

14   *"And so Master Peter ended his days"*
 1. Tr. in Clanchy, *Abelard.*
 2. Tr. in Radice, *Letters.*
 3. Tr. ibid.
 4. Tr. ibid.
 5. Tr. in Waddell, *Epithalamica* (adapted by author).

Epilogue: Fame
 1. Peter Dronke, *Abelard and Heloise in Medieval Testimonies* (Glasgow: Univ. of Glasgow Press, 1976), 51.
 2. D. W. Robertson, *Abelard and Heloise* (New York: Dial Press, 1972), esp. 219–22.

Bibliography

Books by Abelard and Heloise in English translation and works containing
partial translations:
Abelard, *Carmen ad Astrolabium,* unpublished typescript, ed. Brenda
    Cook, tr. Sylvia Barnard (1993).
    Confessio fidei universis, tr. C. S. F. Burnet, *Medieval Studies,* vol.
    48 (1986), pp. 111–38.
    Confessio Heloisae, in Betty Radice, tr., *The Letters of Abelard and*
    Heloise (London: Penguin, 1974).
    Ethica (Know Thyself) and *Dialogue Between a Philosopher, a Jew,*
    and a Christian, tr. Paul Vincent Spade, in *Peter Abelard, Ethical*
    Writings (Indianapolis: Hackett, 1995).
    Glosses on Porphyry, tr. Paul Vincent Spade in *Five Texts on the*
    Problems of Universals (Indianapolis: Hackett, 1994).
    Hexaemeron, tr. Eileen Kearney, in Thomas, *Petrus Abelardus*
    Problemata Heloisae, tr. Peter Dronke, in Thomas, *Petrus*
    Abelardus
    Sic et Non (introduction), in James Harvey Robinson (ed.),
    Readings in European History (Boston: Ginn & Co., 1904–6),
    pp. 450–51.
    The Hymns of Abelard in English Verse, tr. Sister Jane Patricia
    (Lanham, MD: Univ. Press of America, 1986).
Abelard (or Heloise), *Epithalamica,* tr. Chrysogonus Waddell,
    "Epithalamica," *Musical Quarterly,* vol. 72 (1986), pp. 239–71.

Abelard and Heloise, *Early Letters*, tr. Neville Chiavaroli and
  Constant Mews, in Constant J. Mews, *The Lost Letters of
  Abelard and Heloise: Perceptions of a Dialogue in Twelfth-Century
  France* (London: Macmillan, 1999).
Letters, in Betty Radice, tr., *The Letters of Abelard and Heloise*
  (London: Penguin, 1974).

Primary sources in translation:
Anselm, Saint, tr. Frölich Walter, *The Letters of St. Anselm of
  Canterbury* (Kalamazoo: Cistercian Press, 1993).
Bede, the Venerable, *History of the English Church and People*
  (London: Penguin, 1955).
Benedict, Saint, *St. Benedict's Rule,* tr. Justin McCann (London:
  Sheed and Ward, 1970).
Bernard of Clairvaux, *The Letters of St. Bernard of Clairvaux,* tr.
  Bruno Scott James (Stroud: Sutton, 1953).
Cartulaire de l'abbaye du Paraclet, tr. Charles Lalore (Troyes:
  Collection des principaux cartulaires du diocèse de Troyes,
  1878).
Damian, Peter, *The Letters of Peter Damian,* tr. Owen J. Blum
  (Washington, DC: Catholic Univ. of America Press, 1992).
Guibert of Nogent, *Autobiography of Guibert, Abbot of Nogent-sous-
  Coucy,* tr. C. C. Swinton Bland (London: Routledge, 1925).
John of Salisbury, *Metalogicon,* tr. Daniel D. McGarry (Berkeley:
  Univ. of California Press, 1955).
Louis le Gros: annales de sa vie et son règne, ed. and tr. Achille Luchaire
  (Brussels: Culture and Civilization, 1964).
Lucan, *Pharsalia,* tr. Jane Wilson Joyce (Ithaca: Cornell Univ.
  Press, 1993).
Oderic Vitalis, *Ecclesiastical History,* tr. Marjorie Chibnall (Oxford:
  Clarendon Press, 1969).
Otto of Freising, *The Deeds of Friedrich Barbarossa,* tr. Charles
  Christopher Mierow (New York: Columbia Univ. Press, 1953).
Ovid, *Metamorphoses,* tr. Mary Innes (London: Penguin, 1955).

Suger, Abbot of St./Denis, *The Deeds of Louis the Fat,* tr. Richard
Cusimano and John Moorhead (Washington, DC: Catholic
Univ. of America Press, 1992).

William of St./Thierry, "Letter," tr. J. Leclerq, *Revue Benedcitine,*
vol. 79 (1969), p. 377.

Secondary sources:

Abaelard.de Web site: http://www.abaelard.de.

Adams, Henry, *Mont St./Michel and Chartres* (London: Penguin,
1986).

Bautier, Robert/Henri, "Paris au temps d'Abélard," in Jean Jolivet
(ed.), *Abélard en son temps: actes du colloque* (Paris: Les Belles
Lettres, 1981).

Benson, Robert L., and Giles Constable (eds), *Renaissance and
Renewal in the Twelfth Century* (Oxford: Clarendon Press, 1982).

Benton, John, *Self and Society in Medieval France* (Toronto: Ameri/
can Medieval Academy, 1984).

Berlioz, Jacques, *Saint Bernard en Bourgogne – lieux et mémoires* (Paris:
Les Editions du Bien Publique, 1990).

Braufnels, Wolfgang, *Monasteries of Western Europe* (London:
Thames & Hudson, 1972).

Brooke, C. N. L., *The Medieval Idea of Marriage* (Oxford: Oxford
Univ. Press, 1989).

The Twelfth Century Renaissance (London: Thames & Hudson,
1969).

Brundage, James A., *Law, Sex, and Christian Society* (Chicago:
Univ. of Chicago Press, 1987).

Bullough, Vern L., and James A. Brundage (eds), *Handbook of
Medieval Sexuality* (London: Garland Publishing, 1996).

Buytaert, E. M. (ed.), *Abelard Conference 1974* (Leuven: Leuven
Univ. Press, 1974).

Catholic Encyclopaedia Web site: http://www.newadvent.org/cathen.

Clanchy, M. T., *Abelard: A Medieval Life* (Oxford: Blackwell,
1997).

CNRS Colloques Internationales, *Pierre Abélard – Pierre le Venerable,* ed. Jean Jolivet (Paris: CNRS, 1975).

Cohn, Samuel K., and Steven A. Epstein (eds), *Portraits of Medieval and Renaissance Living: Essays in Memory of David Herlihy* (Ann Arbor: Univ. of Michigan Press, 1996).

Constable, Giles, *The Reformation of the Twelfth Century* (Cambridge: Cambridge Univ. Press, 1985).

Cook, Brenda, "Abelard and Son: Time for a Reappraisal" and "The Birth of Heloise: New Light on an Old Mystery?," in Henri Habrias (ed.), *Abélard à l'aube des universités* (Nantes: Univ. of Nantes, 2001).

"Abelard et Heloise, Some Notes Toward a Family Tree," *Genealogists' Magazine,* vol. 26 (June 1999), pp. 205–11.

Deanesly, Margaret, *A History of the Medieval Church 590–1500* (London: Methuen, 1969).

Delaney, Janice, *The Curse: A Cultural History of Menstruation* (Chicago: Univ. of Illinois Press, 1988).

Dronke, Peter, *Abelard and Heloise in Medieval Testimonies* (Glasgow: Univ. of Glasgow Press, 1976).

Nine Medieval Plays (Cambridge: Cambridge Univ. Press, 1994).

Women Writers of the Middle Ages (Cambridge: Cambridge Univ. Press, 1984).

Dubois, Jacques, *Les Ordres Monastiques* (Paris: Publications Universitaires de France, 1985).

Engelstein, Laura, *Castration and the Heavenly Kingdom* (Ithaca: Cornell Univ. Press, 1999).

Evans, G. R., *Anselm* (London: Geoffrey Chapman, 1987).

Gilson, Etienne, *The Mystical Theology of St. Bernard* (Kalamazoo: Cistercian Publications, 1940).

Glasser, M., "On Violence: A Preliminary Communication," *International Journal of Psycho-Analysis,* vol. 79 (1988), pp. 887–902.

Grant, Lindy, *Abbot Suger of St.-Denis* (London: Longman, 1998).

Hindley, Geoffrey, *The Crusades* (London: Constable, 2003).

Irvine, Martin, *The Pen, Castration and Identity: Abelard's Negotiations of Gender* (Washington, DC: Georgetown Univ. Press, 1995).

Jaeger, C. Stephen, *Ennobling Love: In Search of a Lost Sensibility* (Philadelphia: Univ. of Pennsylvania Press, 1999).

The Envy of Angels: Cathedral Schools and Social Ideals in Medieval England (Philadelphia: Univ. of Pennsylvania Press, 1994).

Johnson, Penelope, *Equal in Monastic Profession: Religious Women in Medieval France* (Chicago: Univ. of Chicago Press, 1991).

Jolivet, J. (ed.), *Nantes Conference 1979: Abélard et son temps* (Paris: Les Belles Lettres, 1981).

Kelso, Carl, "Women in Power: Fontevrault and the Paraclete Compared," *Comitatus,* vol. 22 (1991), pp. 55–69.

Knowles, David, *The Evolution of Medieval Thought* (London: Longman, 1962).

Le Goff, Jacques, *Medieval Civilization,* tr. Julia Barrow (Oxford: Blackwell, 1998).

Intellectuals au Moyen Age (Paris: Editions du Seuil, 1957).

Leclercq, J., *Bernard of Clairvaux* (Paris: Desclée, 1989).

"Literature and Psychology in Bernard of Clairvaux," *Downside Review,* vol. 93 (1975), pp. 15–16.

Monks on Marriage (New York: Seabury Press, 1982).

Leff, Gordon, *Medieval Thought* (London: Pelican, 1958).

Lougnot, Claude, *Cluny: Pouvoirs de l'an mille* (Paris: Editions du Bien Publique, 1987).

Luscombe, D. E., *Peter Abelard* (London: Historical Association, 1979).

The School of Peter Abelard (Cambridge: Cambridge Univ. Press, 1969).

"From Paris to the Paraclete," *Proceedings of the British Academy,* vol. 74 (1988), pp. 247–83.

Maddox, Fiona, *Hildegard of Bingen* (London: Hodder Headline, 2001).

Marenbon, John, *The Philosophy of Peter Abelard* (Cambridge: Cambridge Univ. Press, 1997).

McGuire, Brian P., "Heloise and the Consolation of Friendship," in Wheeler, *Listening to Heloise,* pp. 303–22.

McLeod, Enid, *Heloise, a Biography* (London: Chatto & Windus, 1938).

Mews, Constant J., *Abelard and His Legacy* (Aldershot: Ashgate, 2001).

"In Search of a Name," *Traditio,* vol. 44 (1988), p. 194.

"List of Heresies Imputed to Peter Abelard," *Revue Benedictine,* vol. 95 (1985), pp. 73–110.

The Lost Letters of Abelard and Heloise: Perceptions of Dialogue in Twelfth-Century France (Basingstoke: Macmillan, 1999).

Moore, R. I., *The Formation of a Persecuting Society* (Oxford: Blackwell, 1987).

Moos, Peter von, "Le silence d'Héloïse," in CNRS Colloques Internationales, *Pierre Abélard – Pierre le Venerable,* pp. 425–68.

Murray, A. Victor, *Abélard and St. Bernard* (Manchester: Manchester Univ. Press, 1967).

Newman, Barbara, *From Virile Woman to Womanchrist* (Philadelphia: Univ. of Pennsylvania Press, 1995).

North, J. D., "The Astrolabe," *Scientific American,* January 1974, pp. 96–106.

Oldenbourg, Zoë, *St. Bernard* (Paris: Editions Albert Michel, 1970).

O'Shea, Simon, *The Perfect Heresy* (London: Profile, 2000).

Perkin, Harold, "The Rise and Fall of Empires," *History Today,* vol. 52, no. 4 (April 2002), pp. 17–24.

The Third Revolution: Professional Elites in the Modern World (London: Routledge, 1996).

Pernoud, Regine, *Heloise and Abelard* (London: Collins, 1973).

Robertson, D. W., *Abelard and Heloise* (New York: Dial Press, 1972).

Russell, Bertrand, *History of Western Philosophy* (London: George Allen & Unwin, 1961).

Sikes, Jeffrey G., *Peter Abailard* (Cambridge: Cambridge Univ. Press, 1932).

"The Conflict of Abailard and Bernard," *Journal of Theological Studies,* vol. 28 (1927), pp. 398–402.

Simson, Otto von, *The Gothic Cathedral* (New York: Princeton Univ. Press, 1956).

Southern, Richard, *Medieval Humanism and Other Essays* (London: Harper & Row, 1970).

The Making of the Middle Ages (London: Arrow, 1953).

Spade, Paul Vincent, *Survey of Medieval Philosophy* (Bloomington: Indiana Univ. Press, 1985).

Thomas, R. (ed.), *Petrus Abelardus: Person, Werk, un Wirkung,* Proceedings, International Colloquium at Trier, April 17–19 (Trier: Trierer Theologishe Studien, 1979).

Turlot, F. C., *Abaillard et Héloïse, avec un aperçu du XIIème siècle* (Paris: Janet et Cotelle, 1822).

Vernarde, Bruce L., "Praesidentes Negotiis: Abbesses as Managers in Twelfth-Century France," in Samuel K. Cohn Jr. and Steven A. Epstein (eds), *Portraits of Medieval and Renaissance Living: Essays in Memory of David Herlihy* (Ann Arbor: Univ. of Michigan Press, 1996).

Waddell, Helen (tr.), *Medieval Latin Lyrics* (London: Penguin, 1929).

Peter Abelard (London: Constable, 1933).

The Wandering Scholars (London: Pelican, 1927).

Waldman, Thomas G., "Abbot Suger and the Nuns of Argenteuil," *Traditio,* vol. 41 (1985), pp. 239–72.

Wheeler, Bonnie (ed.), *Listening to Heloise: The Voice of a Twelfth-Century Woman* (New York: St. Martin's Press, 2000).

Williams, Paul, *The Moral Philosophy of Peter Abelard* (Lanham, MD: Univ. Press of America, 1980).

Appendix

Selections from the "Early Letters"

What follows is a selection from the collection of letters that is thought by many scholars to comprise excerpts from the notes on wax tablets that Heloise and Abelard exchanged daily during their affair. To read at least some of the letters in their entirety gives an impression of what information can be gleaned from the letters, of the possibilities for future interpretation, and of what remains (and will probably always remain) mysterious.

The letters are contained in a fifteenth-century manual of letter writing compiled by a monk called Johannes de Vepria. The final section of his book is entitled "From the Letters of Two Lovers." Vepria's aim was to provide examples of good writing, not to tell a story, so he vigorously edited the text he had in front of him. The first extracts consist almost exclusively of the beginnings, or salutations, from the correspondents. Later on he seems to have relaxed his rules and allowed a little more of the content to be included. From the start he was conscientious about noting where he had not transcribed a section of the text and he is also very clear about whether it is the man or the woman who is writing – he gives no clue as to whether he himself knew the identity of the couple.

It is plain from the start that both the man and the woman are clever and educated. The language is impressively erudite but Vepria's editing leaves only scant information as to the specifics of the relationship:

To her heart's love, more sweetly scented than any spice, from she who is his in heart and body; I send the freshness of eternal happiness as the flowers of your youth fade.

. . . Farewell my life's salvation. (Woman)

Amori suo precordiali omnibus aromatibus dulcius redolenti, corde et corpore sua: arescentibus floribus tue jubentutis, biriditatem eterne felicitates.

. . . Vale salus bite mee. (Mulier)

※

To a singular joy and the only rest for a weary mind. The man for whom life without you is death sends what is more than himself as far as his body and soul are able.

. . . Farewell, my light for whom I would willingly die.

(Man)

Singulari gaudio, et lassate mentis unico solamine, ille cuius bita sine te mors est: quid amplius quam seipsum quantum corpore et anima balet.

. . . Vale lux mea, bale pro qua mori belim. (Vir)

※

To her most pure love, worthy of the closest fidelity; through the state of true love I send the secret of precious faith.

. . . May the Ruler of Heaven mediate between us and may He be the friend of our faith. Farewell my sweetest one and

may Christ, King of Kings, save you for eternity. Farewell in the name of Him who governs all things. *(Woman)*

Purissimo amori suo, et intime fidelitatis digno, per bere dilectionis statum, care fidei secretum.

. . . Celi regnator sit inter nos mediator, et sit socius fidei nostre. Vale, et Christus rex regnum, te dulcissimum salbet in ebum. Vale in illo qui cuncta gubernat in mundo. (Mulier)

To one who is sweeter from day to day, who now is as much as possible and is always to be loved more than anything. Her only one sends the same unchanging constancy of sincere faith. *(Man)*

De die in diem dulciori et nunc quam maxime dilecte et semper super omnia dilligende, singularis eius: eandem et immutabilem sincere fidei constanciam. (Vir)

To my joy and my hope; I send my faith and my very self with all my devotion as long as I live.

May the giver of every art and the bountiful source of human talent fill the depths of my breast with philosophical skill so that I may greet you in writing, dearest, in the way I intend. Farewell, farewell, hope of my youth. *(Woman)*

Jocune spei mee: fidem meam, et cum omni devocione meipsam quamdiu vivam.

Tocius artis largitor, et humani ingenii largissimus dator, mei pectoris interna philosophie artis impleat pericia, quo te possim dilectissime ita salutare scriptis, ad consensum mee voluntatis. Vale vale, spes juventutis mee. (Mulier)

⸻

To my brightest star whose rays I have recently enjoyed. May she shine with such unfailing splendor that no cloud can obscure her. (Man)

Clarissime stelle sue, cuius nuper radiis delectatus sum: ita indeficienti splendore nitere, ut nulla eam nebula possit offuscare. (Vir)

⸻

Despite the couple's undeniable inventiveness their terms of endearment do become a little saccharine after a while. In the next letters the couple themselves seem to admit that they are aware of the problems of repetition. There also seems to be some unvoiced problem referred to in this little exchange that also confirms for us that we are looking at messages exchanged by the ephemeral medium of the wax tablet.

. . . My mind, bound to you always by duty and by gratitude, has not up to now been able to send you all the greetings that it wished. It has remained silent, lest by listing several it might seem to undermine them all. I think it neither a burden

for you nor difficulty for me to write to you often, repeating the same things again and again, for just as I love you as my very self, so do I not neglect to love you with all my heart.

. . . Farewell, dearer to me than life. Know that in you lies my death and my life. *(Woman)*

. . . Grata mentis mee benibolencia, pro se et officio suo tibi semper obnoxia, cum omnes quas bellet salutes expedire non potuit permultas, et iam siluit, ne plures enumerando, offendere sibi bideretur unibersas. Sepe me tibi scribere, eadem iterum atque iterum repetere, nec tibi onerosum reor, nec michi est difficile, quippe quem sicut memetipsam dilligo, ita te toto cordis conamine dilligere non negligo.

. . . Bale carior bita. Scias quod in te mea mors est et bita. (Mulier)

If I may keep your writing tablets a while longer sweetest, I would write many things, just as many things would come to mind. For even if I could write to you continuously so that I did nothing else, I would undoubtedly still have enough subject matter: your merits, which for me are so many that I could not count them. Farewell my surest hope. *(Man)*

Si tabulas tuas dulcissima diutius retinere michi licereet, plurima scriberem sicut plurima occurrerent. Nam si semper scribere possem, ita, ut nichil aliud facerem, suffiicentiem sine dobbio materiam haberem: tuam scilicet probitatem, tua merita que circa me tanta sunt, ut quanda sint estimari non possit. Vale certissima spes mea. (Vir)

To his heart, her most faithful. I wish you an unclouded night. Would that it were spent with me. Farewell my soul and my rest. (Man)

Cordi suo, fielissimus eius: coctem candidam, et utinam mecum. Vale anima mea, quies mea. (Vir)

To his inexhaustible vessel of all sweetness from her most beloved. May I gaze endlessly at you alone, ignoring the light of day.

Since day was turning into night, I could not contain myself any longer from obeying the call to greet you of my own accord — something which you have delayed doing. Farewell and know that without your good well-being, neither health nor life exists for me. (Man)

Inexhausto tocius sue dulcedinis basculo, dilectissimus eius: neglecto celi lumine, te solam indesinenter aspicere.

Cum dies in noctem bergeret, ulterius me continuere non potui, quin salutandi officium ultro arriperem, quod tu tarda distulisti. Vale et scias quia sine tua balitudine, nec salus nec bita mea consistit. (Vir)

From an equal to an equal, a reddening rose under the spotless whiteness of lilies. I send you whatever a lover gives a lover.

Although it is winter my breast blazes with the fervor of love. What else shall I say? I would write more things to you but a few words instruct a wise man. Farewell, my heart and body and my total love. (Woman)

Par pari, rubenti rose sub immarcido lilliorum candore: quidquid amans amanti.

Quamvis sit hiems in tempore, estuat tamen pectus meum amoris fervore. Quid ultra? Plura tibi scriberem, sed sapientiem pauca fervore. Quid ultra? Plura tibi scriberem, sed sapientam pauca monebunt. Vale, cor et corpus meum, et omnia dilectio mea. (Mulier)

Indeed your words are few, but I made them many by re-reading them often. I do not measure how much you say, but rather how bountiful is the heart from which it comes. Farewell, sweetest. (Man)

Pauca quidem verba tua sunt, sed ea plura feci sepe relegendo, nec ego penso quantum dicas, sed de quam fecundo corde procedat quod dicis. Vale dulcissima. (Vir)

As Vepria became more interested in the content of the letters we see more evidence of the emotional background of the relationship: there are references to the secret nature of the affair and, although details are unclear, we see unmistakable signs of a substantial tiff, followed by a reconciliation:

Terrified by the lord's judgment, which says, "It is hard to kick against the goad," I send you this unadorned letter as proof of how devotedly I submit myself to your instruction in all matters. There is a great distance between East and West, but faith is repaid with faith for those separated for long periods of time — yet not for one second will they be distant if the bond of true love keeps them chained together. For in whatever region they may linger, they will still be joined in soul and mind. I had many things to say, but am hindered by too much bitterness of mind. I would like to be next to you and be talking with you for an hour. I could bear some sadness but I sigh all the more when I consider that times set aside for work are completely abandoned because of you. But of those many things I had to say, I do one: I greet you with a kiss of true peace. Farwell and give me license to go. (Woman)

Domenica sentencia perterrita per quam dicitur: "difficile est contra stimulum calcitrare," has inormatas litteras tibi mitto, earum probans indicio quam debote in omnibus me tuis preceptis subicio. Multum distat ortus ab accidende, sed fides rependitur fide per multa temporum spacia disiunctis, nec puncto distabit si eos binculum bere dilectionis concatenabit. Quamcunque enim morantur parte, anima tamen juncti erunt et mente. Multa habui loqui, sed nimia mentis amaritudine prepedior. Vellem ad horam tibi collaterari, et tecum confabulari; nam parva liceret tristicia, sed plura cordis increscunt suspiria, dum studiosa mei laboris tempora, in te funditus perpendam neglacta. Unum autem de multis ago, te saluo vere pacis osculo. Vale, et licenciam eundi michi concede. (Mulier)

To his only delight. I send whatever is the most delightful thing in life.

. . . I give up on words; they are like the winds. What could I do that might be a price for such remarkable delight? If I were to cross the sea in the hope of such benefit it would be a paltry effort. If I were to climb the Alps in the bitterest cold or risk my life searching for you in the midst of fire, I would consider that I had done nothing. Therefore I humbly beg for your indulgence and ask that you do not measure the letter by the extravagance of my promises.

For some time now, my beautiful one, you have doubted the faith of your beloved because of certain words which I wrote, provoked by an unexpected reproach, while in the very throes of sorrow. I wish I had never written them, for you have etched them too deeply into your memory. I ask you to erase them from your heart and not let them establish roots inside you. God knows I never let them do so: as soon as they had left my hands

I immediately wanted to call them back. If only a casual remark had the ability to make its own way back home.

I am the same to you as I always was; look not to words but deeds. You are not stale to me but each day renewed in my heart, just as pleasant a season of the year is always renewed by the coming of spring. The season itself favors us with its compliance, let us enjoy the opportunities. We shall be able to love wisely, because we shall shrewdly look out for our reputation while mixing our joys with the greatest delight. The fire which is sheltered burns more strongly than the one left to burn freely. Farewell my loveable delight. (Man)

Unice suauitati sue: quidquid in uita suauissimum reperiri potest.

. . . Verba omitto que uentis similia sunt: quis labor, quod opus, tanti sint, ut tam admirandam suauittatem sufficienter mercari possit? Si mare in spe talis bone transiam, exiguus labor est, si Alpes in asperrimo frigore transcendam, uel si de medio igne, cum uite discrimine te petam, in omnibus his nichil fecisse uidebor. Rogo igitur suppliciter graciam tuam, ut litteras istas secundum promissa mea non metiaris.

Aliquanto iam tempore formasa mea de fide dilectissime tui dubitasti propter quaedam uerba, que subita impulsus contumelia, in ipso doloris cursu dictaui, et utinam non dictassem, quia tu nimis ea memoriter signasi, que rogo ut a corde deleas, et apud interiora tua radicem non figant, sicut ego ea deo teste, nunquam fixi, sed ubi ea a manibus dimisi, statim reuocare uolui, si uox emissa reuerti nosset.

Idem tibi sum qi fueram; noli berba sed facta consulere. Non michi betus es; quotidie corde meo innobaris, sicut anni iocunda temperies, equaliter semper ingruente bere, noba est. Tempus ipsum nobissua commoditate blanditur, temporis oportunitate fruamur. Sapientier amare poterimus, quod tamen rarum est, cum quidam dixerit: "quis unquam sapientir amabit?" Nos bere sapienter amare poterimus, quia et fame nostre sollereter consulemus, et tamen gaudia nostra cum summa suabitate miscebimus. Ille ignis fortius estuat qui tegitur, quam ille cui exundare conceditur. Vale amabilis delectacio mea. (Vir)

———∞———

To the dearest chain that binds all things; your most constant friend sends the most complete consummation of love.

The hand of this writer is unable to express how close you are to me. A feeling of inner sweetness impels me to make you my special beloved above everybody else. And so I am unable to reveal to you in any way at all just how greatly my feeling burns for you. . . . Truly I admit, most beloved, that many times I would have halted like an idle sheep along the way, if the masterly skill of your instruction had not kept calling me back to the proper path. "But now let us block the streams, the fields have drunk enough." My intention has decided this: that further conflict between us should cease. The words we have thrown at each other have already stirred up dreadful anger. . . . Why do I linger with long-winded ramblings? May you grant one of my requests: that you never think that I am troubling your soul with my uncertainty. Farewell, my bright star, golden constellation, jewel of virtues, sweet balm for my body. (Woman)

Cunctorum vinculo amoris alligantium carissimo certe sodalitatis amica: integerrime dilectionis summam.

Quam intime carus michi sis, plene nullatenus denudare valet scribentis manus, quia interne dulcedinis me hortatur affectus, ut sis michi pre cunctis specialis dilectus. Quantus igitur erga te meus ardeat affectus, ullo modo tibi manisfestare nequeo. . . . Vere fateor dilectissime quod multociens ut pecus ignavum via subsisterem, nisi magisterialis instiucionis tui sollercia, me prono digressam assidue revocaret tramite. "Nunc autem claudamus rivos sat prata biberunt." Decrevit hoc mea intencio ut cesset ultro alterna contencio; satis iam dire iactis mutuo sermonibus intumuere ire. . . . Quid proxilis moror ambagibus? Unius michi peticionis annuas effectum: ut scilicet me animam tuam tali nunquam ambiguitate inquietare presumas. Vale mi stella clara, sydus aurem, gemma virtutum, corpori meo dulce medicamentum. (Mulier)

A little later in the sequence, however, we find Heloise still concerned about the relationship. Vepria has unfortunately left us only a fragment of Abelard's reply:

To the imperiled boat which lacks the anchor of faith from she who is not moved by the winds of your inconstancy.

You are not being fair with me. You have changed your ways and now trust is not secure anywhere. I regret in no small way having fastened on you alone over everyone so firmly in my heart, because it is wasted effort when nobody responds to the exertion. Suspended in hope, I can barely keep hoping. What good has expectation been to me when it has brought me no result? Farewell. (Woman)

Navi periclitanti, et anchoram fidei non habenti, illa quam non movent ventuaosa que tue infidelitati sunt congrua.

Tu non equo mecum senitis animo, sed mutasti mores; idcirco nusquam est tuta fides. Penitet me non modice, quod te solum pre omnibus cordi meo tam firmiter affaxi, quia frustra laborat, cui laboris mercedem nemo recompensat. Pendula expectacione vix expectavi. Sed quid hec spes michi profuit, que nullum profectum attulit? Vale. (Mulier)

To half my heart and part of my soul: what I am I entrust to you. I am yours as long as I live.
Farewell even though you send me no greeting. (Man)

Cordi dimidio, parti anime mando, quod sum: tibi sum dum vivo.

Vale quamvis nullum miseris miche salve. (Vir)

The next letters seem to reflect the continuation of a less troubled relationship but just occasionally they do finish with a sting in the tail. Abelard apparently feels the need to reassert that he has not changed as well as, on one occasion, to refer to the need for discretion.

To the sweetest of lovers I send the foundation of a stable friendship. May you never know the darkness of faithlessness; may you become neither cold nor lukewarm in the sweet-flowing fire of our love, but rather blaze more ardently than ever; may you always carry me close in your breast without tiring.

My wishes are of no use to me because I and everything I have are worthless to you and because you have borne the pleasure of desired joy as if angry. (Woman)

Tyroni et amantium dulcissimo: fundamentum stabilis amicicie infidelitatis fusca nescire, frigidum neque tepidum fieri in dulcifero nostri amoris ardore, sed solito more ardentius estuare, meque promerentem amicabili formite pectoris semper sine tedio gestare.

Mea bota nil michi prosunt, quia ego et mea tibi bilescunt, et delectcionem desiderati, tu quasi iratus sustulisti. (Mulier)

———

To one who knows well and is best equipped in the rules of love; I am the same friend that I have always been and I send the constancy of eternal love. (Man)

Amoris leges bene scienti et optime implimenti, amicus idem qui fuerat: eandem unici amoris constanciam. (Vir)

⸻

Faithful to faithful, I send the knot of intact love never untied. It is right that a possession should be used attentively by its owner. It should not be made worthless in his heart by neglect but should grow greater every hour. (Woman)

Fidelis fideli: nodum qui nunquam denodatur amoris integri. Dignum est et benefactum ut possessio que possidetur a possessore attentcius exerceatur, neque in corde eius bilescat, sed magis as magis omni hora crescat. (Mulier)

⸻

To his starry eye, may it always see what is pleasing and never what is displeasing.

I am the person I have always been. Nothing has changed in me concerning my ardor for you, except that every day the flame of love for you rises even more. I admit this change alone, this alone do I concede, that it grows in love for you within me in every season. If you care to note, I am now speaking to you more cautiously; shame tempers love; modesty checks love, lest it rush out in its immensity. This way we can fulfill our sweet desires and gradually stifle the rumor that may have risen about us.

Farewell. (Man)

Sidereo oculo suo: semper bidere quod placat, nunquam sentire quod displiceat.

Ego sum qui fui. Nichil in me de tuo amore mutatum est, nisi quod in maius quotidie flamma tue dilectionis exuberat. Hec sola mutacio fatenda est, hec sola iuste conceditur quod tuo amori apud me in omni tempore proficitur. Cautius modo te alloquor si notare bis, cautis aggredior, pudor se amori contemperat, amorem berecundia cohibet, ne in immunsum proruat, ut et nostris dulcibus botis copiam demus, et famam que de nobis orta est paulatim attenuemus. Vale. (Vir)

To one flowing with milk and honey. I am the whiteness of milk and the sweetness of honey and I send the outpouring of every delight and the joy of redemption.

Most loved and most cherished in my heart, so much suited for my love and the complete answer to my prayer, I hope with the greatest intention of my heart that you may always fare well and always live in sweetness. The most precious thing I have to give you, myself, firm in faith and love, stable in desire for you and never changeable. Farewell, rejoice, may nothing upset you nor hurt me through you. (Woman)

Lacte et melle mananti, candor lactis et dulcedo mellis: liquorem tocius suabitatis et augmentum gaudii salutaris.

Te dilectissimum cordique meo amantissimum, amori meo aptissimum, boto meo conbienientissimum semper balere, et semper dulciter bibere, summa opto cordis intencione. Quod preciocissimum habeo, tibi do, scilicet meipsam, in fide et dilectione firmam, in amore tuo stabilem, et nunquam mutabilem. Vale, letare, nil te offendat, nec me per te ledat. (Mulier)

———∞∞∞———

Later still, it is again apparent that all is not well. Vepria has left out the beginning of the letter but he plainly regarded the middle as significant. Abelard expresses the pain of a lover who begins to realize that something is wrong.

. . .There is nothing worse than a foolish man blessed by fortune. Now for the first time I realize the good fortune I previously enjoyed, now I have the opportunity to look back on happy times, for hope is fading. I do not know whether it is ever to be recovered. I am paying the price for stupidity, because I am losing that good thing of which I have been completely unworthy, that good thing which I have not known how to keep as I ought. It is flying elsewhere, forsaking me, because it realizes that I am not worthy of having it. Farewell. (Man)

. . . Nichil insipiente fortunato gravius est. Nunc primum ante actam fortunam recognosco, nuc leta tempora respexisse vacat, quia spes recedit nescio an unquam reuperanda. Ego precium ob stulticiam fero, quia bonum illud quod retinere sicut decuit nescibi, quo utique indignus fui, illud inquam bonum perdo, alio avolat, me relinquit, quia me sua possessione indignum recognoscit. Vale. (Vir)

———∞∞∞———

A few letters later harmonious relations seem to have been restored but there is some sort of change of circumstances: they are able to see each other legitimately every day. Are they now married, or is this some other, unrelated change of fortune? Even though the exchanged letters may be from now on no longer strictly necessary it is revealing that neither of the lovers is entirely reconciled to giving them up.

Since each of us is able to see the other in a moment now, our letters do not need a greeting. Nevertheless I want you to be well, clothed with the grace of the virtues, covered with the jewels of wisdom, endowed with the honesty of behavior, and decorated with complete composure. Farewell font of refreshment. Farewell, flower of the most pleasing scent. Farewell, memory of joy, end of sadness. (Woman)

Quia uterque nostrum alter alterius conspectui modo in momento presentari balet, littere nostre salutacione non indigent. Cupio te tamen esse salbum, birtutum decore indutum, sophie gemmis circumtectum, morum honestate preditum, omnisque com- posicionis ornatu decoratum. Bale, fons refrigerenti. Bale flos odoris gratissimi. Bale memoria leticie, oblibio tristicie. (Mulier)

⁓⁓

To his only one; I send joy which no sickness can destroy. God is my witness, most beloved, that every time I begin to read your letters I am flooded with so much delight inside that I am often forced to go back over the letter I have read because the extent of my happiness takes my attention away. So you can easily imagine how joyful for me is the very presence of your so pleasing person and how important are your living words when just a word sent from afar makes me happy. Farewell. (Man)

Unice sue: gaudium quod nulla egrritudo corrumpat.

Deo teste dilectissima qotiens tuas legere litteras incipio, tanta interius suauitate perfundor, ut litteram quam legi sepe cogar repetere, quia attencionem michi magnitudo aufert leticie. Facile ergo perpendere potes quam iocunda michi sit ipsius gratissime persone tue prescencia et quantum in se ponderis habeant biba uerba tua, cum tantum me uox eminus missa letificet. Uale. (Vir)

⸺◈⸺

If we believe that we have been looking at the letters of Abelard and Heloise then it follows that at some stage we are likely to confront the last letters exchanged between them before their enforced separation and Abelard's castration – none of the letters seems to be reacting to a catastrophe quite on that scale. The final exchange shows signs of strain and sadness. Was Heloise already pregnant? Had they not yet agreed on the idea of her moving to Brittany? Or is some other event referred to of which we have no indication because Abelard did not include it in his autobiography? The sequence ends poignantly with a declaration from an exhausted Heloise.

Where there is passion and love there always rages effort. Now I am tired, I cannot reply to you because you are taking sweet things as burdensome and in doing so you sadden my spirit. Farewell. (Woman)

Ubi est amor et dillectio, ibi semper fervet exercium. Jam fessa sum, tibi responder nequeo, quod dulcia pro gravibus accipis, ac per hoc animum meum contristaris. Vale. (Mulier)

Index